THE LIBRARY OF HOLOCAUST TESTIMONIES

Have You Seen My Little Sister?

The Library of Holocaust Testimonies

Have You Seen My Little Sister?

JANINA FISCHLER-MARTINHO

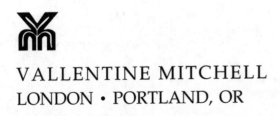

VALLENTINE MITCHELL
LONDON · PORTLAND, OR

First published in 1998 in Great Britain by
VALLENTINE MITCHELL
Newbury House, 900 Eastern Avenue
London IG2 7HH

and in the United States of America by
VALLENTINE MITCHELL
c/o ISBS, 5804 N. E. Hassalo Street
Portland, Oregon 97213-3644

Website: www.vmbooks.com

Reprinted with amendments 1999

British Library Cataloguing in Publication Data
Fischler-Martinho, Janina
    Have you seen my little sister?
    (The library of Holocaust testimonies)
    1. Fischler-Martinho, Janina   2. Holocaust, Jewish (1939–1945)
    – Personal narratives   3. World War, 1939–1945 – Children –
    Poland
    I. Title
    940.5'318'092
    ISBN 0-85303-334-X
    ISSN 1363-3759

Library of Congress Cataloging-in-Publication Data
Fischler-Martinho, Janina, 1930-
      Have you seen my little sister? / Janina
    Fischler-Martinho.
        p. cm. -- (The Library of Holocaust testimonies)
      ISBN 0-85303-334-X
      1. Fischler-Martinho, Janina, 1930–   2. Jews—Poland—Kraków–
    –Biography.   3. Jewish children in the Holocaust—Poland—Kraków–
    –Personal narratives.   4. Kraków (Poland)—Biography. I. Title.
    II. Series.
    DS135.P63F56   1997
    943. 8'6—dc21
    [B]   97-30612
                                                                        CIP
                                                                        r97

Typeset by Regent Typesetting, London
Printed and bound in Great Britain by
The Cromwell Press, Trowbridge, Wiltshire.

Contents

Contents

List of Illustrations

Biographical Note

Janina Fischler-Martinho, a Jewish child, was born in Cracow, Poland in 1930 – the second of three children. Her parents, their three children and a vast clan of close, dearly-loved relations were drawn into the Cracow Ghetto in 1941. By the winter of 1942, only Janina and her brother, Joseph, were still alive. The others had perished. On the morning of 13 March 1943, during the first hours of the 'Ghetto Liquidation Aktion', 19-year-old Joseph led 12-year-old Janina out of the Ghetto's 'snapping jaws' through a sewer.

Janina survived on her own on the Aryan side; her brother in various concentration camps. They were re-united in Cracow in August 1945.

A year later, in the autumn of 1946, they arrived in Scotland. Janina became a pupil at a boarding school in Edinburgh. She came to London in 1949. She qualified as a teacher at Avery Hill Teacher Training College in South London. She taught in both inner London and Croydon schools. She read French as a mature, part-time student at Birkbeck College, London. Janina and her husband live in Croydon. Their daughter Eva and 8-year-old grandson Daniel live nearby.

Joseph, with his wife and daughter, lives in London.

The Library of Holocaust Testimonies

It is greatly to the credit of Frank Cass that this series of survivors' testimonies is being published in Britain. The need for such a series has long been apparent here, where many survivors made their homes.

Since the end of the war in 1945 the terrible events of the Nazi destruction of European Jewry have cast a pall over our time. Six million Jews were murdered within a short period; the few survivors have had to carry in their memories whatever remains of the knowledge of Jewish life in more than a dozen countries, in several thousand towns, in tens of thousands of villages, and in innumerable families. The precious gift of recollection has been the sole memorial for millions of people whose lives were suddenly and brutally cut off.

For many years, individual survivors have published their testimonies. But many more have been reluctant to do so, often because they could not believe that they would find a publisher for their efforts.

In my own work over the past two decades, I have been approached by many survivors who had set down their memories in writing, but who did not know how to have them published. I realized what a considerable emotional strain the writing down of such hellish memories had been. I also realized, as I read many dozens of such accounts, how important each account was, in its own way, in recounting aspects of the story that had not been told before, and adding to our understanding of the wide range of human suffering, struggle and aspiration.

With so many people and so many places involved, including many hundreds of camps, it was inevitable that the historians and students of the Holocaust should find it difficult at times to grasp the scale and range of the events. The publication of memoirs is therefore an indispensable part of the extension of knowledge, and of public awareness of the crimes that had been committed against a whole people.

Martin Gilbert
Merton College, Oxford

In memory of my parents, Henryk and Ewa Fischler,
and eight-year-old brother, Bartuś Fischler,
deported from the Cracow Ghetto on 8 June 1942.

1 • *Mamma's Family*

My maternal grandmother, Helena Weinreb, née Riegerhaupt, had brought nine children into the world. Five boys and four girls who must have all been bonny babies, for they grew up into fit and healthy adults. She had, also, given birth to twin baby girls, Sophie and Helen, who were still-born. I remember their names because my grandmother mentioned them from time to time, always followed by a long, wistful sigh. I was much intrigued by the term 'still-born' of which I would have greatly appreciated a full and clear explanation. Unsolicited, my grandmother would never offer one. Solicited, she would not refuse, she would not fob me off . . . But it would be as brief and non-committal as she could make it. She was a quiet person – not given to criticism, gossip or comment. She was naturally economical with language as with everything else.

Some families like to reminisce, to discourse at leisure, about what has been. Stories are told about forefathers and their deeds great and small; about days gone by, torrid summers and harsh winters, places lived in and occupations followed. About the successes and failures of life, its joys and its sorrows. About friendship and romance, old age and death . . . These topics were not discussed in my family, the past was rarely recalled. Sometimes a droplet here, a crumb there, allowed to stray in an unguarded moment, like the still-born twins' names, seeped through to me and my permanently pricked-up ears would seize it and put it in storage for 'later on'. Only there was to be no 'later on'.

I was an inquisitive child always badgering whoever happened to be around, 'Tell me a story . . .' And once I understood that some stories were made up, whereas others were true, I loved nothing better than a 'true' story, with the members of my family, the people I knew and loved, as the narrative's principal characters. I wanted to be told about events and incidents that had actually taken place – that there were people still alive, as I am today, who had witnessed them with their own eyes, experienced them at first hand.

FISCHLER/WEINREB FAMILY TREES

The FISCHLERS

Samuel = Leiba Heim
(? – 1923)   (? – 1942)

Henryk = Eva Weinreb
(1894–1942) (1896–1942)
Joseph (1923–)
Janina (1930–)
Bartus (1933–1942)

Rose = Adolf Feldmaus
(? – 1942)   (? – 1942)
Zygmunt (1923–)
Sophie (1926–1944)

The WEINREBS

Maks = Helena Riegerhaupt
(1864–1939) (1872–1942)

Salomon = Josephine Krautwirt
(1894–1941) (? – 1945)
Irena (1926–1942)
Adam (1929–)
Stefan (1931–1944)

Eva = Henryk Fischler
(1896–1942) (1894–1942)
Joseph (1923–)
Janina (1930–)
Bartus (1933–1942)

Regina
(? – 1942)

Anna = David Rostal
(? – 1942) (? – 1945)

Sally
(? – 1942)

Izydor = Annie Infeld
(? – 1945) (? – 1944)
Maria (1940–1942)

Marek
(1908–1973)

Zygmunt
(1913–1971)

Arthur
(1915–1978)

So many topics were censored and found unsuitable for children, that I often met with the same discouraging response: 'There is plenty of time . . . You are not old enough . . . When you are older . . .' Sometimes even a sharp: 'Don't bother your head about things which don't concern you . . .'.

As my family was not communicative and as I could not help bothering my head about things which did not concern me, I seldom received satisfaction in my 'quest' for family lore. I might have pestered harder, I might have been more of a nuisance, had I not been led to believe, in the best of faith, that there was a boundless stretch of time in front of us, that I would not need to wheedle information out of my relations. One day, when I was older they would voluntarily and graciously pass it on to me, for safe-keeping, as it were, and I would become the repository of the family annals. Had time been on our side I would now have, in spite of the passage of more than half-a-century, all that 'arcane' knowledge at my fingertips. But time was running out fast for us, only we did not know it.

I have a photograph of my maternal grandparents – it is a copy of a copy, and quite small. The original itself, which I have never seen, cannot have been of very good quality and when the copy was taken it was, no doubt, already bleached by time. It shows a man and a woman, a couple of modest background, dressed in their Sabbath best, posing for a rare, official photograph. It is an occasion. What occasion? I do not know. I can only make a reasonable guess. A wedding anniversary? Perhaps the twenty-fifth? My grandparents appear to be in their late forties – my grandfather, perhaps, in his fifties . . . They are both dark-haired – I see no silver threads – my grandmother's abundant hair is drawn back and piled on top of her head in the Edwardian fashion. Her features are regular and the face which would have been totally free of artifice is still pretty, but the expression upon it is sad – pinched. The eyes are large and luminous, but there is no smile in them. She is not tall, and the con-tours of the upper part of her body are those of a mature woman who has borne and breast-fed many children. She is simply dressed; the only concession in her attire to feminine frivolity is a white frill round the shallow V-neckline of her long-sleeved blouse. No trinket adorns her person, no string of beads around her neck, no ear-rings in her ear-lobes. She has placed her hand, in rather a touching gesture, on her husband's shoulder, so that one can see the tips of the fingers of her left hand resting on his right shoulder. It seems to be, at once, a gesture of reliance and of protection – of partner-ship.

Her husband, my grandfather, is very much taller than she, but not disproportionately so. Still, he towers above her, a tall, slim man – he appears rather narrow-shouldered – who holds himself ramrod straight. He is soberly dressed in a dark three-piece suit and a white shirt with a stiff wing-collar. The ends of his neatly knotted, narrow tie tucked inside his waistcoat. One can see the best part of his right hand, the thumb hooked in between the buttonholes of his waistcoat – the tips of the fingers only just hidden by the edge of his jacket. Just above his hand, there gleam the first few links of a double Albert chain. His cranium is well covered; the hair, rather coarse, was of a reddish-brown colour, I remember, and the slim, oval face is kindly, but I discern a certain slackness in it, he was not cerebral. His dark eyes, under well defined eyebrows, are not afraid to meet another's gaze and there is just the merest hint of a smile under his thick moustache.

These are the outer people posing for a memento photograph, long before I was born. The inner people? I lost them, all of them, when I was still a child, before they had fully revealed themselves to me as human beings and before I was fully able to appreciate them as such. I scan their faces. I look for signs to interpret. I do not see sadness or timorousness in the husband's face – both of which emotions appear in his wife's features. The spouses are not looking at each other – perhaps it was considered indecorous in those days – not deriving comfort and confidence from each other's presence in that way, but looking straight in front of them at the camera and the person operating it.

My grandfather was a carpenter; my grandmother a housewife. I know that as newly-weds, they set up home in a small village – Zastów – within the shadow of Greater Cracow and it was there that their first two children were born: Salomon in June 1894 and Eva, my mother, in February 1896.

When exactly they moved from Zastów I do not know, but by the outbreak of the Great War the family was well settled in a large suburb of Cracow – Czerwony Pradnik – and their last child, Arthur, was born there in 1915. I believe that my grandparents had turned to trade and ran a general grocery store throughout the Great War and for some years after it. When my parents' first child was born, in 1923, my elder brother Joseph, a very comfortable and snug sleeping place was prepared for him whenever he was brought on a visit to his grandparents. He was put on top of a pile of sugar-filled sacks, so that his life might be sweet. . . . This is one of very few snippets of family lore I possess about a period of my grandparents' and their children's lives, which must have covered many years.

The upbringing and education of nine children must have imposed a great strain on my grandparents, for their resources were always very meagre – this I understood quite early on in my life. Again, I know little about the children's schooling but a little more about the daughters' than the sons'. Of the four sisters – Eva, Regina, Anna and Sally – all, except Regina who remained at home and looked after the household in conjunction with her mother, went onto Secretarial College after leaving High School to prepare themselves for earning a livelihood. This testifies, I think, to an enlightened and far-sighted attitude on the part of both parents and daughters.

All four sisters were good-looking, shapely young women, but Eva, the eldest, who would one day become my mother, was the prettiest of them all. She was also gifted. She was sensitive to language and read widely. She liked poetry and, having an excellent memory, possessed a great fund of it off by heart. When I was a little girl, she used to sit by my bed in the evening and either read a fairy-tale or recite a poem to me. I preferred the latter. I used to say: 'Mamma, tell me a poem . . .' and the words would trip off her tongue – strange, beautiful, wondrous words – so smoothly, so musically. Yet, as far as I remember, I never saw anyone reading a book in the daytime; it was not the time for story-telling in my family. There were so many practical tasks and chores to be getting on with that those two activities, of which I was so fond, were confined to the evening, and even then 'dispensed' in very measured doses. They were looked upon, I think, when indulged in during the daytime, as a sign of indolence . . .

My mother wrote as nicely as she spoke and although she was very modest about it, I believe that she received the Polish Language End-of-Year Prize in her final year at High School. She sometimes let me look through her High School photograph album which she treasured. It contained a collection of informal individual and group photographs of young ladies, sometimes with an older lady, the teacher, amidst them, sitting on a lawn or under a tree, their light-coloured, ample skirts dappling the dark grass with white asymmetrical patches. Their young faces tender, their eyes bright with noble ideals, faith and hope – young women on the threshold of life . . . Not one of those photographs remains – they were all consumed in the conflagration that swept across Europe during the last war.

My mother was also an exceptionally fine needlewoman – a skill to which she would turn one day to feed her three children. As a young girl, she used to earn a little pocket-money for herself by helping with the sewing, lace-making and embroidery required in the preparation of a trousseau or a layette.

My mother and those of her siblings closest to her in age were bilingual, for learning in the educational establishments of the day was conducted in the country's official language – German – Franz Joseph's Empire having spread the enormous span of its wings far and wide. The knowledge of that language would, ironically, prove useful to both my parents later on, towards the end of their lives . . . My mother's secretarial training did not go to waste either, for she earned her living, for some years after the Great War, as a secretary. She did not marry until 1922, when she was twenty-six years old.

I remember her talking once about her journey to work – one of those rare glimpses for which I was so avid. Her place of work was a considerable distance from her home, and she travelled to it in an electric tram which she caught every morning at exactly the same hour. In that same tram, every morning, there travelled a tall, slender priest muffled from neck to foot in his black cassock. He was very young and very shy, she believed he had only just been ordained. The first time my mother saw him, they found themselves sitting opposite each other on the tram benches. The young Catholic priest raised upon the young Jewish girl a gaze of such extraordinary purity and sweetness that she felt her heart melt within her breast. After a few moments he modestly lowered his eyes either mindful of his calling in life, or else dazzled by the young maiden's beauty, for my mother was very lovely in the full freshness and innocence of her young womanhood. And although every morning they continued to be aware of each other's presence, he never again allowed his gaze to feast upon the young woman's face and form.

Of the five brothers – Salomon, the eldest, was conscripted into the army in the Great War. He was a fearless soldier – serving under Marshal Piłsudski – who distinguished himself in several battles and in 1918 received Poland's highest military award – The Virtuti Militari (the equivalent of the British Victoria Cross) – for bravery in the battlefield. Once discharged from the army, he secured the post of an official at the Cracow Jewish Council, in which he remained for the rest of his short life. Sometime in the 1920s, he married a nice Jewish girl, Josephine, who bore him three children. He was, also, one of the pioneer builders of Auschwitz, for when he arrived there as one of a group of political prisoners early in the ferocious Polish winter of 1941, there was not even the most primitive shelter awaiting the prisoners; they had to set to and build their hut from scratch.

The next brother, Izydor, was the only one of the nine children to go to Cracow University, where he read mathematics. In 1939, he too married a nice Jewish girl, Annie, and in 1940 became the proud father of a baby daughter. Zygmunt (Siggie) the fourth and the best looking of the brothers, was a salesman. The other two brothers, Marek and Arthur, became dental technicians.

My grandparents were well into their middle age when they stood in front of the camera posing for the photograph at which I have looked, time without number, in an effort to reach, to decipher the inner persons. My grandfather would die in October, 1939, aged seventy-five years. My grandmother's life would be terminated in the autumn of 1942, when she was seventy years old. Did my grandfather live in the tranquil knowledge of a natural death and a peaceful resting place in the Cracow Jewish Cemetery? Is that why the expression on his face, when two-thirds of his life are behind him, is one of contentment? Is my grandmother's heart oppressed with a sense of foreboding and dread? Does the expression of sadness on her face denote a prescience of her own, her children's and her grandchildren's fate?

A long time ago, when the war was in its third year and I was still a child, I understood, once and for all, that the dead do not write letters. They do not recount experiences. They do not complain about anguish, indignity and torment. They remain silent. But I remember them and feel the need, before I too am silenced forever, to speak of them and for them. I have, therefore, woven together with the very few scraps of family lore I possess, a tiny scant thing – a coverlet barely large enough for a baby. For the weave of my scraps is loose, the thread fine and apt to snap – when I speak of my mother, her parents, her brothers and sisters before I knew them. I have held onto this handful of scraps – which has been hard – not letting them shrink or fade. I would like to be able to endow those I have loved and mourned with the substance of human beings whose lives had a beginning, a middle and an end within the natural span of human existence. But the images I possess of their beginnings, their youth and middle-life are too few, too incomplete, bristling with question

7

marks and yawning with gaps . . . I wanted to separate my family, my loved ones, because they were part of me, as I am part of them – and we were bound by the finest of all human emotions, love – from that tragic, nameless, tomb-less human mass. To snatch them out of the anonymity of an ocean of ashes and breathe life into them again, if only on the written page . . . I cannot reconstruct what I do not know, what I have not witnessed – all I can attempt to do is to write my family's epitaph . . .

2 • Father's Family

By the time I was born in April, 1930, my parents had been married for eight years and my brother, Joseph, was already a seven-year-old schoolboy. I know next to nothing about the early years of their married life, except that their circumstances were comfortable. My own earliest childhood memory, I was not three years old at the time, is of my mother packing a suitcase for a 'playing away' match. She had placed it on the table and I had climbed onto a chair standing by it to watch her. She told me my father was going to play in a football match away from home, away from Cracow. My father was a footballer. I believe that for many years, in the 1920s, he was very popular with Jewish Cracow, being a footballer in the 'Maccabi' team. How I wish I had one of those photographs of which, again, there were so many at home. They, too, just like my mother's treasured snaps, turned to ashes in the gigantic bonfire that consumed my world. He appeared in these photographs clad in shorts and striped shirt, hugging enormous bunches of flowers to his breast. A tall, lean, athletically built man, his dark-brown hair tousled by the breeze, his eyes sparkling, his lips smiling . . .

Many years later, in the 1960s, in London, when my husband and I were buying our first home, a solicitor of Polish extraction was doing the conveyancing for us at his office in Chancery Lane. It turned out that he was a Jew from Cracow who had left the country in the late 1930s. Realising, at one point, in the course of a rather general conversation that I, too, was from Cracow and Jewish, he said, 'May I ask your maiden name?' 'Fischler' I replied. 'Oh' he said, 'when I was a lad, there was a footballer in Cracow by the name of Fischler. Never missed a match when he was playing. A fine footballer . . . Any relation of yours?' My whole being flooded with joy, I replied, 'Yes, he was my father.'

I always felt happy when my father and I were walking along the road together. He held my small hand – it felt so snug in his large one and I felt safe and special and all warm and good inside.

9

My father was a gentle man, incapable of hurting a fly and I soon became conscious, even at that early age, of the natural ease with which he related to people, of his good will and courtesy towards them. And he loved women, all women . . . He had that gift, which some men possess, of making a woman feel, irrespective of physical attributes and age, a queen, simply by virtue of belonging to the gentle sex . . .

One warm summer afternoon we were walking, holding hands, along a street in the pre-war Jewish Quarter of Cracow. When we reached the corner there sat, on a little canvas folding-chair, an old lady; a large wicker basket, nicely lined with a square of white muslin, full of freshly cooked broad beans standing by her side. There were many vendors in the streets selling all manner of home-made delicacies – baked, cooked, fried, boiled, steamed, roasted – but I was particularly fond of cooked broad beans and I knew that my father would buy me a bagful, just as in winter he always bought me a bag, only much smaller, of roast chestnuts. As we approached the old lady, a pair of lively dark eyes peered at us from under a ker-chief that covered her whole head and only just stopped at her eye-brows. She exclaimed with unfeigned pleasure, 'Henio!'. My father's first name was Henry, its affectionate diminutive being 'Henio'. 'Auntie Hannah!' My father took her work-worn hand in both of his, as if he were holding a most precious, a most fragile object. She was no relation. Just an old lady who knew and remembered him from his boyhood days. They chatted for a while of things past, of people they knew, of her children who had not done well in life and whom she was trying to help make ends meet by selling cooked broad beans. And she filled her tin measuring mug to the brim: 'A special measure for your little girl, Henio', and let them slide slowly and carefully into a newspaper cornet. My father put a coin in her hand, 'Oh, no need for change, Auntie Hannah.' We thanked her and walked away a little sad because of her troubles, a little glad because we were together and I was already popping the delicious beans into my mouth. Again, it was a lesson in human relations and, although at the time I did not understand it as such, it has remained with me.

My father was by nature and inclination a *bon viveur*. A loving husband and father, a man of courage and extreme kindness towards all living creatures, he was not by temperament and again, inclination, a family man. The confines of domesticity were too narrow, too binding for him. His expansive, naturally convivial nature would not be contained within domesticity's clearly marked borders. The world where he was most at home, fully at ease, truly in his element, that is apart from the football pitch, was the world of the café – I use the word advisedly in the broadest, most cosmo-politan sense – in the sense it had for me as a child. My father's favourite café in central Cracow, the one at which he spent most of his waking hours – and those varied greatly depending on whether he could, or wished, to leave the gaming table – was very much like, and offered the facilities of, a good club.

It was pleasant to enter its portals in late mid-morning, immacu-lately groomed, one's hand-made shoes snug about one's well-tended feet, to greet and be greeted by friends and acquaintances and to ensconce oneself in a deep leather arm chair. The day's news-papers, in their bamboo frames, were nicely laid-out, all ready for perusal. The waiter – who knew his clients, I dare say, better than they knew themselves – appeared instantly, as if at the touch of a magic wand, offering his services. As if on paws of velvet, he re-appeared in no time at all bearing upon his tray good, strong coffee and a glass of some other, more powerful, fine beverage, ready to flicker his lighter the moment my father's hand went in search of his cigarette-case. And as one sipped these beverages a delicious warmth and confidence spread through one's body dimming, obliterating even, the existence of domestic problems. As the day wore on the fine cuisine, the relaxed, quietly companionable atmosphere, the stimulating conversation with the additive of a little gossip, a little scandal, a mordant anecdote or two, the latest witty Yiddish joke, a few tips about this and that – rumour which was fast acquiring the weight of authenticity – made time slip by. The discreet wall-lighting was already adding its glow, dusk having in the meantime dropped its dark cloak over the city, to the general glow of well-being experienced by the habitués. My father was well liked and much appreciated by his companions for his *bonhomie*, his urbanity, his genuinely sympathetic ear when needed, his largesse when in a position to exercise it and his accomplishments which were always to hand. The evening might be spent at the billiard table, for my father was an accomplished billiards player, or round the supper table – a small, but intimate gathering of companions regaling each other with piquant appetisers, filling and re-filling each other's glasses with sparkling wine, adding yet more zest to the conversation. Often well into the evening and then late into the night, a serious game of poker would develop, and my father was a consummate poker player. How often have I heard those words as a child: 'If only I had been called away from the gaming table at three, even at four (in the morning) when I was winning hand over fist . . .?'

In the spring of 1933, when I was just three years old, we moved house. We went to live in Clean Street. I remember the move well for I was allowed, as a special treat, to ride, accompanied by a much older cousin, in the removal van which was transporting our chattels. I was very conscious of the fact that we were moving to CLEAN Street. My cousin enjoyed the ride immensely by making it thoroughly miserable for me; she would not stop teasing and tormenting me. 'Hmmm, Dirty Street . . . You did say you are moving to Dirty Street . . .' I protested. 'What did you say the name of the street you are moving to was?', she asked repeatedly – 'Clean Street . . .' 'Oh no, you are wrong; it is Dirty Street . . .' 'Oh dear, what a shame, imagine having to tell people "I live in Dirty Street . . .!" ' 'You did say you are moving to Dirty Street?' 'Clean Street', I would repeat emphatically yet again. 'Oh no, you didn't get the name right, you are only little, it is Dirty Street . . . I know, I heard the van driver say: "We are moving these people to Dirty Street." ' I was very upset by her taunting me in this merciless manner and as soon as we had arrived at our destination and the driver had set me down on the pavement I asked him, 'What is the name of this street, please?' 'Oh, it is Clean Street', he replied without a moment's hesitation. 'You see,' I said triumphantly to my cousin, 'it is Clean Street.' 'Oh no, you are wrong' was my cousin's prompt response, 'The driver probably can't read, lots of people can't, but I can. Some people don't even know where they are going. They just know the way, but they can't read the street names: You can't, can you?' I had to agree that I couldn't.

The move to Clean Street, to smaller, more modest accommodation placed us as a family on the slippery slope. In August of the same year – 1933 – whilst we lived in Clean Street my parents' third child was born, a baby brother, Bartuś. We had become a family of five. Within a year or two of the blue-eyed, fair-haired little boy's arrival, the football career, which had been slowly guttering – my father was forty years old – burnt itself out bringing about the natural progression of a family on the downward gradient. Times were hard. At the age of five I understood quite well the meaning of those words. My father, however, remained true to himself – he remained a free spirit. He would not be shackled by prosaic domesticity, nor extinguished by a staid nine to five job. His life-style continued albeit precariously; ours diminished, steadfastly . . .

I know nothing about my father's childhood, adolescence and young manhood. He was twenty-eight years old when he married my mother – I do not even know how they met – but it was, indeed, a love-match. His antecedents were very modest, even more so I think than my mother's. Neither of my parents was in the least religious, although in that respect their backgrounds differed, for my father had been brought up in a strictly Orthodox home, by strictly observant parents. Yet, like all other encumbrances, he eschewed his Orthodoxy and was every inch as assimilated as my mother. Deep down in their souls, however, both my parents were wholly Jewish.

My father liked to take me out and I loved being taken out by him. The world was a lovely, safe place when we were walking abroad together, my hand almost lost in his. I often accompanied him on his regular visits to his mother. I refer here to the late 1930s when I was already a schoolgirl, eight or nine years old. I sometimes felt that my father's love and tenderness for his mother were tinged with sadness and sorrow and perhaps guilt.

I know little about my paternal grandmother, but enough to realise that my life, compared to hers, has been so abundant in every kind of human experience that it is hard for me to believe that her blood flows in my veins. I cannot but marvel that this simple, self-effacing, almost childlike woman, so devoid of all ambition and aspiration, either material or spiritual, had engendered in some distant past a grandchild as avid, as eager for all experience that constitutes living as I have been. Looking back upon her life and mine, it seems that aeons of light-years divide me from this progenitrix of mine instead of a mere half-century.

My paternal grandmother came from Niepołomice, a small town, situated on the Vistula, with a large Jewish community known for its abject poverty. Grandmother Heim – she was always referred to by her maiden surname (I do not know why) for in fact, she was Leiba Fischler – was an orphan. She must have lost her parents when very young and, having no siblings or close relations, she left Niepołomice when she was twelve years old. She made the journey to Cracow in search of work on foot, crossing the wild and dangerous Niepołomice 'Jungle'. Instinctively, she made for the Jewish Quarter of Cracow for her first tongue, although she spoke Polish perfectly freely, was Yiddish, and the Jewish faith, strictures and traditions the only way of life she knew. There she found employment as a 'live-in' domestic help.

In the fullness of time, she met Samuel Fischler who had come from Vienna, also in search of work, and they were married. They started their married life in a small, rented room in that tangle of narrow streets and dark alleys, of gaunt, sunless tenements and squalid, hunch-backed little houses, that constituted the pre-war Jewish Quarter. But they were amongst their own. There, their three children came into the world in quick succession. Their first child, a son, who would become my father, was born in February, 1894; then came a baby girl, Rose, and then a baby boy who died in infancy. By the time I knew Grandmother Heim, she had been a widow for many years, my paternal grandfather having died in 1923.

Grandmother Heim lived with her daughter, Rose, her son-in-law, Dolek, and their two children – Siggie and Sophie. She kept house for them. 'Kept house' is rather a grandiloquent expression in this context, for rarely have I known people, who were relatively well-off, to live in such ignoble accommodation. Having entered No. 15 Sebastian Road – one of the bleakest, dingiest tenements in the Jewish Quarter – one crossed a dark, malodorous passage to find oneself in a circular inner courtyard. A courtyard whose naked intimacy was not unlike a bulging belly ripped wide open, its entrails hanging out in heavy, scarlet bunches. Narrow wooden staircases led from the courtyard to cramped little landings. Three tiers of wooden balconies – festooned with plump goose-down comforters and square, lumpy pillows in blood-red ticks slung over their rails to air – enclosed the gloomy, clammy courtyard in a tight embrace.

Sometimes, as we were about to climb the stairs – our relations lived on the first floor – the front door of the ground floor flat would creak open and remain slightly ajar. Two pairs of brown eyes, with whites like translucent porcelain, would shine brightly in the almost palpable obscurity around them. Two small boys with wispy cork-screw curls, their heads covered with skull-caps, peeping out through the gap in the open door – their curiosity, at the sound of footsteps, having got the better of them. I was as curious about them as they were about me. I understood well enough the poverty in which they lived, but only dimly perceived their exclusion from the rich stream of a child's life. I have often thought of those two grave, nameless faces glimpsed through a crack in the door. I doubt if a single person living in that tenement at the time survived the war – my family, with one exception, certainly did not. They, those children who would die having barely lived, would constitute with their parents and relations in the not too distant future the staple diet, the grist of the mills of death. The rich, the assimilated, those with a 'good' appearance and correct social connections were sometimes able to defer, occasionally even to escape, the death sentence passed upon them '*In absentia*' – but not the poor, Orthodox Jews – they were wholly and irrevocably doomed. Those children would vanish, as the breath that leaves the body vanishes – without a trace . . .

The familiar smell of onions, garlic and simmering giblets accompanied one's progress up the rickety, wooden staircase. Aunt Rose's flat had no entrance-hall or vestibule of any kind. One walked straight from the landing into the kitchen which was long, narrow and poorly lit. Its one window gave onto the wooden balcony, which itself was enclosed and dark, so that the light which filtered into the kitchen was already clotted with shadow and cold. Under the window stood a large wooden kitchen table at which, as often as not, Grandmother Heim would be standing kneading dough, or doing the ironing. Her face would light up as soon as she saw us. My father would hold her close to him and kiss and stroke her hair, and she would pass her hands over his head and face like a sightless person seeking, through touch, to reassure herself. She must have, once, been a big woman, tall and spare of bone. I had to stand on tiptoe and crane my neck to plant a kiss on her withered cheek. When I knew her, she was already in her seventies. To me, a young child, she looked ancient and bowed down, as she was, with age and a lifetime of hard work and care. She always wore the same sombre, loosely fitting, shapeless garments. As I became older and vain, I often wondered if she had any clothes 'for best' as I did, but I never saw her 'dressed up'. With the top button of her blouse undone, her sleeves pushed above the elbows, the skin of her neck and forearms was very creased and had that sickly, grey pallor of flesh which is never exposed to sun and wind and fresh air. Sometimes, as she shuffled around the kitchen, her swirling skirts would reveal a glimpse of her thick, swollen ankles. But it was her hands I marvelled at. They must have been magnificent hands, robust and capable with long, slender fingers. Their discoloured skin was now threaded with thick, black veins and the knuckles and joints stood out like hard round pebbles. Yet the fingers did their work with marvellous precision and swiftness.

15

The greeting over – my mind having registered the fact that the kitchen, as always, was spotlessly clean and smelt of good wholesome home-cooking – she would lead me to a small windowless passage, between the kitchen and the bedroom. There on the flap of an old Singer sewing machine sat a round wicker basket full of fresh, crusty rolls. She would hold it out for me to choose a roll. . . . Grandmother Heim had no conversation, not even small-talk; I would stand by the table, munching my roll, and watch her work. My father and she having exchanged all their brief items of news in Yiddish at the outset of the visit, she got on with her work. She might be plaiting a *challa*, her fingers moving with extraordinary agility and sureness. Her dough was so light, so malleable she could make it do anything she wanted. She would then dip a goose quill in a saucer of beaten up egg-yolk, smartly brush the *challa* up and down with it, and pop it into the oven to bake. Or she would be doing her ironing, the heavy, ember-filled iron gliding effortlessly over a garment. She always had a small bowl of water to hand, tinted the palest blue and from time to time she would dip a little white rag in it, squeeze it out, dab at an obstinate wrinkle or two and then apply the sizzling iron over it. And the stack of perfectly laundered, exquisitely ironed and folded shirts would rise . . .

Looking back and remembering that the only sanitation in the flat was a primitive water tap in the kitchen, not even a sink, I am now, as then, filled with infinite admiration for my grandmother. How I wish I had plied her with questions about her childhood, her youth, her life as a young wife and mother . . . I never did . . . She gave me no encouragement, for in her innate modesty and self-effacement she did not think herself, or her life, interesting enough to chat about. She never volunteered to speak about herself.

Her generation, just like the children in the ground floor flat, was doomed. An old woman, an Orthodox Jewess with pronounced Semitic features and as guileless as a new born babe, she did not have the slenderest chance of survival – and I know, she would not have wished to live in a world in which there was no room for her children, her grandchildren, her people. She would tread the same path as the children – 'tread' methaphorically, for when the time came to follow that path she would have to be borne along it, for she was both too old and too frail to walk . . .

Aunt Rose, my father's younger sister, and her husband, Uncle Dolek, were publicans who ran a prosperous pub in one of Cracow's roughest districts. It was something of a mystery to the family how

16

they managed to do it successfully, for they were both, but particularly Uncle Dolek, timid, unassertive people. Uncle Dolek would not have known how to say 'boo' to a goose. He was a big, flabby man; his eyes lacked lustre, his nose was large and fleshy, his clean-shaven chin weak. He was a gentle, kindly man whose whole life was his family. He lived, as much as worked, only for them. Whatever personality they had as a couple was embodied in Aunt Rose. She was tall and slim and must have been a strikingly good-looking girl with her delicate complexion, dreamy blue eyes and a mop of extraordinarily luxuriant, curly, auburn hair. She dressed fashionably and wore perfume. I do not think that she had ever needed to so much as lift a finger in running her home. She was waited on, as were the children, hand and foot, by her mother – Grandmother Heim.

Aunt Rose adored both her children, but Siggie, the first-born son, was the apple of her eye. He could do no wrong, although the daughter, Sophie, as time and circumstances proved, was a singularly sweet and unselfish person. Aunt Rose, it was felt, generally had ambitions and aspirations for her children far above the parents' station in life and, perhaps, far outside the children's ability to fulfil. The children were pampered, cosseted and molly-coddled to a degree that drew great disapprobation from the family. My father was extremely fond of his sister, as she was of him, and whenever he dropped in on her – as he did often, mostly at the pub, for she relied on his counsel and needed his emotional support, and he appreciated the pleasure and affection she manifested on seeing him – she never failed to send a parcel of sweetmeats to us, the children.

Our existence became very precarious – really a hand-to-mouth existence. My father – I find it infinitely painful to write about my father; my heart contracts with grief – grief for which I have no words . . . There are things in one's life which one has acknowledged to oneself and accepted as being immutably true; but to reveal them, to impart one's knowledge of them to the world at large, is quite another matter. To tell the truth, the whole truth and nothing but the truth is a brave undertaking and I have never been brave. My acts of courage, such as they have been, were always motivated by fear. The whole truth? I shuddered at the very idea. I feared the censure, the disapproval, the raised eyebrow, individually and collectively, of the world at large. I feared them for him and when I was young and vulnerable and mindful of the world's opinion, by implication for myself. The thought that I, his dearly loved child, should tarnish his name, bring opprobrium upon his person in the eyes of the world, whose good opinion always seemed so desirable to me, was unthinkable. But now, that one's view of the world has fully crystallised only the truth, stark, naked, often ugly, seems worth revealing . . . For if one makes up one's mind to reveal, one must possess, I think, the courage to hold back nothing. Until now I have lacked that essential ingredient . . . I believe, now, that truth and shame need not go hand in hand.

Many years ago, over half-a-century ago, I drew a veil over certain events in my life. I struck a tacit agreement with my subconscious to remain silent, to lie still. I would not probe its murky depths for fear of dredging up that most painful wreck – the loss of my parents, brother, family . . . In spite of the passage of time, I have never stopped smarting from that loss. It is only now, when the sands of my own life are running out, that I have found the courage to plunge my hand into the turgid waters of that subconscious and draw out, into the broad light of day, that tragic wreck, so that it may yield up facts, memories and impressions which I find, when the shrouds and layers of time are peeled away, well preserved and intact, as if time itself had taken a rest these last fifty years.

Literature often describes parents and relations with total open-ness and candour. The father figure not infrequently looms large in such descriptions. The father's character, with all its weaknesses and strengths, and its attendant consequences upon the wife and children, is explored at great length and described in minute detail. Sometimes the father emerges as a figure of fun; sometimes as a figure of pathos. He may be a ruthless business tycoon, merciless in the sight of men, tender and lenient with his own family. Not infrequently he is a feckless, irresponsible man who leads his family a 'terrible dance'. There is virtually no end to the possibilities and permutations . . . A writer worth his salt will paint a convincing picture and elicit from the reader the desired response. It is perfectly valid, I think, to aim to obtain a particular response or responses – often matching one's own feelings. All the techniques employed to elicit the emotion, or emotions, which the writer himself has felt, still feels, are again perfectly valid when the father has ended his days in what we accept as a 'natural occurrence' – a natural death. The pain tugs at my heart and the question rises up time and time again: 'Do I have the right? Does anyone have the right?'

Six million human beings perished. As a statistic that multitude has always appeared in my mind's eye as a broad, endless, greyish-black band, rather like a colourless rainbow . . . A neutral, opaque stripe runs through its centre; like a fresh, white page not yet written upon – representing the children – those who have not left a ripple upon the waters of life. That central stripe is caught along its outer edges between two much broader stripes, speckled grey-black, like a scattering of ashes. The outer stripes represent the young, middle-aged, old men and women . . . people . . . some of whom were truly good, even saintly . . . But on the whole, they were just people who had lived, or who had had, at least, a taste of life, however bitter, however sweet and who were endowed with all the failings that flesh is heir to . . . The sun has set in my rainbow. It is night-time. They march in rows of five. They have the meagre, shadowy outlines of phantoms . . .

The Cracow Jews went to their death in rows of five.

3 • At My Grandparents'

By the time we had moved to Clean Street, my maternal grand-parents and their three unmarried daughters had been living in central Cracow for some time. No. 3 Wielopole was a seven-storey apartment block. It had no lift. The rent for that reason was within the family's reach. They lived on the sixth floor. Wielopole was an interesting address to have – for it was Cracow's Fleet Street. No. 1 was a large, tall, imposing corner building, the nucleus of pre-war Cracow's press industry.

Grandmother, who was by then in her middle-sixties, descended and ascended the six floors of stairs at least once, sometimes twice, a day. She did and carried, in person, all the family shopping. Daily, she went to a nearby market for her vegetables, fruit and all fresh produce. Dry, long-term provisions she obtained in Wielopole itself from a well-stocked, very much a nineteenth century general store, owned and run by a slow, ponderous, elderly Jew. Grandmother and he got on very well, for he understood perfectly, every turn, twist and bye-law of applied economics. Climbing the six storeys of stairs, laden with heavy, bulging shopping bags cannot have been easy for her. I never heard her complain – neither about the stairs, nor about the volume or weight of her shopping. Nor have I ever known her to be unwell or to have a 'lie in'. The adjective 'indis-posed' was never used in the family. Grandmother got up, every morning, at the crack of dawn and was at her post, as it were, clean, neat, unruffled, but busy, the aroma of freshly ground coffee waft-ing from the kitchen. She was totally devoid of feminine vanity. I am certain that her lips had never known the silken touch of a lipstick, nor her cheeks the caress of a powder-puff. She considered herself old. She seemed very old to me.

The apartment at Wielopole was spacious, the rooms whose doors were folded back in the daytime giving on to each other rather like a picture gallery. It was modestly furnished – except for my grand-parents' room which contained a very fine, sombre bedroom suite –

with an assortment of old sticks of furniture, all greatly cherished and regularly dusted and polished. Its appeal lay (I liked it immensely) in its impeccability, its warm, unpretentious home-liness, its pleasant feminine touches. Genteel poverty? Perhaps. I did not see it in that light then.

The kitchen, which gave onto the back of the building and from which one could see the printers at their presses, had a very large balcony. In good weather there were colourfully striped deck-chairs disposed about it in which I liked to sit holding a newspaper, most likely upside down, pretending to read. The hub of all domestic activity was the kitchen. Grandmother ran a very tight ship indeed, as far as house-keeping went. She was the most frugal housewife I have ever known, yet a good manager. She succeeded in stretching her modest house-keeping allowance and somehow made ends meet, so that one was not aware, when the family sat down to a meal, that the month was coming to a close, as was often the case in other households.

The whitewashed kitchen was roomy, cheerful, full of light and warmly welcoming. The pine-wood floor was scrubbed every morn-ing by Grandmother and Aunt Regina working in tandem – their hitched-up skirts tucked into their waistbands. All meals were taken in the kitchen at the large family table which, at times, accommo-dated a dozen of us. There was always enough food to go round, even when one or two of the children or grandchildren turned up unexpectedly as sometimes happened. Everyone in the family knew that Grandmother's house was the one place where you could always count on a hot, wholesome meal.

Grandmother herself never sat at the table with her children. She had a small folding-table all to herself near the stove. I suppose she was none too nimble with a knife and fork, whereas her children were. I remember the everyday tablecloth so well. It was the same one every day and, yet, it was fresh every day. How and when it was washed, dried and ironed I do not know. What I found so attractive about it was that it had no wrong side to it. One side was red with white flowers; the other side was white with red flowers.

Aunt Sally, one of the two bread-winners, sat at the head of the table. Grandfather, who sat at the other end facing her, was more skilled in the use of 'new-fangled' table implements and liked to eat with his children. Aunt Anna, the other bread-winner, sat on Grandfather's right and I, opposite her, on his left. He used to cut up my food for me, but he never needed to urge me to eat up. I loved

Grandmother's cooking. Uncle Izydor, the eternal student, was often present and, towards the end of the month, when the shortage of funds was keenly felt and spirits generally flagged, one or two of the other sons would also put in an appearance. A good solid meal fortified not only the body, but also uplifted the soul.

Lunch was always a three-course meal. We started with a nourishing soup, served piping-hot; there was no end to Grandmother's inventiveness in that domain. The main course was either meat or farinaceous; if the former, then mince meat; again, under so many different savoury, richly-spiced guises; if the latter, the variety of grandmother's pasta products, their lightness and texture, their fillings and sauces, all home-made, testified to pure culinary genius. The puddings of my childhood! The cool, tangy fruit mousses in the summer; the hot, creamy rice pudding garnished with sweet, fleshy prunes in the winter; the apfel-strudel, at all seasons, the raisins tumbling out like small amber beads, the sprinkling of brown sugar and cinnamon having turned into a rich, burnished glaze. My mouth waters to this day when I remember how I waited, already pleasantly replete, but still with ready appetite, for the two large pudding dishes or platters, from which we served ourselves, to be placed at each end of the long table . . . Very little talking was done at the table. Aunts Sally and Anna were immersed in their library books, the only time when reading was not looked upon askance. Uncle Izydor, who enjoyed special privileges in that respect, always ate with his textbook propped up against the water jug.

One of the rooms in the apartment contained a discreetly positioned couch where Uncle Izydor, a permanent non-paying guest, whose very meagre and uncertain income was derived from tutoring wealthy parents' offspring, spent his evenings and nights burning the midnight oil.

By the mid-thirties, officially, the apartment was inhabited by the parents and their three daughters – two of whom – Aunts Sally and Anna, were earning a livelihood. It was upon their shoulders that the whole fragile edifice of maintaining the home and a modest, but civilised, way of life rested. Today, I would say that my grandparents and their daughters were perfect examples of *petit bourgeois* respectability, dependability and integrity. Rent and bills came first and foremost – it was a matter of honour – and then the coat was cut, most prudently, most economically, according to what was left over.

And still only two of the nine children were married; the eldest son, Salomon, and Eva, the eldest of the four daughters, my Mamma.

To marry off four daughters, none of whom carried even the most modest dowry, was no small, no easy matter. Give or take a year or two, the young ladies were approaching that critical age, as far as matrimony was concerned, of being thirty years of age. In the 1930s the marriage market was not only volatile, it could afford to be extremely whimsical. The silver-tongued marriage brokers had their work cut out; they had to use their natural talents with great sagacity and tact to earn a commission, even when the young lady herself was an appealing proposition. Not having a dowry, not being in her early twenties any more, a young lady could find herself described, not within her own, or her parents' hearing, of course, in the marriage broker's crude parlance as 'difficult merchandise to shift . . .' Parents worried greatly about their daughters' future – and many an unhappy and unsuitable marriage was contracted under the pressure of that worry – especially when the freshness, the fine bloom of youth began to fade.

I knew none of this at the time and I would not have understood any of the implications which having three unmarried daughters, no longer tenderly young, signified emotionally, economically, socially. With hindsight, however, I think that their daughters' protracted maidenhood must have constituted a source of both grief and concern for my grandparents. But griefs and concerns were not given vocal outlet, certainly not within a child's hearing, and although I would come to plumb, and witness, the greatest depths of human suffering, the early years of my childhood were free from it. Our life was hard, but it was the only life I knew. I was a loved, cherished child. I belonged.

Aunt Sally, the youngest of the four sisters, although generously endowed with physical attractiveness and the qualities, in abundance, which would turn her into an excellent wife and mother, knew that her parents could offer nothing in the way of incentive beyond the intangible gifts of blessing and prayer. A fact which greatly diminished her chances in the marriage market. Young men sought and appreciated, as they are wont to do, that initial gesture, a dowry, to render the grave venture into marital bliss and the attendant responsibilities a little less onerous. Sally was an emancipated, self-supporting woman. She had worked for her livelihood all her adult life – being a legal secretary in one of Cracow's oldest and most respected Jewish law practices. Although a very independent and self-reliant person, she lived at home with her elderly parents and two unmarried sisters. In that distant past, young women did not set up on their own; they lived with their family and hoped that, in the fullness of time, a suitable husband, heaven-sent, would materialise.

Both by nature and from conscious choice Sally was a pillar of respectability. She took pride in the fact that the domestic mechanism, of which she was one of the two chief supporters, functioned like a perfectly tuned, well-oiled engine. She took pride in the fact that the rent and bills were paid on time, that all commitments were met when due. She liked a well-ordered, well-planned, predictable life.

Aunt Anna, the second bread-winner of the household, was also a legal secretary. At that stage of my childhood she was a closed book. She said little and she did not seem to have much interest in very young children. Yet, she was aware of my presence, as I was aware of hers, each of us for a different reason. She was strict, even hurtful, at times, although all corrections and admonitions addressed to me were delivered in a quiet, even voice. She would say: 'sit up, don't slouch,' or, 'don't talk with your mouth full,' or, 'tuck your tummy in,' and invariably, 'are your hands clean?' I enjoyed looking at her. She was a very attractive, elegant, self-possessed young woman. Starting with Mamma, I lived among good-looking, fashion-conscious, vain women of slender means. Anna was, perhaps, the vainest of the four sisters. Although I most often saw her in the same tobacco-brown fine-wool dress – immaculately brushed and pressed – I noticed that she contrived to give the old dress every so often a new, discreetly eye-catching touch which made me contemplate her with added pleasure: a snowy white piqué collar, a modest, but charming, ivory brooch, a neatly knotted silk scarf, its subtle colours complementing her smooth, creamy complexion; a nicely crafted belt around her trim waist. I see her to this day in all her loveliness – Anna, my tragic, much loved Aunt.

The third sister, Regina, a sweet-natured, generous woman, was perhaps the best suited of all four sisters to wifehood and motherhood. There was nothing she was more adept at, nothing she enjoyed more, than creating, with wisdom, affection and innate understanding, a home within which a close-knit, devoted family thrived. I never saw Grandmother evince preference for one or another of her children, but as Regina stayed at home and shared all its chores, tasks and cares with Grandmother, a special, very close bond developed between mother and daughter and, in the light of future events, I understood that Regina was her favourite.

24

Regina waited on us at table, thoughtfully and graciously. She, herself, would only sit down to eat when we had all finished and the table had been cleared of debris. Whilst Regina was eating, Grandmother was already tackling the washing up of which there was an enormous stack. Regina, having finished her meal, gave a hand with the drying.

My earliest, most concrete memory of my grandparents' home and of my relationship with my aunts dates back to the summer of 1933 – a year which proved to be a watershed for European Jewry. In August of that year my younger brother, Bartuś, was born. He was going to be born at home because, as I believe, clinic or hospital fees were outside my parents' reach. Arrangements had been made for my elder brother and myself to stay with relations for a few days. Our home was not large and it just did not do for young children to be about during a confinement and a period of convalescence following it. I was farmed out to my maternal grandparents. The three maiden sisters shared a bedroom. It was known as the 'Young Misses' Bedchamber'. The only room to be furnished and decorated entirely in white. It was as clean, neat and fresh as a bandbox. It fell to Aunt Sally's lot to share her white, virginal bed with me. I have retained a shadowy impression that the prospect of having a restless, wriggly little creature in her bed, night after night, did not please her. One could hardly blame her. She needed a good night's rest. She had to be up early every morning. She wished to be fresh and wide-awake at the office. It was a long working-day which started at eight o'clock in the morning.

I liked my aunts' room. I liked the bed I was to sleep in. It was an exciting change, but I was not happy. Every evening I climbed into Sally's cool, comfortable bed and she tucked me up for the night; she did not cuddle me; she did not kiss me; she did not tell or read me a story. 'Goodnight' was all I got. I missed Mamma sorely. Perhaps it was a foretaste of the yearning, of the sadness that ten years hence would have become an integral part of my being, an inseparable life's companion . . .

When my baby brother was about twenty-four hours old, Sally – armed with a nicely arranged sheaf of fresh flowers – and I travelled to Clean Street. She went to offer her congratulations to her sister and to see the new baby; I to receive a hug from Mamma and to give a kiss to my baby brother. That was how Sally explained things to me. I was throbbing with excitement. When we arrived, we went straight to Mamma's bedroom. I was taken aback to see Mamma in bed, for it was still daylight. Sally had not prepared me for that and I had already understood that being ill, tired, taking a nap in the daytime was not encouraged in my family. What rendered me even more shy and awed was the sight of Grandmother Heim in her shabby finery, sitting stiffly on a high-backed chair, her poor, work-worn hands folded in her lap, by Mamma's bedside. The only time, in the twelve years during which I knew her, when I saw her sitting down; the only time when I saw her outside her kitchen; my earliest, unblurred memory of her.

I approached the bed and bending forward buried my face in Mamma's hair. She said: 'Give Grandmother Heim a kiss and then go and see little Bartuś – he is a dear little boy.' I kissed Grandmother Heim lightly on the cheek, but she held me to her stroking my hair. She then let me go saying: 'You must be impatient to see your new brother.' I tiptoed across the room to the corner where the basinet stood. The open bedroom door hid it from view and, shutting out the daylight, rendered the corner shadowy. My own face just above the edge of the basinet, I saw a puckered little face framed by a bonnet and two tiny clenched fists. Bartuś was peacefully asleep sucking on a dummy. I put out my hand and tore it out of the tiny mouth. I drew on it frantically a couple of times. His eyelids did not even flutter. I put it back in his mouth and his lips closed round it. My one pang of jealousy had spent itself never to reappear. Standing on tiptoe, leaning forward I brushed his soft, warm cheek with my lips. He did not stir. I gazed at him unable to get my fill, when Sally joined me. She bent down and inspected the baby closely. She said: 'A good baby, look how peacefully he sleeps.' Gently, she drew her finger across his cheek. He slept on. We would, all, love him dearly. He and I became great playmates.

The windows of our flat in Clean Street gave onto a square, paved courtyard. It was good for skipping. I used to come down with my skipping-rope. Mamma could keep an eye on me just by popping her head out of the window. There was her small daughter, safe and sound, skipping, skipping, skipping . . .

There was in the courtyard a stout wooden door heavily chained and padlocked. It intrigued me. I asked the caretaker about it and he said: 'It's a private store-room.'

One day when I came down to do my quota of skipping, I saw that the chains and padlock had been removed – the twin-leaved door flung wide open revealed a group of men working inside the store room; they were sweeping, brushing, scrubbing, distempering.

Some days later a van pulled up outside our building and huge crates were unloaded and carried into the store-room one after another, and then, after a while, carried out again – empty. They contained ice-cream making equipment. A handful of men appeared, black-haired, sun-tanned, with liquid brown eyes and wide, friendly smiles. They spoke a musical foreign language; they sang and whistled whilst they worked using their hands with quick, round movements. We had an ice-cream factory in our courtyard. The men running it were Italian. Mamma said the Italians had left their wives and children behind in their beautiful country, in Italy. They had come to Cracow to earn a living. I was strictly forbidden to approach the factory door. I still did my daily skipping practice, but in the most distant corner of the yard. One of the Italian men would come out with a tightly packed cornet of the most delicious ice-cream and hand it to me smiling. I was not even able to say '*grazie*'. Mamma said they missed their wives and children.

Bartuś was a two-year old toddler when we found ourselves on the move again. We were a family of five, but we gravitated between accommodation suitable for two, at best three. Rent constituted a very large chunk of my parents' limited and uncertain income. Landlords did not like letting a small flat to a large family. After years of manœuvring and staving off, Mamma, upon whom fell the painful and onerous duty of finding new, cheaper accommodation, adopted a procedure which, in time, became standard. She would rent a flat for a family of three. Bartuś and I would stay with relations whilst our parents and Joseph were moving in. After a 'decent' settling in period had elapsed, I would be 'smuggled in'. Then, some weeks later, via the same circuitous route, Bartuś would join us. Invariably the landlord acquiesced with the injunction that 'we behaved quietly and did not disturb the other tenants . . .'.

The move to 'The Officers' Village' was our last voluntary move. It was to be our happiest home; the one in which we would live the longest; the last one we entered as free human beings to continue our ordinary, harmless existence. Four years before light ceded to darkness.

27

4 · The Officers' Village

'The Officers' Village', a residential suburb of Cracow, derived its name from the many military establishments, administrative offices, barracks and quarters situated on its fringes. It was in this very pleasant, as yet, sparsely populated area that my parents rented a small, brand-new flat. The blocks of flats which were modern, airy and human-scale were inhabited in the main by white-collar workers with their families and young couples setting up their first home. There lived, also, a fair sprinkling of elderly, retired people. The villas, spacious and gracefully proportioned, were inhabited, mostly, by high-ranking officers and their families. They were set in large, well-kept gardens. The streets and avenues were wide, the grass verges trim and stately old trees lived cheek by jowl with brush green saplings.

'The Village' was bright and spick-and-span; the very sky had a pale luminosity and the air a soft freshness which I had not known before. There was nothing to remind one of the dark, dank, fetid tenements of the Cracow Jewish Quarter. Its atmosphere, unhurried and unharried, was one of lightness. The suburb was dotted with many large, vacant lots overgrown with coarse grass, speckled with dandelions and bristling with thistles and stinging-nettles which smote and stung our legs, as we ran and played in them. And there was a shallow, clear river, running across not too distant meadows, in which we paddled in the summer. We had never lived close to nature before and discovering it, we, the children, found ourselves in wonderland.

We lived in a long road planted with acacia trees whose heady fragrance and delicate foliage were part of the ease, the well-being the roominess of the suburb – named after a bishop whose piety and good works had become a legend in his own lifetime. The pace of life was dignified, even and predictable. The seasons, clearly delineated, followed each other and each wore its rich mantle of beauty with justifiable pride. Respectability seemed to be the keynote of the suburb. Its inhabitants were cordial, quiet people – friendly, but not inclined to meddle in the affairs of others. Even though our family circumstances were extremely modest, life in the suburb appeared, to me, sweet and smooth. I had not yet learnt about putting a brave front on a troubled mind or a grieving heart, but it was a time of learning, both time and learning being of the essence.

All our needs were catered for within the suburb. There was a school (St Anne's Primary School for Girls which I started attending) a church, a public library, a cinema, a cemetery and a number of shops. As is common on the Continent, the ground floor of a block of flats often contains a shop. And so it was in our road. Mr Blochmann – a man with singularly Semitic features and a singularly devout convert to Catholicism, kept a grocery store just a few doors away from where we lived. I would pop into the store to get the day's shopping for Mamma. The Blochmanns were an interesting family and I did not mind waiting, however long it took, my turn to be served. Mr Blochmann was a cripple, having had a leg amputated as a result of a serious wound sustained in the First World War – 'Laid on the altar of my own, personal patriotism' – was how he used to put it, but moved about on his crutches with greater speed and agility than many people did on two perfectly good legs. He had a terrible temper, which he seemed unable to control. Whenever he was angry the blood would rush to his face and black veins, thick as rope, would stand out on his temples. He also liked to speak his mind; his outspokenness cost him dear. He would lash out, preferably at his son, but if he was not around then at humanity at large, and not infrequently at a customer who had incensed him for some reason, calling upon his adopted God, in irascible tones, to be his witness. Both character traits not only lost him customers, but earned him not a few enemies.

Mrs Blochmann, who used to help her husband at peak periods, was as slow and lethargic in her movements, as he was brisk and energetic. She was a stout, flaccid woman with bovine, blue eyes and tightly permed hair. They had two children. The boy, who had taken after his mother, was a perfect Aryan specimen, blue-eyed, blond, built like a bullock – with brains to match. He was permanently in the dog-house with his father who resented his laziness and rudeness. He hung around the shop ready, the moment his father's back was turned, to plunge his hand into the till, or, at least, into a jar of sweets. He was fleet of foot and, generally, slippery as an eel. It was not easy for Mr Blochmann, encumbered as he was by his crutches, to pin the lad down, but he had his technique and sometimes it paid off. He would corner his offspring, make him bend over a barrel of salted herrings or sauerkraut and one crutch firmly embedded in his armpit, lay into his son with the other with positive glee. We, the youngsters, listened to his howling with relish, for he was a bully and generally disliked. His sister, quiet and timid, bore the brunt of her father's Jewishness. She was a female edition of Mr Blochmann and her antecedents were written, quite plainly, across her brow. The Blochmanns' had been a love match. He had embraced his wife's faith, whilst they were courting, to prove himself worthy as a prospective son-in-law. He was very fond of regaling his customers with the details of their, even for those days, extremely decorous courtship and how he had been, after all kinds of arduous character tests, finally, admitted into the bosom of his wife's Gentile family. He always referred to his wife as 'A better class of person' – a phrase which, I noticed, often called forth an ironical smile on the part of the person he was addressing. Mr Blochmann was always very nice to me, perhaps out of a lingering sentiment for his own Jewish background and family.

It was I, often helped by Joseph, who did the family shopping. Mamma very rarely set foot outside the house before late afternoon. She was a very attractive woman, if a little plump, and extremely *soignée*. She would not have dreamt of descending the stairs and venturing out into the open, into the public gaze, before every 'i' had been dotted and every 't' had been crossed as far as her appearance was concerned. Only in the late afternoon, freshly bathed, carefully corseted, discreetly *maquillaged* and in spite of her slender means, for she was a most accomplished needlewoman, quietly, but fashionably dressed, did she sally forth. She did so to pay her daily, ritual call at her parents' house, in the heart of Cracow, where an informal social gathering took place every evening.

Although I did not realise it at the time, looking back now and examining events, actions, words with meticulous care, I believe that Mamma was loath, in those days, before her world, her life had been shattered beyond repair, to have dealings with tradesmen. Not only did she see it as demeaning, but also because our very meagre shopping list reflected our very meagre way of life. Had it been sumptuous, had she had a servant to carry her shopping basket, had it been filled to the brim with high quality provisions, she might have felt differently about the daily shopping expedition.

Mamma looked after her household herself, with only occasional domestic help, but when she appeared in public she looked, as she was, every inch a lady. I do not think that her social status was an issue on which she would have been prepared to compromise and thus place it in jeopardy. In fact, she had none, except by virtue of her appearance, her personality, her innate refinement. She had a fertile imagination which, to some degree, I have inherited and her social 'standing' was purely a figment of that imagination.

I loved to watch Mamma getting ready to go a-visiting. I found the 'abracadabra' of that ritual spell-binding. The jars, phials and bottles that accompanied it seemed to contain magic potions. She must have laid her plans very carefully, in the course of the day, as she went about her daily tasks; what she would wear, what final effect she wished to achieve – for when she started to implement them it was plain to see that they had been meticulously worked out in her head, as she proceeded, step by step, to turn a vision into reality. The prelude to the ritual was a set of pale, lace-trimmed undergarments laid out on the bed.

Mamma had a lovely face with a healthy, clear complexion. Her nose was short and straight and perfectly Aryan; the nostrils delicately fashioned. I was conscious of the merest hint of a sepia shadow playing in their corners. Her eyes were very fine – large and green – their expression grave, almost sad, when her face was in repose. She wore her straight, black hair combed back from her round, smooth forehead and temples and twisted into a heavy chignon over the nape of her neck. Mamma never varied that rather severe hairstyle. Her mouth was full, sensuous and when her lips parted in a smile revealing her magnificent, gleaming teeth – of which she was justly proud – I felt I was basking in the warmth of the sun. It was family lore: 'Eva has never needed a filling . . .'. She was of medium height with a feminine, well-rounded figure. Mamma was vain of her hands; they were small and elegant, the skin unusually white and soft, the nails, carefully tended, like rose petals. She had a reciprocal arrangement with a Jewish manicurist. They had known each other for years. She used to drop in on Mamma once a week 'to do' her nails. In exchange, Mamma would carry out for her some alteration or refurbishment to a garment. We used to say that Mamma had 'Golden Hands' for there was no feminine skill they did not possess or could not learn to acquire. I remember, vividly, every one of her outfits – she did not have many – quality rather than quantity was what she believed in.

She had donned my favourite outfit; an austerely tailored grey suit, an immaculate white blouse peeping from under the jacket and against the deep blackness of her hair there glowed a cherry-red, soft velour deer-stalker worn at the merest suggestion of a rakish angle. There was an added inducement to looking good this evening: her sister Sally was being courted and the young man in question would be present at the gathering.

I loved Mamma most tenderly and I gloried in her loveliness. When I close my eyes very tight and concentrate very, very hard, I can still call up that dearly loved image from the pitch-black, bottomless well of time. Her face floats into view – sometimes as it was before the mirror had cracked, but more often as I saw it during the last few months of her life . . .

About this time, in the late 1930s, Sally was being very discreetly courted by a young dentist – Lolek – a presentable and ambitious young man. I liked him very much. He used to tell me the most gruesome stories about teeth he had extracted, teeth he was going to extract. He wished to establish himself in a good residential quarter of Cracow where he would come to be recognised and appreciated, as an able dentist and a man of integrity. He hoped, in time, to enjoy the fruits of a successful career together with a secure, happy family life.

To set oneself up in practice, however, at a good address with a fully equipped modern surgery required a great deal of money – money which he did not possess. His parents, people of modest means, having parted with all their savings to provide him with a higher education, were unable to offer further assistance. He sought to combine, in marriage, true affection with financial advantage. That he was genuinely attracted to Sally, truly fond of her was indisputably obvious to everyone, yet the head triumphed over the heart and he stopped courting her as discreetly as he had begun.

In the meantime, our own life took on a slightly rosier, a slightly more hopeful hue. Mamma, in person, was the very best advertisement for her skills and talents; her truly professional craftsmanship, her quiet, unerring taste. Gradually, word got round The Village that the attractive, elegantly attired lady, who picked her way, daily, to the late afternoon tram to town, could 'create' an outfit to make one's friends view one with new, increased interest . . . That she was reliable, helpful, very nice to deal with and . . . reasonable in the matter of emoluments. Little by little Mamma won over a clientele and established herself. The officers' wives were gracious and grace-ful women. Whether young, middle-aged or elderly they spared no effort to enhance and preserve their appearance. They were fashion-conscious women who led lively social lives, who needed, and liked, to ring the changes in their apparel. A dressmaker who could pro-duce a garment at reasonable cost, was already a find, but one who possessed style and flair, whose products had the cut and finish which stamped them with a touch of distinction, a touch of class, was indeed a treasure. And the ladies had daughters whose first serious dress was, invariably, the first Holy Communion dress. Mamma's Holy Communion dresses were pure floating dreams – demure, light, delicate – they were as beautiful as gentle white doves poised for flight; they were much admired. The ladies, who were also practical, did not seem to mind that they had been pro-duced by Jewish hands. They had the same understanding relation-ship with Mamma as Grandmother had with her grocer at Wielopole. They were gentlewomen, the officers' wives, delicious to look at, agreeable and beautifully mannered. And they were principled, honourable women who paid their bills on time ... After a time, Mamma took on an assistant, a country girl, 'a natural', Mamma said, whose stitches were so small, even and neat as to be virtually invisible and she did not mind giving a hand with the household tasks.

The Jewish families living in The Village could have been counted on the fingers of one hand, but, as it happened, there were two in our apartment block: Ourselves on the second floor and Mr and Mrs Haas, a young, newly married couple, on the first floor. Mr Haas was an engineer. His bride who, I remember, blushed very easily, was painfully shy. They were both quiet, reserved people very much aware of their Jewishness. The travelling iceman used to deliver huge, frosted-up slabs of ice at their door. Nobody else I knew availed themselves of that facility.

In the autumn of 1939, after the outbreak of hostilities and the partition of Poland, our neighbour, Mr Haas (who since the occupa-tion had become somewhat more voluble) confided to Father that he and his wife intended to cross over to the Russian side. Thus, one evening, after dusk had fallen, they slipped out of the building, taking not even hand-luggage so as not to draw attention to them-selves, and walked away into the darkness. They left behind their comfortable and tastefully furnished flat, which I was to know so well, with its entire contents. I do not know what happened to Mr and Mrs Haas, but nobody bothered about the flat. It was theirs, they had the keys to it. They could come back one day.

My maternal grandfather was a lucky man. He passed away in October, 1939 – a month after the German troops had marched into Cracow. He was seventy-five years old. We were all very saddened by the loss. He died in the Cracow Jewish Hospital ministered to by dedicated medical staff and visited daily by a loving, devoted family. He had a traditional Jewish burial at the Cracow Jewish Cemetery, at which a local Rabbi intoned the prayers and dirges in a deep, sonorous voice. His widow, his children, his grandchildren and a bevy of relations gathered round the graveside on a peaceful, warm autumn afternoon mourning his passing. Yet, in the light of future events, we should have rejoiced, not wept. No other member of the family would have such a splendid, dignified funeral as grandfather – 'splendid', again, in the light of what was to come, for almost every member of that vast clan assembled there, that day, would perish anonymously within the next three years . . . their corpses tossed onto primitive pyres or incinerated in ramshackle crematoria. But we had no inkling of our fate, as we stood there, under the benevolent Cracow sky, united in grief.

By the winter of 1940 – the first of the occupation – the world had turned upside down. The invader seemed to have found his feet and was already feeling very much at home in Poland, in Cracow. We, the Jews, were very keenly aware of this. One of the very first laws to be promulgated concerning the Jewish population was that all Jewish citizens wear, outdoors, a white brassard with a blue Star of David in its centre. Thus, straightaway, the sheep were segregated from the goats; a lot of confusion was avoided; everybody knew who was who and Jew-baiting and persecution were rendered that much simpler. Also, the Jewish population census, taken at this very early stage of the occupation, made it much simpler to requisition a Jewish home and to confiscate Jewish property.

Misfortune, fear, privation were fast becoming daily companions. With the outbreak of war, Mamma's source of income and what she hoped would become a thriving little business, instantly dried up. The September débâcle also brought despair and tragedy to the officers' wives' lives. Some of these ladies, especially those with young children, found themselves in very straitened circumstances indeed. Their husbands killed in action or missing; or taken prisoner of war and despatched to camps in Germany. Or having found themselves in the Russian occupied territories – their remains would be disinterred, a few years later, in the communal graves of the infamous Katyn Forest. They proved to be plucky, resourceful women who faced up to their new lonely, austere existence, burdened with awesome responsibilities, with courage and determination.

At the same time, Father's café-life ground to a halt. Almost from day one of the occupation, the Jew served as a means of sport, relaxation and a break in the daily tedium of barracks routine. Two places in which amusement was guaranteed to be found – without getting one's gleaming boots muddy in the insalubrious Jewish Quarter – were the synagogue and the café. Better sport, richer pickings were to be had, it seemed, at the latter. The Jews who congregated in the cafés were different in type from those of the synagogue. They were assimilated men of the world holding liberal views. Tormenting them, breaking them was, perhaps, more of a challenge, more psychologically satisfying, required more sophisticated expertise. With all routes of escape smartly blocked, these café round-ups provided an afternoon's entertainment and not so much as a speck showed on one's elegant pearl-grey gloves . . . All the café needed, like a plum tree laden with ripe fruit, was a shake, a puff of the wind, and the fruit tumbled down straight into the bag – the odd lorry or two parked by the kerbside. Often the *habitués*, as well as the staff, were never seen or heard of again . . .

These developments did not entirely deter Father and his friends from meeting at each other's houses – ours was not suitable and too far out – where a few rubbers of one card game or another would be played, whilst the host saw to it that innocuous beverages and modest refreshments were served. And the news. They all came eager to discuss the bad, bad, bad news . . . They, literally, turned it inside out; they argued from every conceivable perspective; they put forward the most imaginative interpretations; they subjected it to the most cunning, so they thought, analyses. An eye had to be kept on the clock, which imposed a certain restraint on their deliberations, in view of the curfew. The friends scattered in the early evening, everyone hastening homeward softly and inconspicuously; the muffler wound round the lower part of the face, the hat pulled well down over the forehead, the coat collar standing up straight – to cast a shadow over the face, but particularly to play down the proboscis. The first harsh winter of war . . .

Strangely enough, whereas more and more Jewish men and women were being, daily, thrown out of their employment, Father's skills became very much in demand. Right, left and centre, the Cracow Jews were writing humble petitions, lodging meekly-worded appeals, substantiating gentle pleas. Father's German had been acquired in Franz-Joseph's rigorous educational establishments. I believe it was excellent. He possessed just the right admixture of the formal, the bureaucratic and the ornamental. And he wrote a beautiful hand, copper-plate at its finest. The capital letters with their elaborate strokes and curlicues were works of art.

With the wheels of the machinery of destruction gathering speed, the first family casualty, Mamma's eldest brother Uncle Salomon, fell victim to it. He was a respectable and respected official at the Cracow Jewish Town Hall. He was also a great patriot, early to join the Cracow Underground Movement. His 'cell' listened to foreign radio broadcasts – an action unambiguously forbidden by the new régime. It printed and distributed news-sheets – a most perilous enterprise. He was denounced by a fellow Jew, arrested, classed as a 'political' prisoner and incarcerated at Cracow's Montelupich prison.

Mamma was very attached to her eldest brother and, having recently lost her father, felt this blow very acutely. Life, which had become very grey and bare, was now underpinned by hopelessness, anxiety and fear; the only distraction, the only little corner of a 'silver lining' were those 'get-togethers' at her widowed mother's house. She continued to frequent them even more assiduously, in spite of the armband, in spite of the curfew, in spite of their much subdued tone. The freedom, the spontaneity, the lively conversation, the delicious snippets of gossip had ceded place to one topic and one topic only; the war with its infinite ramifications.

This was the spring of 1940 – the Star of David armband was a compulsory article of a Jew's apparel. Mamma chose to flout that command, time and again, and leave the house not wearing it.

I had always been respectful of authority. I was now afraid. Such frightful, spine-chilling stories were in circulation about the new régime – its brutality, its cruelty, the fearful punishments it was meting out to people for the slightest infraction of the new laws. Not to wear one's armband was one of the most hazardous infringements. I knew that the Jews were their favourite target. These stories were not meant for my ears, but I was for ever eavesdropping, for ever adding two and two together, not necessarily getting four of course, but, at times, something close to it . . . I knew that the fate that lay in store for a Jew caught in the streets of Cracow without his armband was terrible, or rather I thought I knew; in fact, I had no idea, neither the scraps of overheard conversation, nor my imagination came anywhere near the stark, naked truth. Mamma's daily outings caused me terrible anguish.

There was a dark corner in our kitchen, a sort of niche, right behind the tiled kitchen stove. As soon as the door had shut behind Mamma, I would creep in there, sit on the floor, my knees drawn up to my chin, my frock draped round my legs, my imagination running riot. I was believed to have a vivid, fertile imagination. I found years later, that in that extreme war climate, it was quite barren, a positive desert, in fact. Not even faintly did my imagination approximate the facts . . . I sat there, wound into a little ball of fear and trembling for Mamma's safety. Quite often when my parents returned, for Father, too, had taken to dropping in at Grandmother's, in the late evening, they would find me there, behind the range, fast asleep. Father would gather me up and carry me to bed in his arms. Drugged with fatigue, I would open my eyes just enough to see the two dearly loved faces.

5 • *Frau Liselotte Berger*

The doors of State Education closed to Jewish children in the spring of 1940. I loved school. I felt cut off from a life-giving source. There was still the Public Library – I could read at home. A few months later that, too, came to an end and with it the beginning of the end of my childhood. I was exactly ten years old.

In the early summer of 1940 when the victors, intoxicated by their military successes, were crushing us underfoot harder and harder, a strange incident occurred in our road. It was about eleven o'clock in the morning and as there was no school for me any more, my younger brother, Bartuś, and I had drawn a hopscotch court on the pavement outside our building and were about to start playing, when we saw a bright-red sports car turn into our road and come down it slowly to stop at our gate. A car of any kind was a rare enough occurrence in our road, but one as dinky, as pretty, as colourful as a new toy made us quite dizzy with wonder. We stopped playing and just stood and gawped. A German Air Force officer got out of the vehicle and smartly came round to open the passenger door. I saw a pair of shapely legs, clad in fine silk hose, shod in smart black court shoes, swing neatly to the ground and a young lady emerged from the automobile. Accompanied by the officer, she walked briskly into our building. A few minutes later, she and her tall companion appeared on the Haas's balcony and stood there for a while surveying the neighbourhood and chatting. Within days of this preliminary visit, quietly and unobtrusively, the young lady took possession of the Haas's flat. Their name-card was removed from the tenants' register in the entrance lobby and replaced by one bearing the name: 'Frau Liselotte Berger'. I liked the sound of her name, particularly the Christian name, it was foreign and somehow evocative.

We saw very little of Frau Berger and knew nothing about her except that she was German and thus had every right to appropriate a Jewish flat. I noticed, too, that the caretaker put a little more elbow

38

grease than she was wont to into the polishing of her doorknob and letter box; that they shone that little bit more brightly. Also, it struck one that when her name was mentioned a note of special deference would creep into the speaker's voice. These were merely impressions registered by a child's inquisitive consciousness. They were in no way indications of what was to come. I accepted the events as a matter of course, without question, surprise or resentment. I had long understood that we were second-class citizens: now, not even that.

Since school had ceased for me, I had been feeling a sense of isolation and alienation. I felt now, every day, the way I used to feel before on Sundays. I did not like Sundays in the Village. The church bells would start pealing early in the morning. It was not that I did not like their music – I did – but I associated it with loneliness and a sense of separateness. Soon, the inhabitants of the Village would start coming out of their houses in family groups and slowly, decorously, cross the large green opposite our building on their way to church, to mass. All were dressed in their Sunday best, conscious of the great honour, of the great privilege of being summoned by the bells to the House of God – clutching their prayer books firmly in their hands. The parents had large, black missals, the children small, white, gilt-edged prayer books. As I watched them, my heart grew heavy: I did not like being excluded from the herd.

In June, 1940, I saw Mamma weep as I had never seen her weep before. It was as if an inner barrier had given way. Her whole body shook with the sobs and Father, equally grief-stricken by the news he had brought from town, stood by powerless to ease her sorrow, to stem the flood. She covered her face with her hands, but the tears still fell thickly. Her whole being trembling uncontrollably, she hiccoughed, stuttered out – 'Paris has fallen . . . They are in Paris . . .' I did not understand of course the implications of that news, but my parents did, only too well. And Mamma wept as if the sorrows, anxieties, humiliations, hardships and dashed hopes of her whole life had formed a torrent of grief inside her body which that final calamity – 'Paris has fallen' – had released. When I was a child, nothing affected me as much, nothing made me as achingly unhappy as Mamma's pain, whatever form it took. For Mamma to be crying like this, I knew, it must be serious.

In the summer of 1940, Frau Berger was joined by her family from Lübeck, for that was her home town. The newcomers were four in number: an elderly lady, a young lady and two little boys; one a lively three year old, the other a baby. Very soon after their arrival, our caretaker stopped me on the stairs saying that she had a message for my mother from Frau Berger. Could she come and deliver it? I said, 'Yes, of course, I'll tell Mamma to expect you . . .' We were very apprehensive. What could she, a German, possibly want from us, Jews? It could only be trouble. But they seemed such nice ladies! Anyway, the caretaker did ring our doorbell a little later and told Mamma that Frau Berger would be grateful if she, Frau Fischler, would call on her in the late afternoon. Mamma thanked her, but did not enquire if she, the caretaker, knew why this invitation had been issued. We were now very puzzled. 'Grateful? Call on Frau Berger?' What did it mean?

Mamma looking very charming in a fresh, crisp blouse said she wanted me to accompany her – this was to become standard practice. My frock was clean, my hair neatly plaited, my hands freshly washed. Frau Berger opened the door herself and bid us enter. She shook hands with Mamma and smiled at me. She led us to a comfortable, cheerful room where further introductions followed: the elderly lady, her mother; the young lady, her elder sister; the toddler – Jurgen – her sister's little boy; the baby, Hans, her own little boy. Mamma was invited to sit down. Our hostess spoke in German and was pleased to discover that there was no language difficulty. She had invited Mamma, she explained, to ask her if she would become her own, personal dressmaker. Mamma, only just believing her ears, smiled her full, radiant smile, which was not lost upon the three ladies and said something which contained the word 'natürlich' – the only one I understood. Everybody seemed perfectly satisfied.

There was a tall, old-fashioned, not very wide, cupboard standing against the wall. Frau Berger went up to it and using both her hands pulled the door plate vigorously towards her. The doors parted and swung sideways revealing an Aladdin's Cave. An expression of wondrous disbelief registered on Mamma's face; on the other lady's the possessor's just pride. Frau Berger invited Mamma to approach, to look more closely at the treasure, the cupboard's mind-boggling, belief-beggaring contents. Shelf upon shelf upon shelf of fabrics arranged with methodical care. Stack upon stack, upon stack, symmetrically perfect, of tender, plain silks, and, bursting with colour, patterned silks; fine, soft wools and heavy, sombre wools; velvet as black as night; richly embossed brocades; chiffon in all the colours of the rainbow; jewel-coloured taffetas; moiré – a pool of shimmering silver; lace as fine as spun moonlight; lace as rich as whipped cream; and muslin and cotton and shantung . . . The finest products of Lyons, Bruges, Amsterdam, the spoils of Europe reposing quietly in the Haas's family heirloom of a cupboard. Mamma and Frau Berger continued to chat in front of the open cupboard, the latter's finger pointing to this or that stack; softly stroking this or that fabric. After a while we said 'Gute Nacht' and Frau Berger saw us out.

We tiptoed upstairs quietly. Mamma looked very pensive. Whilst we were getting supper ready, she said: 'You know these fabrics are uncommonly fine. Exquisite. I feel apprehensive. I said as much to Frau Berger. I said I should like to start with a relatively simple outfit, made out of fabric which was not too precious. She replied, "Yes, I need a linen suit, a plain skirt and a striped jacket."'

For the next two years Mamma worked exclusively for Frau Berger, although she also made the odd garment or two for the mother and the elder daughter. Neither of them was accustomed to a great deal of choice in the matter of dress; neither of them hankered after it. They were 'Kirche, Kinder, Küche' women.

The mother was very likeable. She was slim with quick, energetic movements. Her face was like a rosy apple, her blue eyes twinkled behind her steel-rimmed spectacles and her short hair was silver white. These features made her appear old to me, although, at the time, she may not even have been fifty years old. Back in Lübeck, she told us, she was a railwayman's wife. She liked to chat and it gave her pleasure to be able to communicate freely, with Mamma, in German. She knew we were Jews and she must have been exposed to a good deal of propaganda, especially in the last ten years or so, but she was, I think, as she must always have been, without prejudice. Whenever we came down for a fitting and Frau Berger was not quite ready, she would invite us into her spotless, warm kitchen. Mamma would be offered a cup of coffee – real coffee – and I a slice of home-baked 'zwieback' and a glass of milk.

We learnt, in due course, that Lt Berger was not baby Hans's father. His daddy had been a *Luftwaffe* fighter pilot. His plane, seriously damaged in action, had plunged into the sea on the return journey – she did not specify where he was returning from and Mamma did not dare ask – before he and Liselotte had had time to be married. It was she who was bringing up baby Hans. Both she and her husband, she said, loved him dearly.

Louise, the tall, plain-faced, elder daughter was married to a

41

Wehrmacht officer. She was quiet and homely, always busy with her needlework. Mamma said that Louise had an extraordinarily beautiful figure and superb carriage. 'She moves like a queen and just as unselfconsciously.' But, of course, our benefactress, our daily crust of bread as it were, was Frau Berger. We knew that she was an ardent Nazi; that she had been moulded with zealous thoroughness and total dedication – which she wholeheartedly reciprocated – in the ranks of the *Hitler Jugend*. She had been fully, consciously, willingly indoctrinated. Her mother, very delicately, made that clear too. She was very young, only twenty-two years old when Mamma first started ministering to her needs.

Frau Berger was different from her mother and sister. The relationship between Mamma and her was placed from the outset by her, since she was calling the tune, on a strictly impersonal, business footing. Mamma had something to sell which she wished to purchase and she was prepared to pay for it, generously I must add. She was polite and straightforward; she knew what she wanted and when she wanted it. The conversation between Mamma and her never strayed outside, not by so much as a fraction of an inch, the realm of the business in hand. She knew she belonged to the Master Race – there was none better.

Right at the beginning of the 'mutually convenient arrangement', Frau Berger showed herself to be a practical, astute woman, fully alive to the advantages that can accrue, to both parties, from an ably conducted, shrewdly executed business transaction.

Appearances can be deceptive. Frau Berger was not tall and was slight in build. Nor was she conventionally pretty. She had a clear, fresh complexion, very round green eyes, a pert nose and a toothy smile. She was dainty and feminine. Her figure was slim, her movements supple and she knew how to wear clothes to effect. Today, with hindsight and the revelation of her true nature which nearly cost my brother, Joseph, his life, I would say that she was an ambitious, calculating woman and that under the soft, alluring exterior there dwelt a hard-headed, determined, singularly grasping woman.

She worked, a civilian, at Cracow Airport, for which 'The Village' was most conveniently situated, but what post she held there we never learnt. She liked male company; she liked a good time; she liked Cracow; she liked where and what she was. She was prospering, her life was shaping up nicely. Vistas were opening up before her; she was going places. She possessed the cool ability to become totally disengaged, totally detached in her dealings with people. Only those who could be of use to her mattered and only when they were being of use. Yet, she did apply 'the brakes' in her race to the goalpost. She did not take advantage of those who served her.

She asked Mamma at the very beginning of their negotiations if payment in kind would be acceptable to her. Mamma's reply was, 'Yes, perfectly.' Again, I must add in fairness to Frau Berger, that Mamma never felt herself to be exploited. 'In kind' meant receiving the most extraordinary 'goodies', a bag of lemons (about 25 of them), a bottle of 'Armagnac', packets of fine coffee beans, tea, Portuguese sardines. All of which items were readily disposable and fetched a good price on the black market. We almost never kept or used any of these luxury items – and to us they were luxuries – which Mamma received from Frau Berger. We sold them, and with the proceeds we bought bread, vegetables, flour, lard. For two whole years, till the summer of 1942, Mamma would work for Frau Berger who, like it or not, became an integral part of our existence. All our hopes, plans, calculations took Frau Berger's patronage into account.

In the meantime, great changes had taken place at Grandmother's house, in Wielopole. Of course, Grandfather was no longer there, but we all came, in time, to recognise and acknowledge the fact that he had been one of God's chosen few.

Uncle Izydor having completed his studies before September, 1939, had finally vacated 'the pallet' under the window. He and his fiancée, Annie Infeld, the handsome, sturdy daughter of well-to-do parents, were married some weeks before Grandfather's death. They moved to a flat provided by Annie's father.

My lovely Aunt Anna received and accepted an offer of marriage in the spring of 1939 from a tall, bright, but extremely shy and gauche, young barrister. The law practice in which they had both worked was dissolved by the New Masters, and they were both relieved of their posts within the first few months of the occupation. David, Anna's fiancé, returned to the small town, outside Tarnov, from which he came and where his family still lived. He wrote to her daily, urging her to join him, so that they could be married. She was torn. It was hard to uproot herself; to leave her widowed mother, her sisters, family and friends – all she knew and loved. Eventually, she packed her bags and departed for Tarnov. She left the contents of her bottom drawer at home – life had lost its pattern of permanence and predictability – for she was not sure what she would find at the other end. She joined David in the spring of 1940 and they were quietly married in his home town.

The atmosphere at Wielopole changed. It stopped being a busy 'metropolis'. The three ladies, Grandmother, Regina and Sally, suddenly became three small peas in a very large pod. Grandmother's three bachelor sons, Siggie, Marek and Arthur, decided to leave Cracow and cross over to the Russian side. Many Jews, circumstances permitting, were doing just that. They attempted in all earnestness to prevail upon their mother and sisters to leave Cracow, to come with them and to allow themselves to be looked after. The three ladies declined the offer in one strong, unanimous voice which would brook no discussion. How could they, they asked, leave their home, their possessions, their life, and set out for the unknown? They continued to keep open house, and the evening gatherings, albeit reduced in size and changed in character, still took place. Misfortune, it seemed, united people and various wealthy relatives who, up to now, had maintained a certain aloofness, a certain distance, now called on the three ladies wishing to express sympathy: Grandmother had not long been widowed, her eldest son continued to be detained at Montelupich Prison. They felt the need to talk, to ask questions, to compare notes; they wished to commiserate and to be commiserated with.

No great changes, however, had taken place at Grandmother Heim's in Sebastian Road. Aunt Rose and Uncle Dolek were still running their pub. There was no shortage of people wishing and needing to drown their sorrows. Business was brisk. Up to now, in spite of so many Jewish enterprises having been confiscated, expropriated or totally wiped out, the pub was thriving and no member of the Master Race had, so far, darkened its threshold. Father now actively helped his sister and brother-in-law.

Grandmother Heim continued to run the household as efficiently as ever, quite unaware of the apocalyptic storm brewing outside her kitchen walls. Officially, there was no more school for Siggie and Sophie, just as there was none for Joseph and myself. Our cousins were fortunate in that respect. Well-to-do Jewish parents were quick to find suitable private tutors and organise small, private study groups. Siggie and Sophie continued to attend classes and to do homework.

Joseph, my elder brother, had become a young man of seventeen. Good-looking and well-built, he had inherited Father's love of sport and Mamma's sensitivity to language, as well as her 'Golden

Hands'. It was becoming vital for young Jewish males to be equipped with 'positive' skills. No fripperies. No embellishments. Just solid, useful, everyday skills. Suddenly Cracow's Jewish 'Golden Youth' were all eager to learn carpentry, plumbing, mechanics . . . Apprenticeships were few and competition was stiff. It was some time before the young people fully grasped, fully understood their future prospects. They would form part of the vast slave-labour force that was to perish, just like the one-time Roman slaves, in the building of the 'thousand-year Empire'. My brother, Joseph, would make his contribution.

My younger brother, Bartuś, should have started primary school in the autumn of 1940. If one of us three youngsters was to benefit from private tuition, we were all agreed that it should be Bartuś. We reasoned that once he had mastered the three 'Rs' he would possess the key to the door, he could read for himself. He joined a small group of Jewish children and Mamma somehow managed to pay the fees for these classes.

In the late autumn of 1940, the family was dealt a very painful blow. Round-ups in the Jewish Quarter, in the streets of Cracow, had become a daily, regular feature of life. Jewish males were the prime target. On a quiet autumn afternoon, whilst Grandmother and Regina were busy in the kitchen, the table covered with all the paraphernalia required in bread-making and baking, Wielopole was cordoned off. The green-uniformed soldiers, weapons at the ready, leaping from slowly cruising lorries, burst into houses. Somebody was ringing Grandmother's doorbell with frantic urgency. The two ladies working in the kitchen looked at each other anxiously and Regina said, 'I'll go . . .' She opened the front door to be faced by a fear-frenzied neighbour screaming, 'We are surrounded! They are everywhere! They are coming!' Grandmother, summoned to the door by the noise and commotion, found Regina lying on the floor – unconscious. But they never came up to the sixth floor; in fact, they did not enter Grandmother's block of flats at all.

Regina had suffered a stroke. She became paralysed down one side of her body. The elderly Jewish doctor who attended her was an able, dedicated man, but already very frightened and none too pleased to have to climb to the sixth floor each time he called. He recommended quiet and rest and every time wrote out a prescription. He assured Grandmother that time and loving family care would do the rest. Regina lay on the snow-white bedding – her body inert, her eyes closed, her mouth twisted. Grandmother, who was naturally pale, now became ashen-faced. Moving about soundlessly, so as not to disturb her rest, she waited on her daughter hand and foot. Sally, who had lost her employment – the law firm where she had worked was taken over by an Aryan partnership and she received her 'cards' forthwith – became her mother's right hand. She did the housework, cooked, shopped and pored over her 'accounts' in an effort to balance her meagre budget. They took turns to sit at Regina's bedside for they watched over her, at this early stage of her illness, almost twenty-four hours a day.

The sadness, the burden of the second winter of war was felt by everyone, as was the shortage of food and fuel. The three ladies huddled together in one room to economise on wood and coal, for the weather was as sharp as the Masters' whip, lashing out long, cruel strokes. It was during that second winter of war that a new word entered my vocabulary. A strange word – soul-less and colourless – it did not please the ear, it did not stir the imagination: 'ghetto'. Rumours were circulating amongst Cracow's Jewish community – hard times were ahead of us.

6 • *The Interview*

By the winter of 1940, Uncle Salomon had been held at Montelupich Prison for close to a year. During this time, his wife, Aunt Josephine, did all within her power to obtain his release. It was a brave undertaking and under her quiet, rather shy, exterior she proved to be both courageous and resourceful. It was a very costly venture and there was little ready money to hand as they were educating three children. Paws had to be greased – large, grasping, expensive paws at that – right, left and centre. To obtain an interview with someone who wielded genuine power or carried genuine influence, many doors had to be opened, many thresholds had to be crossed. To grease all the palms stretching out to help her along her thorny path, she embarked on the process of 'dismantling' her home. She started by disposing of valuable, dispensable articles and worked her way through to necessary, everyday objects.

She knew the prison time-table down to the minutest detail and spent hours, in all weathers, waiting outside in the hope of catching a glimpse of her husband at slopping out time or on his way to or from the exercise yard. She also got to know some of the prison warders, who were not unsympathetic to the prisoners' plight and organised, at a price, a food parcel service to supplement the meagre prison diet. She left no stone unturned.

Her hopes were raised many times and just as many cruelly dashed. She continued to battle on to the bitter end, showing unexpected grit and tenacity for a person who had led a quiet, sheltered life and who had never had to meet the harsh, external forces of life head on – but did not succeed in obtaining her husband's release.

Early in 1941, a convoy of lorries carrying male political prisoners, Uncle Salomon amongst them, left Montelupich prison for the railway station at Prokocim – the Auschwitz line . . . They were wearing prison fatigues marked with a large white cross chalked across the back – a fitting emblem of the martyrdom for which one and all had

47

been singled out; they were being transferred, in the depths of the harsh Polish winter, to a camp called 'Auschwitz'.

We knew the town, on the edge of which the camp was situated and whose name it bore, as Oświecim – its rightful Polish name. A small town in the south of Poland, an insignificant backwater, whose name translated into German would become synonymous with the darkest, the most heinous deeds humanity has ever known. But we were not to know that, nor would we have understood it, at the time.

I do not think that anyone in the family had the slightest inkling of what the name stood for then, or what it would come to stand for in the years to come. A camp! The whole concept was a new experience; the function it would eventually perform was not even a concept, it was not something we could have grasped, or for that matter believed, in the winter of 1941.

Uncle Salomon was one of the pioneer builders of Auschwitz. We learnt much later, that when his particular batch of prisoners arrived at the camp, it was a vast, snow-covered wasteland with the ground frozen solid and a biting wind whistling shrilly under a heavy, yellow sky. There was a handful of modern, well-equipped build-ings housing the SS personnel manning the camp, but no shelter for the newly-arrived prisoners. They were ordered to set to and build their huts from scratch in the white wilderness.

We also learnt that Uncle Salomon was assigned to sewage exca-vation work. He stood in a ditch in below zero temperature breaking up soil as hard as rock. He was then in his middle-forties, a tall, well-built man.

Within a month of her husband's transfer to Auschwitz, Aunt Josephine received a censored, sparingly-worded, printed post-card. It carried the briefest of messages: 'I am well. I want for nothing. All my love. Slamek.' The post-card was passed around at a family gathering and handled reverently as it travelled from hand to hand, everybody sighing and repeating to everybody else, 'He is well . . . Thank God; he wants for nothing . . . Thank God; can't be too bad . . . Thank God . . .' There was no reason to disbelieve its contents and although his wife could not write back to him, that meagre message, a sign of life, succeeded in allaying her fears.

Six weeks after the receipt of the Auschwitz post-card, well into the winter of 1941, Aunt Josephine received another printed post-card – this time from No. 2 Pomorska Street – the Cracow Gestapo Headquarters. She was asked to present herself at the headquarters on a given date, at a given time for an interview in a given room. No reason was offered for the interview, but she felt that it must have some bearing upon her husband's incarceration and she was filled with great apprehension. To comfort herself, she kept repeating, like a silent prayer, the scanty content of his message from Auschwitz.

Aunt Josephine was still a handsome woman and perhaps, a trifle vain. On the appointed day she took great pains over her appearance, just as she used to do in the days when she appeared, on her husband's arm, at family gatherings or official functions. She put a light dusting of fine, fragrant powder, a delicate dab of rouge, a touch of glowing lipstick – all discreetly and judiciously applied – a modest string of pearls at her throat and as she met her reflection in the looking-glass she was almost, except for the greying hair, her pre-war self.

She found her way, on a raw winter's morning, to the Gestapo Headquarters. Although fearful of being late, she had arrived a little too early. She was immediately led to the room indicated. She knocked gently and was instantly invited to enter. And here, with hindsight, the mind seizes. The year was 1941 and Aunt Josephine a Jewess. Yet, she was received with exquisite, old-fashioned courtesy by a Gestapo officer. A young man, the product of an old school, who meticulously adhered to a protocol which had, long ago, ceased to apply as far as official negotiations between the Jews and the German Authorities were concerned. She had barely set foot in the room, when this tall young man, in full uniform, sprang to his feet and clicked his heels. 'Frau Weinreb?' he asked, and as she assented, he pulled out a chair for her and said 'Pray, be seated.' He then went round to his side of the desk and opened a file on which she could read, upside down, her husband's name. She knew then that her premonition had been right. He took a long time to find what he was looking for, bracing himself for the grim task in front of him, postponing the moment when he would have to meet her honest, steady gaze. He found it hard to have to face her.

He had addressed her very courteously by her name, pre-fixed with her marital status – Frau Weinreb. Because of his youth and extreme deference towards herself, she felt less ill at ease, less conscious of her heart-beat. Having thumbed through the documents in the file, he found what he was looking for. He lifted a sheet of paper out, holding it in his hand, his eyes fastened upon it. In the ominous silence of the room, as she waited for him to speak, to tell her why she was there, her heart began to beat faster again, her breath came more quickly, her mouth felt parched. And then he spoke enunciating every syllable, every word slowly and distinctly, allowing for her halting school German. His voice was soft and gentle. Slowly, he brought his gaze to rest on her face and said quietly and evenly, 'I am afraid I have bad news for you.' There was genuine commiseration in his voice. He was not enjoying his task. 'Your husband, Frau Weinreb, has died . . .' From the very bowels of the building a long, piercing wail, like the desolate cry of a captive bird muffled by a thousand walls, but still swollen with pain, reached her ears. It jolted her. Her face was wet. She produced a wisp of a handkerchief, the finest white lawn edged with delicate lace, carrying her favourite scent of wild flowers and dabbed at her eyes, as she had been taught to do, like a lady. He did not rush her. He let her take her time. It was difficult to repress the sobs rising in her throat, to think clearly, to concentrate. And then, emboldened by his obvious sympathy, she said timidly, 'But my husband was so strong, so healthy . . .' He, unable to meet her gaze this time, spread out his hands, palms up, in a gesture of human impotence and said, 'Even the strongest and the healthiest of us have to die. The urn containing the ashes will be sent to you.'

The interview was over. She stood up and, feeling weak at the knees, she took her time fastening her coat, drawing on her gloves. He understood. He opened the door and stood aside for her to pass. The last thing she heard was the even click of his heels.

The porter was hovering in the corridor to guide her out of the building. The sharp, frosty air hit her full in the face. She stood on the steps for a minute or two breathing it in. She knew she had to be strong; she had three children to bring up single-handed. Somehow, she found her way home.

Again, after some time, she received news of her husband through the 'grapevine' – acquaintances who knew somebody who knew a prisoner who had been released from Auschwitz. He had worked alongside her husband, had seen him daily and passed on what was fast becoming legal tender, a stock phrase, ephemeral and enigmatic, imponderable and tenuous, the last memento of a dear one to which the family would cling, 'He had shown great courage and dignity to the last.' Again, the phrase was handed round in hushed, awed tones by relatives and friends and did, to some degree, its work as a palliative.

I have had time, aeons and aeons of time, half-a-century and more and with the full knowledge of the role Auschwitz has played in the annals of human suffering and destruction to ponder the content of that message brought long ago, out of human-created hell, to a family desperate for solace. I have parsed and analysed that sentence time without number. I have dissected the meaning, the purport, the significance of each word singly and collectively, in context and out of context. I know, now, that the words it contained were scooped out and drained of their conventional meaning, for how was it possible in Auschwitz to maintain dignity, to show courage as we, those who have never been there, understand them? And yet, I believe, I know, that they were maintained and shown on the grandest, on the most dazzling scale there, in Auschwitz, if one knew how to read, how to measure. There may well have been truth in the epitaph brought home to the wife, to the children, to the mother . . .

7 • The Cracow Ghetto

The area designated for the Cracow Ghetto was situated on the right
bank of the Vistula. It was within easy reach of the river which, at
that point, was spanned by Cracow's busiest, most important
bridge, 'The Third Bridge'. It was a barren area. There were no trees,
no greenery, no strip of grass to alleviate its harshness and squalor,
to relieve its monotonous greyness. Yet, it was cunningly chosen
with an eye to the future, for it lay within walking distance of two
Jewish cemeteries, which could be levelled out, as indeed they were,
to serve other purposes, as well as a suburban railway station to
'The East'; attributes which must have been considered eminently
desirable by the planners. They had the merit, too, of being quietly
tucked away so that the city of Cracow need not know, need not be
involved; neither as spectators, nor as witnesses, in the activities
taking place on the right bank of the river and beyond.

Although the area in the sense of acreage was small, to encircle it
with a high brick wall with large gates for entry and exit of heavy
transport and small gates for pedestrian traffic – as well as suitably
equipped guard-rooms, by those gates, for those who would
guard the future Ghetto – was an ambitious undertaking. The work
on the wall started early in 1941. I did not see it in the process
of being built, only when it was fully completed and ready to
receive Cracow's Jewish population. The masons must have been
experienced, industrious men who toiled daily to meet a deadline,
as the wall was solidly constructed and ready in good time. The curtain came down, as it were, on 20 March 1941. The gates were
snapped shut and navy-blue uniformed Polish policemen took up
the duty of guarding them day and night. The very top of the wall
was crenellated – a decorative motif – that was how it appeared to a
child's eye. I never really gave it any thought, nor did I ever hear
anyone comment on that finishing touch. Only many years later did
I realise that those crenellations, one and all, were the most exact, the
most faithful replicas of Jewish tombstones. A touch of humour? A

touch of irony? A sinister message – simple enough to interpret for us Cracow Jews. But how many of the Ghetto's inhabitants interpreted it correctly? My family failed to do so . . .

The move to the Ghetto applied, in the first instance, to Jews living in Inner Cracow. They had a choice, however, or so it appeared. The German cat played a very sly game indeed and the Jewish mice, already scared out of their wits, did so wish to believe him. They could move and 'escape' to Outer Cracow or to the country proper. Inner Cracow was to be cleared of Jews, lock, stock and barrel, by 20 March 1941. Many chose not to enter the Ghetto, but they still had to leave their homes. This resulted in a desperate, feverish quest for accommodation in the outer suburbs and villages around Cracow. The rent, even for modest, often primitive, lodgings, soared to the skies. People scaled down the size of their homes and fine furniture, carpets and all manner of household chattels, were to be had for a song . . . There was endless to-ing and fro-ing between Inner Cracow and the suburbs; between Inner Cracow and the distant, outlying villages. Horse-driven peasant carts, the most common conveyance and means of removal, were in great demand and could be seen crossing and criss-crossing Cracow, laden with furniture, bedding, suitcases and various carefully wrapped objects in every direction. These moves and the new, exorbitant rents were on the whole only within the reach of the more affluent Jewish families.

The Jewish poor, bent like beggars under their heavy sacks and bundles, were to be seen crossing the Third Bridge under a slate-grey sky, in the teeth of an icy wind rising from the river, into the Ghetto . . . The elderly, in long, threadbare coats and pitiful footwear, often made of cloth, their bare hands purple with the cold, were to be seen shuffling across the Third Bridge carrying grips, parcels and bags into the Ghetto . . . Closely huddled family groups, trundling their meagre possessions in hand-carts and old prams, were to be seen in Cracow's cold, wind-swept streets. The father furtively glancing to left and right, as he carefully steered the hand-cart; the plodding, patient mother – so weary, so anxious, her fear-filled gaze darting from one child to another – as she struggled with the over-laden pram . . . The children, drab little figures, with dark Murillo eyes burning in wan, passive faces – clinging to the cart, to the mother's coat, all silently, submissively treading their way across the Third Bridge into the Ghetto . . .

As 'The Officers' Village' was situated in the outer suburbs, the edict to vacate one's home and transfer to the Ghetto did not apply to us. We could stay put. We counted ourselves very fortunate.

Aunt Rose and Uncle Dolek decided to give the Ghetto a miss and to move to the suburbs. Thus, they, their children and Grandmother Heim came to live in Olsza – a rural suburb right next door to the 'Village'. They succeeded in renting a room in a bungalow with a pleasant front garden. The transplant was very painful for Grandmother Heim. She mourned having to leave her old home, her kitchen, the familiar world in which she had lived for the last sixty years. The blue sky, the sun, the fresh air, the greenery were no compensation for the uprooting she had suffered. It struck her that in her old age the world was changing, and not for the better.

Grandmother and her two daughters – Regina still bed-ridden, but less inert, less helpless – followed the only path open to them into the Ghetto . . . Space in it was already at a premium and decent accommodation in the area selected for it very scarce indeed. Grandmother and her daughters had struck lucky, however. They moved into a comfortable flat in which they had a spacious, airy room, the other room being occupied by the flat's original owner – Aunt Josephine's sister, Lola, with her twelve year old daughter, Irena. The kitchen and bathroom – it was one of very few flats to boast such modernity – were shared by the two families. Later, as the Jews from the outer suburbs and later still, from the provinces, started pouring into the Ghetto – my parents and we three children amongst them – the pressure upon housing increased many fold and living conditions became desperately cramped and primitive. But in those early days, families in basically good accommodation lived quite decently. The three ladies, who were natural home-makers, turned their room into a restful, comfortable home. They now lived on the second floor of an old, but well maintained block of flats. The triple-paned window of their room gave onto Limanowskiego Street, the Ghetto's main thoroughfare. It afforded a glimpse of the world from which they had been banished, inasmuch as 'Aryan' tramcars carrying Aryan passengers coursed up and down it, for there was a heavy traffic entrance and exit gate at each end of this artery. Grandmother's flat was only about fifty paces away from one of these gates and about the same distance from the Jewish Police Headquarters. It was a good vantage point from which to keep a finger on the Ghetto's pulse.

Shortly before moving to the Ghetto, in March, 1941, Grandmother had a passport-size photograph taken to be affixed to her new identity card – the *Kennkarte*. She was then sixty-eight years old. About twenty years had elapsed since the inaugural photograph in which she stands by her husband's side, her hand on his shoulder. It shows the Grandmother I knew and loved and remember – a very old lady. Her silver-white hair is plainly drawn back from her forehead into a bun. Time has tooled the skin of her face with an intricate pattern of wrinkles and lines. The full upper lip bears down hard on the lower one. The gaze is unflinching, but the light in her eyes is glazed over by suffering and life's hard usage. It is a face of mute, resigned acceptance; there is no reproach. A black coat collar, of ample proportions, accentuates its pallor.

During the nine month long remission period, when our relations were already deprived of their liberty, we, the Jews living in the suburbs, still enjoyed a considerable degree of it. Although it was hard to keep body and soul together it was nonetheless a good deal easier for us living in the relative freedom of the suburbs, than for those already penned and isolated within the high walls of the Ghetto. It still required a very skilful balancing act, the credit for it to be chiefly ascribed to our Mamma, for my parents to feed their three children and themselves. I do not remember ever being hungry, so long as our parents were alive. It was different after we lost them. Mamma managed, miraculously, to make ends meet and there was even a little bit left over. It fell to me to carry 'that little bit', almost daily, to our relations in the Ghetto. There was not much for me to do except to draw upon my one great asset – my cast-iron credential – my truly Aryan face. It enabled me to move in Cracow as freely as the wind. I was eleven years old, independent by nature, and naturally resourceful in the art of day to day survival. I would set off for the Ghetto carrying whatever 'crumbs' we could spare in a string shopping bag. Its modest contents were priceless treasures, a few potatoes, carrots and onions; a small bag of sugar; half-a-loaf of bread; a handful of prunes, a few apples. The bag was heavy and I had to cross the whole of Cracow, but I knew every short cut, every turn and twist of the way and I hummed to myself and made up stories in my head, as I meandered along the familiar streets. I kept swapping the bag from one hand to the other; sometimes I blew on my hands to cool them; sometimes I would place the bag on a low stone-wall or ledge and have a little rest.

One day, having slipped into the Ghetto as usual, without any difficulty, I bumped into Aunt Sally in the street. She was pleased to see me and immediately relieved me of the heavy bag. We walked along Limanowskiego Street together. Although it was getting on for spring, the weather was still cold and sharp. Aunt Sally was wearing her black winter coat and a scarlet, beautifully patterned headscarf, neatly knotted under her chin, over her dark hair. I knew both items of apparel very well, but it struck me as we walked cheerily along, like two friends – chatting, how sprucely turned-out my aunt was, how new the old coat looked and what a graceful, fleet-footed woman Sally was. We entered the building and climbed the stairs.

Grandmother and Regina were also glad to see me. All three made much of the gifts I brought. I felt a sense of gratification and warmth spread inside me. Regina, propped up against her pillows, was sitting up in bed sipping a cup of warm milk. She smiled, her mouth a little crooked, listening to the news I brought, following the conversation. Their room was homely and warm and everything in it so nicely arranged. One corner of it had been turned into a 'dinette' with a pine-wood table and a cupboard for kitchen utensils and food storage. All four of us felt safe and peaceful in that room. Time passed quickly. Soon, I had to think of returning to the 'Village', to my parents and brothers . . . before darkness set in. I was not at all apprehensive. I made for the nearest exit gate. I was very familiar with the Polish policeman and his uniform. I had never had reason to be afraid of him. Slipping in and out of the Cracow Ghetto was quite simple; one did not even have to have an official pass – I never did have one. One just had to know the individual policemen. Most of them were decent, kindly men. I already knew them, at least by sight, and if there happened to be a hard-liner on duty – and there were one or two amongst them – at the nearest, most convenient gate, I only had to wait for him to be relieved. His successor was bound to be reasonable and approachable, or make for a more distant gate. I slipped in and out of the Ghetto during its entire two-year existence – except of course during SS conducted *aktions* when it was hermetically sealed – almost at will.

In the early summer of 1941, Mamma and I were invited by Frau Berger's mother to come and see her brand-new grand-daughter, Louise's baby girl. I was sitting on a small wooden stool, facing Louise, my feet resting on its rung, my knees slightly raised, the plate with a wedge of *zwieback* safely entrenched in my lap. The cake was as rich and sweet as ever. The milk fresh and cool. Louise was sitting at the kitchen table, her weeks-old baby girl, her tiny head covered with thick mousy fuzz, firmly and comfortably nestled in

56

the crook of her left arm. Deftly, with the fingers of her right hand, she undid the buttons of her short-sleeved blouse. A maternity brassiere was all she had on underneath. It was exquisite and ingeniously designed. The work of a French seamstress? The cups hooked onto a narrow satin panel directly over the cleavage. She ran the tip of her nail under the flap of the cup and the panel and it parted. The snow-white, lace-encrusted nest yielded its treasure. Louise's breast was large and hard. The creamy, silken skin, like that of a fully ripened fruit, stretched to capacity. A few droplets of milk, as matt and tiny as seed-pearls, appeared on the pale-coral nipple. She placed her hand under the warm, luscious fruit of her breast, her slender index and middle fingers delicately drawing out the nipple until it fitted snugly into the niche formed by them. Gently, she guided it to her baby's mouth. The tiny lips closed greedily around the rich fruit of Louise's breast. Her rather commonplace features became transfigured by perfect serenity and fulfilment. I was spell-bound by the ritual I had just witnessed. I was at that time only dimly aware that in Louise nature had cunningly contrived to pro-duce a perfect female body; that the chemical components which went into the creation of her – for she had been created, not made – had been most meticulously, most censoriously weighed and measured, balanced and counter-balanced. Louise was a shy, retiring person. She performed this oft-repeated ritual with an unselfconscious, perfectly natural grace. I found it moving like a beautiful poem, or a beautiful picture.

One day, when I dropped in on my Ghetto family, in the summer of 1941, they were receiving a visitor – Sally's friend, a married lady in her thirties, who had managed to obtain a pass to visit her family and friends in the Ghetto. Jews in the suburbs were able to obtain a pass, from time to time, to visit relations in the Ghetto. These were group passes for twenty to thirty persons who came in and out on the one pass, having been counted at the gate on entry and on exit. She brought the three ladies a princely gift, a huge, unwieldy bunch of field flowers, cornflowers and poppies and large white daisies wrapped in green fern leaves. Their strong, vibrant colours glowed richly against the sombre wood and furnishings of the room. She brought with the bunch of flowers, into the grass-less, tree-less, concrete desert of the Ghetto the magic of fields, meadows, woods and orchards. The smells, sights and textures of a world from which the Ghetto Jews were already barred.

A child of eleven, as I then was, did not bring judgment to bear, particularly moral judgment, upon her elders and betters. She did not criticise or evaluate their actions, she certainly did not analyse them. These mental processes were as alien to me then, as was the language in which I write today. I believed my family, my grandmother and aunts to be above reproach as human beings. I was too young, I suppose, to allow for the frailties and weaknesses of the human race. This is not to say that I was not aware of some imperfections in some human beings; I simply believed my immediate family not to be afflicted by any. Yet both the ability and the desire to pass judgment were implicit in my reaction to the scene that followed, a reaction which I stowed away in the very back of my mind, but did not forget. I do not know if I would have been able to put into words what I felt, or how strongly I felt it, but my aunt's conduct produced a deep sense of shame in me. My aunt has been dead for over half a century now and whenever I think of her my heart fills with infinite pity. Whatever shortcomings she may have had, she redeemed them a thousand fold by the manner of her death. I did a great deal of heart, mind and soul searching before putting pen to paper. I would like to be able to say fine and noble things about her, but if I did I would not be true to her or to myself. I would be sketching a cardboard character, and Aunt Sally's most outstanding attribute to my mind was her vitality. If I stripped her of her shortcomings I would strip her of that immense, surging vitality that pulsed and throbbed in her and which I very consciously admired. A vitality stemmed in full tide.

My aunt's friend had a slight cold, but as she said, a slight cold was not going to prevent her from seeing her friends. And who knew if she would be able to obtain a pass again. Every so often she blew her nose in a discreet, lady-like manner. After a while she started sneezing rather as if she were suffering from a bout of hayfever. In no time at all her handkerchief was soaked right through; though she still carried it to her nose, dabbing at it delicately. She was embarassed and we were conscious of her embarassment. There was only one thing to do. Borrow a handkerchief. But she would not ask. One just did not vocalise certain physical, physiological or even emotional needs; it was not seemly. The ball was in Sally's court. She had to make the gesture. She had to offer to lend her friend a handkerchief. She took her time making the offer. In her mind and in her heart, for her emotions were as much engaged as her sense of ownership, she was weighing up the advantages of possession against the disadvantages of non-possession. There was only one conclusion she could reach. Even so, she made the supreme gesture. Her offer, which was made in rather a tight voice, as if it needed oiling, was humbly and gratefully accepted.

My aunt took a couple of steps across the room and stood pensively in front of the twin robes which I have since come to term, in my mind, as 'Fort Knox'. It was indeed a pair of very large, very solid, very splendid mahogany bedroom wardrobes. They had always been in the family, for they formed part of Grandmother's bridal suite and part of the dowry she had brought her husband. They were greatly cherished and shone brilliantly from regular dusting and polishing. One wardrobe had shelves and the other a long metal clothes rail. Both only just managed not to spill their contents, so crammed were they with possessions. The word 'crammed' suggests, perhaps, dilettante or haphazard arrangements. That is not the impression I wish to convey. It is simply that nothing material was ever discarded or considered superfluous in Grandmother's household, and it sooner or later found its way into one or other of the wardrobes. Their internal arrangements were in fact perfect models of perfect neatness, planned and executed with such cunning ingenuity that the wardrobes assumed, at least for me with the years, almost human qualities. They seemed to expand, they were willing to accommodate, they were a little smug about their well-filled bellies and nicely padded contours.

I am now more than old enough and reasonably able, I believe, to appraise possessions. For I too, am very attached to them and I too, experience a pang of sorrow when parting with an object of mine, however modest. I know now that those two wardrobes contained very little of any intrinsic value. I know too what significance possessions assume for us and how, through them, we believe, quite erroneously, to have a firm grip on life. So long as the two wardrobes, gorged beyond satiation, cast their protective shadow over the room and its inhabitants life went on, life made sense, life had a silver lining to it. Aunt Sally was now turning the key. It was always a treat for me to catch a glimpse of the interior of the wardrobes – particularly the one with the shelves, where the arrangements were more elaborate, more imaginative and the contents more varied. Those contents, which were as dear to my relations as the blood in the veins of their bodies, on which so much time, effort and tender care was lavished, comprised household and personal linen. Every item had gone through, time without number, washing, boiling, rinsing, starching and ironing processes. Every item, or nearly, bore marks of patient, skilful repairs, like so many surgical scars. There was hardly a sheet there that did not have a perfectly matched, exquisitely stitched patch on it; hardly an undergarment that had not been mended or darned with loving care. And the clothes, too, had been taken in and let out; taken up and let down; refurbished, altered, re-styled, dyed and re-dyed and eventually, when they were all but threadbare, they were passed down to the children in the family to be cut up, cut out, and made to fit them. And even then, when the children outgrew them and they had become virtually transparent, they were cut into neat squares, some to be used for trimming, some as dusters or rags for polishing the floor.

Aunt Sally's hand unerringly made for the right spot on the right shelf and there it hovered hesitantly for a minute or two. There were several stacks of handkerchiefs graded, as it were, according to age, condition, quality and even lineage – for some of them had a background and a history. Many considerations were passing through Sally's head, the uppermost being, as I well knew, that the handkerchief she parted with should be the oldest, the plainest, the least valuable. She soon found what she was looking for, extracted it from the stack and passed it to her friend. The lady left soon afterwards.

In the late summer of 1941, we learnt from Frau Berger's mother that Lt Berger, her son-in-law, was due for a spot of leave. A great flurry of activity was under way in his honour; a second spring-cleaning; mounds of delicacies being cooked and baked; a vase of fresh flowers on every table. As it turned out, he only had three days' furlough and I was the only one, by pure coincidence, to catch a glimpse of him.

It was late afternoon. I was returning from my daily trip to the Ghetto, having by now become the family's only link with the outside world. I noticed the black car standing by our gate. It signified that Lt and Frau Berger, were at home. Half way up the flight of stairs leading to the first floor, I met Frau Berger and her tall husband. As the staircase was not very wide, I stepped aside to let them pass. I said 'Guten Tag', to which they both smilingly responded. Frau Berger looking very elegant and smelling divinely, swept past me in a cinnamon-coloured, close-fitting silk frock. But the Lieutenant, in full *Luftwaffe* regalia, stepping back and raising his fingers to the peak of his cap, courteously indicated that I, standing just a couple of steps below him, should ascend before he would descend. I had never experienced such gallantry before, and from a

German officer and one so easy on the eye. It made me positively tingle with pleasure. I knew that physically, the ideal German was like Louise's toddler son Jurgen; strong, healthy, long-limbed with eyes the colour of forget-me-nots and hair the colour of sun-ripened corn. Lt Berger looked like a Greek god. His ancestors had surely once inhabited the shores of the Aegean Sea. He was a tall, erect man in a uniform which fitted him like the proverbial glove. He had a face to warm the cockles of a woman's heart: dark, smouldering eyes, whose very gaze was a caress; a jet-black whisker along the bronze, clean-shaven cheek; teeth like peeled almonds. A singularly well-favoured officer; a man of charm and impeccable manners. A gentleman was Lt Berger.

Autumn was again upon us. September. The school year had started. It seemed such a long time since I had set foot in the class-room and sat on a form at a desk. I remembered my two precious years of schooling so vividly and with such yearning. I would have been in the 5th Form now. The Polish autumn is beautiful. Truly 'A season of mists and mellow fruitfulness . . .' I was as aware of the changes in nature as I was of the changes in our life. I liked the long, dark autumn evenings when the stove had been lit and we felt snug and sheltered in our home. I lay tucked up in my bed, my book by the pillow, and listened to the howling of the wind and the pattering of the rain. I felt warm and protected. But the autumn of 1941 was different from all the previous autumns of our lives. For many of us it was, truly, the last season but one. And the sharp evening air carried on its chilly breath not only the pungent odours of the demise of nature. It carried the stench of singeing,charring human flesh – for the Jews were already dying, in great numbers, a terrible death.

During that autumn of 1941, some time after Frau Berger's family had returned to Lübeck and she was again living on her own, she made a gesture which revealed that she was not entirely divorced from the reality in which other, non-German, people lived.

The third winter of war was approaching – for thousands of Cracow Jews their last, but we were not to know that, and like all living creatures, we were preoccupied with the practicalities of day-to-day survival. Fuel, particularly coal, with the winter just round the corner, was becoming one of our main concerns. It was difficult to obtain and our purse-strings would not stretch to meet its already prohibitive but still rising price. Our kitchen range was insatiable, but if we were to cook our food and heat our water it had somehow to be fed. Quite unexpectedly, Frau Berger, who kept

Mamma busy enlarging and enhancing her winter wardrobe, asked if Mamma would like a delivery of coal. 'Coal, not slag', she said, 'to be deposited in your very cellar.' The timely offer was readily accepted by Mamma. The promise was kept. Some days later, a cart laden with sackfuls of coal drew up outside our gate. The coalmen, supervised by Joseph, emptied a number of sacks in our cellar. Joseph said it was half full. The coal, which apparently came all the way from Silesia, so the coalmen said, was good quality. In our joy, we planned to smuggle, somehow, a few small lumps, one at a time, into the Ghetto for Grandmother to use during the worst of the winter.

The following morning Mamma and I went down to the cellar to fill our bucket. I carried the old bucket and a small hand-shovel. Mamma unlocked the door and stood on the threshold. There was no need to cross it. Our cellar was empty. There was no coal in it. Not even coal-dust. It had been cleaned out some time during the night. 'What coal for the Jews? Too good for them . . . They can freeze like everybody else . . .' And some tip-toeing neighbour, stealthily and thoroughly, relieved us of it. Mamma and I looked at each other in stunned disbelief. Neither of us was able to utter a word. Mamma was very distressed. The tears glistened in her eyes. We climbed the stairs again, the hand-shovel rattling in the empty bucket.

Our true vicissitudes, which would make those of yore soon appear as a light breeze crinkling the surface of calm waters, were about to begin. The ghostly quiet before the Apocalyptic storm . . . The last weeks before we, too, crossed the Third Bridge and were sucked into the vortex of the Ghetto.

8 · The Basement Room

The latest edict concerning Cracow's Jewish population required Outer Cracow to be cleansed of Jews by December 1941. Again, they were offered a choice, although this time somewhat narrower – the Ghetto or the country proper. Again, there were those who made a mad scramble for the country in the belief that they were choosing freedom as opposed to incarceration. And so they were, for a limited period. Alas, there was no escaping the dragnet as they, too, would discover in a few months' time. The new Edict embraced both the 'Village' and 'Olsza' where Father's family lived. For us, a family of five who only just managed to eke out an existence, there was only the Ghetto . . .

For my parents the two most pressing problems were a roof over our heads in the Ghetto and an income which would enable us, as a family, to subsist. For the moment, the most immediate, the most burning need was to find solid shelter within the Ghetto walls. The building at No. 42 Limanowskiego Street, where Grandmother lived, belonged to Aunt Josephine's father. We knew it was full to bursting, but we appealed to her to intercede with him on our behalf; perhaps he still had some nook or cranny . . . She did. He said he had, although he was loath to offer either, a store-room in the courtyard and a basement room with a window (also in the court-yard). By the time this information reached us, the store-room had already been spoken for by a family of six. There are basement rooms and basement rooms – this was the worst. We took it.

The second equally serious problem was not to forfeit, through the move, our only steady source of income, Frau Berger's goodwill and patronage. The writing of petitions had petered out; the Jews having understood, by now, that it was a fruitless exercise. They were outside the protection of the law and could expect neither justice, nor humanity from the Authorities. Father no longer helped his sister and brother-in-law at the pub. That useful source of income had dried up too. As for winning at cards, even Father, an optimist, had to admit that 'Good Luck' and 'Good Fortune' had packed their bags and departed to distribute their smiles elsewhere, among non-Jews. Mamma spoke to Frau Berger as soon as the opportunity presented itself. She said, in acknowledgment; 'I see. Will you still be able to work for me?' Mamma, immensely relieved at her reaction, assured her that she would.

News that 'the Jews are moving to the Ghetto' spread round the 'Village' swiftly. Neighbours, acquaintances, people we only knew by sight, as well as total strangers, knocked on our door with the question: 'Are you selling anything?' The blouses with the pin-tucks, the pearl-grey suit, the fetching hats, the best part of Mamma's wardrobe found ready buyers. The bedroom wardrobes, the dining-table and chairs, the bedroom ceiling-light, which was like an inverted bowl filled with early morning sky on a sunny day . . . The hall-stand which contained a laundry-chest on which Bartuś and I used to sit whilst I read to him and told him stories . . . A crystal blue and white flower vase – a much treasured wedding gift . . . A rather nice wall tapestry embroidered by Mamma when she was a young girl . . . The best coffee set, decorated with bunches of flowers which Mamma had bought on impulse, something she very rarely did, because we both liked it so much . . . They were all snapped up . . . Possessions which were part of us, as we were part of them, went whilst much-handled, dog-eared banknotes were pressed into Mamma's hand . . .

Fine, frosty snow-flakes were drifting out of the sky, as we followed the horse-drawn cart carrying our much reduced worldly possessions. We were lucky. We had proper winter coats and shoes and gloves. The chestnut mare in between the cart's shafts was clip-clopping sedately. Our chattels were not beyond her strength. Bartuś and I, holding hands, kept an eye on the cart. The most precious object in it, carefully and lovingly padded round with pillows, blankets and goose-down comforters to ensure its safe arrival, was Mamma's 'Singer' sewing machine. Just as for a poor farming family the loss of their only cow means starvation, so for us the loss, or serious damage, of the old 'Singer' would mean the same.

By the time we had crossed the Third Bridge and were waiting at the gate for our papers to be checked and approved, to gain official entry into the Ghetto, an early winter twilight was descending upon Cracow. The cold was piercing. It was completely dark when we reached 42 Limanowskiego Street – tired, hungry and chilled right through. The cart-driver, glum and grumbling openly, helped Father and Joseph to empty the cart and to carry our possessions, by candle-light, down the sixteen steps into the basement room. Father paid him and he went. The room had no stove and no water. We had brought some bread and I fetched a saucepanful of hot soup from Grandmother's. We sat down, in our coats, on the mattresses and ate the bread and soup. Even in the dim, flickering candle-light our parents already looked different – weary and down-cast and aged. Mamma and I were going to sleep upstairs, at Grandmother's, until we had managed to set up a small iron stove, for there was a flue in the corner of the room; we did sleep upstairs for a while, Mamma with Sally, I on the kitchen table, even after the stove was in place.

From December, 1941, till June, 1942, the five of us lived in that dungeon of a room, deep down in the bowels of the building. That winter, my parents' last, was a harsh one and it seemed interminable . . . The yard was full of old sticks of furniture, which nobody wanted, to which everybody assumed they had a right . . . We helped ourselves and chopped them up for firewood. It was almost impossible to get the room warm. The walls remained damp and slimy; the floor-boards, riddled with woodworm, continued to rot. The tiny iron stove, which one of the neighbours helped us procure, was very temperamental and unpredictable. Some days we would manage to get it working; it would get red hot; we would gather round it for warmth and to watch the steam build up under the lids of our cooking pots. Some days, it simply refused to work, no matter how much we coaxed it. It would pour out black clouds of thick, acrid smoke which stung our eyes and made us cough. On those days we froze and there was no hot food. Mamma would then send me to one of the Ghetto's soup-kitchens where various hot, take-away dishes were sold. I would buy two portions of tripe and race back to bring it home hot. We shared it between the four of us, for Father was rarely home at that time, mopping up the thick, spicy gravy with bread. It made a meal.

Aunt Rose, Uncle Dolek, their two children and Grandmother Heim had also come to live in the Ghetto. They found a room, a very spacious one by Ghetto standards, at No. 4 The Square of Peace, in a one-storey tenement which enjoyed a unique position . . . It was on the doorstep of – it fully faced – the Ghetto's only square, its only open space and, as it turned out, the future *Umschlagplatz*. The tenement, too, was only about fifty paces from the Ghetto's busiest pedestrian gate, The Square of Peace gate. Grandmother Heim accepted this second move, as she accepted all things, with total docility. A second move within less than a year . . . At least, she was now back amongst her own people. By the time they came to live in the Ghetto, Aunt Rose and Uncle Dolek had renounced any right to their pub. I believe that they had handed it over, of their own volition and by private arrangement, to a Polish, Aryan owner . . .

On one occasion, when Father and I paid them a visit, and whilst Father was chatting with his mother and sister, I spotted a nice wedge of cottage cheese on a near-by table. I had not seen, never mind eaten, cottage cheese it seemed for an eternity. Quietly, inconspicuously, I edged closer to the table. I broke off a piece and stuffed it in my mouth. It crumbled and melted on my tongue . . . I broke off another piece and another . . . By the time Father and I left I had put the whole wedge away . . . Nobody had noticed – then . . . I believe that Aunt Rose was very angry when she discovered that the cheese had vanished, but Grandmother Heim did not hold it against me . . .

One morning, in January 1942, soon after we had moved into the Ghetto, and whilst Mamma and I were temporarily sleeping in Grandmother's room on the second floor – because of the terrible dampness and cold down in our basement – we were woken up, at the crack of dawn, by a loud torrent of words mounting up from the street. Still dazed by sleep, in our night-gowns, bare-footed, we rushed to the window, Mamma, Sally and I. Down in Limanowskiego Street, directly under our window, a black car, with a loudspeaker attached to its roof, was disgorging an unintelligible message. We threw the window open, and almost stunned by the onrush of frosty air, shivering, we listened intently. The message was in German. The occupants of the car the SS. Mamma, whose German was good, had difficulty in understanding the announcement, the distance and the volume distorting the words. We waited, fearful, for her to interpret. At last, she said: 'They want our furs . . . All furs, all fur trimmings are to be deposited, under penalty of death, by mid day at the "Fur-Depôt" set up in Wegierska Street . . .' Trembling all over, she closed the window and now – more than fully awake – we started dressing. Grandmother, who had not spoken up to now, asked innocently, 'Our furs? What for?' 'All furs – coats, jackets, stoles, trimmings – even fur-lined boots and slippers', replied Mamma – 'by mid day.' Mamma, pale-faced, her eyes large, looked pensive. 'They need our furs. They need them for the Russian front. They are feeling the cold' she said. 'They need Jewish furs to keep them warm . . .' We were non-plussed, rather

66

than frightened, by this direct demand, the first we had experienced, to hand over our possessions just like that, at a moment's notice.

All Mamma possessed by way of 'fur' was a black, pony collar on her winter coat and a grey Persian lamb collar and cuffs on the jacket of her heavy winter suit. It transpired, however, that Grandmother owned a proper, full length furcoat. It came as a bit of a surprise! I had never seen it and Mamma, equally taken aback, did not remember it. We were fully dressed now; Sally was boiling a small saucepan of water on the spirit stove. Grandmother pulled out the bottom drawer of the wardrobe. She drew forth a large, well-filled linen bag. She loosened the drawstrings – producing a voluminous, rusty, pony furcoat with a shawl collar in matching fox-fur. She spread out the garment on her already neatly made bed. She said, a bit diffidently: 'It was quite nice . . . It was passed down to me. I can't remember when I wore it last . . .' We gathered round the bed, hardly believing our eyes. It was a mangy, moth-eaten garment, almost bald, except for the odd patch here and there, showing the pony's original colouring. The fox's nap had gone as well, except for a handful of sparsely scattered bristles. The stitching between the pelts was coming adrift and the coat's lining was full of rents. 'I suppose it will have to be handed in. I was a young girl when I was given it.' She sighed.

Mamma and I went down to our basement. It was Sunday. Joseph was at home. He had managed to light the stove and he and Bartuś were busy heating the potato soup for our breakfast. Mamma took her coat and jacket out of the cupboard. She proceeded to unpick the trimmings. She was neither sad nor upset. Just thoughtful. She passed them to me saying, 'Hand them in with Grandmother's coat.'

I stuffed the trimmings inside the furcoat's pockets and slinging it over my arm came out of the building. It was a raw January day. People must have found it hard to part with a warm, snug furcoat on a day like that. As it was Sunday, the Ghetto's entire population was inside the walls.

All along Limanowskiego Street I saw small groups of people engaged in earnest discussion – brows furrowed. On the corner of Wegierska Street, I met Mamma's cousin, Polly, and her husband in their sumptuous fur-lined winter coats. Polly, very preoccupied said' 'We just don't know what to do – all our furs . . . It can't be? What have you got there?' 'Oh, just Grandmother's old furcoat and Mamma's trimmings', I replied. 'Yes. I see.' She was too polite to comment.

I walked into the Depôt with our offerings. There was an SS man, in a greatcoat, cap and gloves, sitting at a table by the entrance. I stopped a few paces away from it. He raised his hand pointing his gloved index finger over his shoulder. I saw a great pile of furs on the floor in the centre of the room, like a gigantic, brindled animal. I approached it and let our contribution slide onto it.

I met Lidka Fajweles and her mother in Limanowskiego Street, in the winter of 1942, soon after we came to live in the Ghetto. 'Lidka', I cried – 'Yasia!' and we threw our arms round each other. Lidka and I used to belong to the same Religious Instruction group for children who attended non-Jewish state schools. I had not seen her since we broke up for the summer holidays in June 1939, before the war. She had changed, grown and filled out, but I would have recognised that magnificent, flaxen plait, her only claim to beauty, anywhere. We used to sit together in class. We liked each other, even though we were as different as chalk and cheese. She was a big, solidly built girl, with a round, pale face and pale eyes, a spitting image of her mother, both unmistakably Jewish in appearance. But she did not have her mother's warm, friendly smile. A quiet, passive girl, an adored only child, she was not spoilt. Her mother was even-tempered and sensible. We had so much to say to each other, but Limanowskiego Street, on a freezing January day was no place to linger in and chat. Her mother invited me to come and see them. 'Yes, come . . . promise?' added Lidka. They, too, lived in Limanowskiego Street, just by the traffic gate, only about three houses away from us and had been in the Ghetto from the very beginning.

I visited Lidka several times between January and June 1942. One entered her flat from a wooden balcony facing the courtyard. She and her mother shared a room with two middle-aged, maiden ladies – they were in no way related, they just happened to be 'lumped' together by the Housing Committee. Her father lived elsewhere. Her parents had had to separate, she told me, because the two ladies would not so much as hear of sharing the room with a male. They said the idea was too preposterous to be taken seriously. Sometimes, I accompanied her when she went to see her father, who lived at the other end of the Ghetto, and we were then able to chat freely and be ourselves, which was impossible in the constrained atmosphere of her room.

Every time I paid Lidka a visit, I was asked by one of the ladies – they occupied the near half of the room by the door, so that one could not avoid crossing their territory – if I had wiped my feet properly. Both of them eyeing, pointedly, my scuffed, well-worn, ankle-high boots. Then the other lady would chip in, just like that, for no obvious reasons 'Ghetto or no Ghetto, we do not intend to lower our standards by a fraction of an inch.'

There was an extraordinary finesse about the two ladies – almost an ethereal quality. Two grey-haired, slight and slender women, attired and coiffured with extreme care, sitting, at their end of the room, in their comfortable easy chairs, by their perfectly made beds, reading . . . They wished to appear totally absorbed in their reading matter, but I do not think they were . . . They never set foot outside their room, so I learnt from Lidka, for fear of soiling their fine footwear in the Ghetto's dirty, littered streets, and to avoid any and all contact with the riff-raff that walked up and down those same streets. Lidka's mother was a gentle-woman and Lidka, herself, a well brought-up, placid girl – yet they were not socially acceptable to the two ladies. To emphasize their separateness from the Ghetto and its life, they employed a woman, a go-between, who came daily to clean, cook and wash for them. She also did their shopping and ran their errands. But, then, they had always had servants. They kept their hands soft and white and delicate . . . Continuing to adhere to the customs and habits of a lifetime reinforced their sense of independence from the Ghetto. They had not knuckled down. They sat there oblivious to and yet acutely aware of, all that went on around them. Two perfectly groomed, prim and proper ladies who prided themselves on being impervious to the 'tremors' of the volcano upon which they lived, passively waiting . . . But it was eerie. Life had been frozen, like assets in a bank, and they were patiently waiting for . . . a thaw. Their every even breath, every punctilious gesture, every perfectly enunciated syllable made one understand that they were quietly waiting. And whilst biding their time, they exercised extreme vigilance over their persons, minds and social accomplishments, so as to be able to return to their place, when the waiting had ended, in civilised society. But, little by little the waiting had ceased to be abstract; it had become almost solid, palpable, odorous; it had become a living organism emanating dreadful fear. One could not stay long in that room without feeling its tentacles fastening upon one.

We sat at Lidka's end of the room, by the window, and talked in hushed tones, conscious that we were disturbing the ladies' reading – encroaching upon their privacy. Lidka's mother plied me with questions about 'The Outside'. She would sigh and say, 'Oh, to stroll along the streets of Cracow with my husband and daughter, free, just once more.' In the end I came to see her as much as Lidka. The two ladies were always present. They never relaxed their rigorous stance. I knew they disapproved of me.

One late afternoon, it was already dark, in the winter of 1942, I came out of the Ghetto's only pharmacy in the Square of Peace having run an errand for Grandmother. She had asked me to collect Regina's prescription. It was very cold; the night's icy fingers were clawing at my face. The silent streets were dark and deserted. A thin, tinny moon stood still in the sky. I saw a tall figure coming towards me, 'Daddy' I exclaimed. 'Yasia', he responded and scooped me up so that my legs dangled in the air. He kissed and hugged me. He had just come out of Grandmother Heim's tenement, which was almost opposite the pharmacy. Quickly I peeled off my glove and put my bare hand in his. He never wore gloves, he just kept his hands in his pockets. His hand was so warm. The night had changed its aspect. The moon and the stars were shining brightly in the velvety blackness of the sky and now it was just a frosty winter's evening.

We entered a house in Targova Street. Father knocked at a door on the ground floor. A woman opened it. The room we entered was warm and well lit and it smelled, unbelievably, of roast goose. The woman was pleased to see us. She addressed Father by his first name and knew mine. She bid us remove our outer garments and sit down at the table which was covered with a lovely white cloth and nicely set for a meal. The woman, in her forties, plump and neat, wearing an immaculate apron over her dark dress, busied herself at the stove. She had just that one biggish, bright, clean room in the centre of which stood the round table at which we had seated ourselves. 'Lila runs a small restaurant, just for friends.' said Father. She turned round, smiled and nodded. She brought each of us a plateful of tasty, piping hot soup. I ate very slowly, because it was scalding my mouth and because I felt a lump rising in my throat. She removed the empty plates, all the while chatting with Father, and presently brought us the main course. I looked at my plate; the food, tantalising in itself, was very nicely arranged on the plate: two slices of roast goose, roast potatoes and red cabbage. A meal like that, in a room like this. The lump in my throat was getting bigger. I did not want to embarass Father or the woman. I did not want to spoil the pleasure of this mouth-watering meal – so beautifully cooked, so daintily served. But I could not swallow. I thought of

Mamma and Joseph and Bartuś, of the cold, damp, bleak room, of the potato soup Mamma was cooking for the evening meal. I wondered if the stove was acting up . . . The woman, very surprised, said, 'Don't you like it, Yasia?' 'Oh, yes, I do, very much.' 'Then why aren't you eating?' 'I . . . I don't seem to be hungry. I don't seem to be able to swallow.' Father looked at me, his kind, blue eyes close to my face. But the woman knew why I could not eat. She came over with a plateful of beautifully sliced goose-breast, each slice trimmed with a ribbon of crisp, golden skin and said, 'Look, I'm going to wrap these up for you to take home to your Mamma and brothers. And there's a loaf of freshly baked white bread to go with them. I'll wrap it all up, nicely, for you to take home. Don't cry, now then.' Father gave me his handkerchief. I blew my nose and dried my tears. We ate.

9 • Saturday and Sunday Jobs

During a particularly cold snap, in the winter of 1942, one of the neighbours in our building approached me with the offer of what I can only describe as a 'Saturday Job'. She asked: 'Do you know how to light a fire?' 'Yes, very well', I replied. Would I be willing to do it, every Saturday, for her friend's daughter? I would be paid for my services. It did not even occur to the neighbour to sound Mamma out on the subject; I was already considered quite autonomous.

I was engaged by a young married woman to light the fire in her room every Saturday morning. She and her husband, only recently married, were a strictly Orthodox couple. I knew that it would have been an infringement of their religious observance, for either of them, to light a fire on the Sabbath.

They were people of considerable means; this was obvious from their life-style. Their room was large and only two of them in it – they must have had influential friends or relations to have obtained such accommodation, all to themselves, in the desperately over-crowded Cracow Ghetto.

Every Saturday morning, punctually, I went to the flat, in which they had their room and found newspaper, matches, wood and coal. They had plenty of the latter, though it was as rare and as coveted as gold-dust, even outside the Ghetto, all neatly prepared. All I had to do was to lay the fire, which I was well able to do, get it going and once it was blazing away, judiciously pile it up with lumps of coal, so that the young couple could enjoy its warmth all day without having to add to it. The money for my services had, also, been put out in advance – for neither of them would handle money on the Sabbath. All I had to do was to scoop it up, put it in my pocket and say 'good-bye'. But I liked to linger over the job. I found the couple and their room spell-binding. They were both tall and dark and strikingly good-looking. They were, also, very elegant in themselves

72

and in their possessions. I often wondered if there was another such room, an island of cleanliness, orderliness, comfort, peace and, to my eyes, luxurious beauty in the quagmire of the Ghetto.

The furniture was solid and glossy; the rugs silky and muted in colour; the pictures and ornaments discreet and yet, glowing with a natural richness. It was the bed, however, that I found the most enchanting – a heaven within a haven. It was the kind of bed in which generations of the same family are conceived, born and die . . . Its elaborately carved, highly polished dark wood was complemented by the loveliest bedspread I have ever seen. It was made of delicate, creamy voile scattered with nosegays of pink carnations, so skilfully embroidered that the buds seemed to be bursting open and the pale-green ribbon, binding them, to be unfurling in the breeze. It was framed, as it were, by broad bands of beautifully crocheted cream lace, carrying the same floral motif, to give it body and to make it hang well at the sides. The palest, pink, silk lining underpinned it. I never got tired of feasting my gaze on the bed and its exquisite appurtenances.

The young couple were kind and considerate towards me; yet there was an aloofness, an impenetrability about them that made me understand that I knew nothing about their world and that this brief, weekly contact with them allowed me a glimpse, reserved for the privileged only, of the inner sanctum of that world and their life.

There was an added bonus to this job. The young couple lived on the second floor. On the first, directly underneath my employers, there lived a family of pastry-cooks who supplied the Ghetto restaurants, pastry-shops and cafés with their delicious, mouth-watering products. The landing windows in that building had very deep inward ledges. On the first floor ledge there stood bowls, dishes, basins, even buckets, put out to cool and stay fresh till required, of mousses, creams, custards, pastes, fillings. The kind of stuff that fairytales and children's dreams are made of and I was only eleven years old.

I would pad up to the first floor as soundlessly as I could and stop for a 'rest' on the landing by the window. The ledge was always laden. Swiftly and expertly, I would plunge my right hand index finger into a container, and draw it out all gooey with raspberry mousse or mocha cream, lick it clean and proceed onto the next and the next and the next container. However many times I dipped my finger in a particular dish, I never left the slightest trace on its surface of any sampling of its contents, but patted it neatly over, so

73

that nobody was any the wiser. I would then climb up to the second floor and ring my employers' bell, already 'high' as a result of the 'tippling' I had done on the way up and was going to do, again, on the way down. My employers must have thought me a very cheerful girl indeed. I was never caught red-handed sampling these glorious fillings. If I did hear a door open, or footsteps in the hallway, I would simply bend down, my back to the ledge and pretend to be tying a shoe-lace.

We did not see much of Frau Berger during the last month of the old and the first month of the new year. What with Christmas, the New Year and the Festive Season, generally, she was caught up in a whirl of social activity which left little time for anything else. And her wardrobe was more than adequately equipped to cover any social occasion, however esoteric.

When Mamma first started working for Frau Berger, she would hand over one length of fabric at a time. But after about a year, or so, of their mutually satisfactory association, she told Mamma that she would prefer her to work on two outfits simultaneously. The initial session – the selecting of fabric, style and accessories was, inevitably, more lengthy than when planning only one garment, but she could have double fittings and save time and bother that way. Although she still enjoyed standing in front of the long cheval mirror in her room turning and twisting this way and that, preening herself, having the fabric draped against her body, singly or in combination with another, flowing over her shoulder, gathered at her breast, the novelty was wearing thin. She had come to rely on Mamma and have confidence in her. Mamma, too, understood her well by now; she knew her likes and dislikes, her quirks, what discreetly emphasized her attributes, flattered and enhanced her slender shape. What really suited her and what did not; what made her feel good, attractive, desirable and ultimately brought out her approving smile.

She was quite happy to listen to Mamma's suggestions and let her use her flair and discretion. And whereas, at first, each garment required two fitting sessions, now much to Mamma's gratification and Frau Berger's relief, one was perfectly sufficient. In that respect, their association had grown, matured and was bearing fruit.

The problem was, however, and it was one of major proportions, that we no longer lived on the next floor from Frau Berger. Not only did we now live at the other end of Cracow, but we lived behind the walls of the Ghetto. For Mamma to move on the 'Outside' legally,

74

she needed an official pass stamped and signed by the Authorities. This she could not obtain, as she was not involved in war-industry sanctioned by them. Hers was a private venture and Frau Berger a private individual. It was one thing for me, a child of eleven, to be slipping in and out of the Ghetto, to be moving, intrepidly, outside the walls; it was quite another for an adult, subject to the multiple restrictions and harshly punitive laws.

As the day approached to pay Frau Berger a call, Mamma and I reached a compromise as far as the trips to the 'Village' and the wearing of the armband were concerned. Neither of us was at all Jewish in appearance – that was the main reason why these trips were at all possible – Mamma was, however, obliged to wear the white brassard with the Star of David on her arm. She agreed to wear it under a long, grey shawl draped round her shoulders – the brassard was thus hidden, it would not draw attention to us outside the walls and, yet, she was not breaking the law, not on that count.

The day came to call on Frau Berger. The day I had dreaded. For Mamma to go 'Outside' was a most perilous venture on a number of other counts apart from the armband. She had no pass. She had to cross the whole of Cracow – it was not unusual for a man or a woman to be stopped in the street by a German demanding to see their papers. To go back to the 'Village', into the very street, into the very building where we had lived for so many years and where everyone knew us, was an added considerable hazard. And where, although we had never crossed swords with anyone, there were people who hated the Jews for all sorts of reasons; sometimes for no reason at all – just on principle. We would not take the tram; it could be stopped anywhere along its route by the German patrols, the entrance and exit blocked, the passengers ordered to produce their identity papers for inspection. Once trapped inside a tram, there was no escape. Sometimes, they were all herded into a waiting lorry and driven away. We would walk. The streets seemed safer. We would time the 'operation', for an operation it was, to arrive at the 'Village' at dusk. Under the cover of darkness, moving with extreme caution, we would steal along the road, soundlessly enter the building and like thieves in the night, tiptoe up the stairs and lightly ring Frau Berger's bell. We had made it one way. There was always the return journey at the back of our minds.

I was fast becoming an old woman of eleven. The more responsibility I took upon my shoulders, the better I understood how much I loved Mamma, how much I feared for her safety. These expeditions where she was flouting the law, exposing herself to the most terrible danger, imposed a great strain upon me. I shook and trembled for Mamma's safety. I clutched her arm tightly; my own body was to be a fortress against the buffetings of the enemy. I much preferred to go out alone. I had no fear for myself. I was neither morally, nor physically brave. I did not even understand, at that time, the concept of moral courage. In my inexperience and ignorance, I naively believed that nobody, not even a German, could be cruel to a child. I was fortunate; having reached the age of eleven, I had never yet been the direct object of any form of physical aggression or cruelty.

It was during our first call on Frau Berger since we had moved to the Ghetto, with Cracow in the grip of a long, bitingly cold winter, that she told Mamma she too was feeling the need of a warm, cosy garment which would protect her from the season's harshness. She explained that she wished to acquire a furcoat, and did Mamma know of anyone who might wish to dispose of a suitable garment? For a moment or two, there was an awkward silence. Mamma had to explain, tactfully and diplomatically, that there were no furs in the Ghetto and why. 'I see' said Frau Berger, rather put out at the inconvenience of it all. Mamma added, however, that she would speak to a furrier who might be able to put her onto someone outside who traded in that sort of commodity. Frau Berger brightened visibly saying, 'It would be nice to have it before the winter is over.' Mamma, understanding her little joke perfectly, lost no time in tracking down a furrier in the Ghetto who was able to put us in touch with an Aryan woman trading in pelts who, as luck would have it, commanded the services of an excellent Aryan furrier. The whole transaction had to take place outside the Ghetto, since no pelts could be brought inside the walls. Neither of these two individuals, with whom Mamma was negotiating, knew that we were Jewish, that we came from the Ghetto. It made dealing with them straightforward and certainly, cheaper.

There was a great deal of to-ing and fro-ing to be done on the 'Outside' in which I played an active part – between the pelts' 'specialist', the furrier and of course the lynch-pin in the transaction – Frau Berger. She selected a set of very nicely dressed rusty pony pelts. She wanted them made up in the style of a military greatcoat, double-breasted, with two rows of buttons and an ample collar, lapels and cuffs. Mamma had agreed with the furrier, who was only too glad to accede to her proposal – he said he had no time for the finicky work – that she would put in the lining, sew on the fastenings and add whatever finishing touches the garment required. We thus delivered the furcoat almost ready, but not quite, to Frau Berger one late, dark afternoon. She liked it immensely, but her mouth assumed a pout of disappointment because she could not ensconce herself in it right away and appear, thus ensconced, before her friends and admirers. Mamma explained that it still required several hours' work, all of which had to be done by hand using an awl, as opposed to an ordinary needle. Of course, she could not take it home to complete. It had to be done *in situ*. Frau Berger, fired as much by eagerness as impatience, hit upon the perfect solution. 'Look', she said, 'why not come tomorrow, as early as you can and spend the night here? You will have the flat to yourselves and I shall leave the larder well stocked up. You need not rush. You can take your time in quiet and warmth'. Mamma agreed.

Did Frau Berger know that harbouring a Jew carried the death penalty? If she did, her facial expression gave no hint of it. It remained inscrutable.

We did spend that one night in Frau Berger's flat. Neither of us felt talkative. Neither of us wanted to pain the other. We were both remembering the same things, I think, the days when we too lived in this very building and how different life then was . . .

I sat up with Mamma for a while, after we had eaten, but she said that she would have to work well into the night – it was slow, arduous work. I lay down on the bed and for a while watched Mamma sitting in the pool of yellow light, her head bent forward, the lower part of her body submerged under the ample fur garment, her nimble fingers plying the awl. When I woke up in the morning, Mamma was lying next to me all warm, breathing softly.

Within a short time of acquiring a 'Saturday job', I was offered a 'Sunday job'. Although it was much less glamorous, it was still satisfactory and profitable. It was, however, very demanding in self-restraint. My Aunt Josephine, my Mother's eldest brother's widow, had a sister, also a widow, who owned a thriving sanitary-ware shop in Cracow. Within a few months of the occupation, a German overseer was assigned to the shop and Hannah, the owner, became a mere cipher in the business. Even so, her presence irked him and cramped his style and he schemed and plotted until she was requested by the Authorities to answer a charge of irregularities in her accounts ledger. She was removed from the shop and detained in a women's prison pending investigation. Aunt Josephine knew all about prison fare from the days when her own husband was incarcerated at Montelupich prison. She still kept, by Ghetto standards, a good table. She and her children enjoyed well-balanced, wholesome, regular meals. She approached me with a business proposition. Would I deliver Sunday lunch to her imprisoned sister? She would pay me in kind. The scraps and crumbs from her table were very tempting, very desirable. It was a cold, hungry winter. Every little helped. I accepted the commission.

Every Sunday, I collected Hannah's lunch from Aunt Josephine. It was a three-course meal; thick, piping-hot soup; a tasty and substantial main course; a mouth-watering pudding. The three courses were placed in neat aluminium containers which fitted over each other and were then slotted onto an aluminium frame with a comfortable wooden handle for easy transportation.

I would slip out of the Ghetto and make my way on foot to the prison. It was the third winter of war. It was bitterly cold. It was Sunday. The Cracow Streets were almost deserted. Only dire necessity drove people out of doors. An almost empty tram would clank by. A pedestrian, muffled up to the ears against the buffeting of the icy wind, would slink by. A group of Jewish women would be clearing the streets of the winter's ballast, chipping and scraping ice off the pavements and sweeping it, in neat little piles, into the gutters; shovelling snow and pommelling it into tall, white mounds at street corners. A chauffeur-driven, black limousine carrying a high-ranking German officer – his face almost hidden by the ample fur collar of his greatcoat – would glide by. And although some part of my brain registered these sights and sounds, my mind was totally preoccupied with the food I was carrying.

Every Sunday, my conscience and I wrestled silently, but nonetheless remorselessly, with each other. I wanted to creep into a quiet, sheltered doorway, out of the cold, out of the wind, out of sight, sit down, unseen, unnoticed, in some dark corner on a flight of stairs and devour Hannah's lunch. Every doorway I walked past seemed to be offering just the kind of haven I was looking for. Every Sunday, I went through the same temptation, the same torment and the same relentless tussle with my conscience.

'But you have no spoon, no fork.' my conscience would point out. I would slurp the hot, aromatic soup; I would tear the rest with my teeth and my fingers, the thought of biting into a roast potato made me almost swoon with desire; the fruity, liquid pudding – I would pour it down my throat; I would lick the containers clean, I would lick my fingers clean; nobody would know. 'But think of Hannah

waiting in her prison cell for her lunch', my conscience would inter-
ject.

I never yielded to the temptation of gobbling up Hannah's
Sunday lunch. Every Sunday, throughout that long, white winter,
her lunch was delivered on time. Then, in the spring of 1942,
Hannah was released from prison, having renounced all right to her
business and to her Cracow home. She went, with her two children,
to live in Bochnia.

Mamma was being eroded by the Ghetto, by our living conditions
and by the desperate struggle to preserve a semblance of dignity; by
the yoke of day-to-day existence. She kept herself and her family
clean and neat; she washed, ironed and cooked. Above all, she sat at
the sewing-machine, under the window, to keep the wolf from the
door. She knew that Frau Berger's 'custom' remained essential to
our survival. Throughout that interminable winter she tried to give
us two hot meals a day, even if it was only soup. It was important to
her to keep the room clean and tidy, for everything to be in its
allotted place. And her hands – she had to keep them soft and cared
for. How else could she handle those fine fabrics? How else could
she work on those elegant garments? The effort took a terrible toll of
her. We, the children, helped as much as we could, but right up to
the end she remained the family bread-winner. Her children looked
to her to be fed.

Father spent a great deal of time at Grandmother Heim's in the
Square of Peace, where living conditions, although modest, were
much more favourable than ours. They lived above ground and still
kept a decent table. Father and his circle of friends still met. They
would meet in a café, or a restaurant, or somebody's room. All they
needed was a corner to themselves; a table, chairs, a pack of cards, a
packet of cigarettes – the respite of a few hours' escape; a degree of
oblivion. One smothered, temporarily, the nightmare of day-to-day
life.

It was during that first winter in the Ghetto that I became almost
obsessed with food; I hankered after plain, homely, hot food in
abundance and bread – good, tasty bread thinly spread with butter.
It was not real hunger, as I would discover later and even then there
were degrees. It was just that I could not stop thinking about food.
My whole body, including my brain, ached with the craving for
food. We had disposed of the best part of our 'estate' when we came
to the Ghetto. Even so, Mamma still found odds and ends to sell. She
would still produce the odd nice piece of household linen, and the

remnants of her wardrobe, shoes, gloves, a handbag. She parted with them one by one. I took them out and sold them on the 'Outside'. They did not fetch much, but enough to buy a loaf of bread, some vegetables, a bottle of milk, a few eggs.

I was returning from one such expedition – the tram having just pulled away from the last 'Aryan' stop. Literally within seconds it would be taking the very sharp corner on entering the Ghetto traffic gate. It was already assuming its concertina shape. Having just set in motion, and being about to negotiate that very sharp corner, it was moving at a snail's pace. The moment to jump off was immediately after it entered the Ghetto; I should have been mentally and physically tensed up for it, before the concertina straightened out and started gathering speed.

But I had missed my cue; I had not been quick enough, not alert enough. I was carrying a well-filled shopping bag. I had to be swift and nimble; it was a manoeuvre I had done many times, and would do many more times. There was no excuse for my absent-mindedness, except that I had, probably, been lost in a day-dream about food. I had to remain on the tram as it drove, close to the pavement, along the even-numbered side of Limanowskiego Street – our side.

Standing on the pavement, right in front of the doorway of No. 42, our doorway, were Mamma and Bartuś. Mamma, the grey shawl draped round her shoulders for warmth, was holding Bartuś by the hand. They were expecting me back and were watching out for me, but they were both, attentively, looking straight in front of them, as if their gaze were fixed on some distant point, visible only to them. What did they see in the distance? What were they looking at so intently? Had they looked up, they would have seen me as clearly as I saw them. We were only divided by the thickness of a tram's window pane, but we may as well have been separated by all the seas of the world poured into one, for our destinies, already charted, were tearing us apart. Of all the images that my mind's eye has preserved of that period of my life – this is the clearest, the most detailed and the most painful. Mother and child – so plainly scarred by the Ghetto – standing in that cold, grey street, vulnerable and defenceless. The child is clinging to the mother for protection, but she is not able to offer it. It hurts . . . Overwhelmed by love and pity, the tears stung my eyes, but a public conveyance was no place to indulge myself.

With the vague promise of spring, for it was late and slow in coming, the Ghetto match-makers came out of hibernation and Sally found herself, once more, the object of their assiduous attentions. A healthy, energetic woman, time was hanging heavy on her hands. She wanted to work and to earn, even if only a pittance. I do not know how the match-makers went about stalking their prey, for it remained a closely guarded secret of the trade, but find Sally they did.

One day, two middle-aged ladies, of very sober aspect, called on Grandmother. Their tactics had changed. They had adapted to the place and the time. 'Was her younger daughter', they asked Grandmother, 'looking for gainful employment?' A great deal of cottage industry had sprung up in the Ghetto they explained. That was true of course. They talked about it at some length, by way of a preamble to the true reason for their visit. They knew a widower, they said – a fine figure of a man – who had been a most devoted husband and father. A good, steady provider and a highly respectable and respected member of the Cracow Jewish Community. He was running a brush-making factory, here, in the Ghetto, a very lucrative enterprise they assured Grandmother. And the gentleman was contemplating re-marriage. Only the best would be good enough and they knew Grandmother's youngest daughter to be a jewel beyond value. That was why they were calling . . .

A meeting was arranged. Courtship, normally, required privacy, the one commodity unobtainable in the Ghetto. The two match-makers were not easily daunted. Sally and her prospective employer met, at their invitation, in the two ladies' abode. Within days of that meeting large sacks of wooden forms, roughly planed and crudely perforated, as well as sacks of bunches of bristles started arriving at Grandmother's address. The gentleman, a portly, kindly man in his fifties, had fallen for Sally hook, line and sinker.

Although spring was just round the corner, the evenings were still long and dark and very cold. But their nature had changed since Sally and the brush manufacturer had come to an understanding. The kitchen table at Grandmother's, which doubled as my bed at night, became a beehive of activity. There were sometimes as many as eight people sitting round it threading bristles into the forms with Sally, at its head, directing operations. She had clever, dexterous fingers and had taken to brush-making like a duck to water. It was a pleasant way to pass those long, dark evenings. The room was warm and well lit. Members of the family, as well as neighbours, came, as did Mamma, Bartuś and I, to help with the brush-making, as much as to be in the warm, in the light, to listen and to talk. Bartuś

81

and I made ourselves useful; we put out supplies; we collected the finished products and stacked them neatly into sacks and generally saw to it that everyone had what they needed.

The couple from the kitchen came every evening. The kitchen in Grandmother's flat had long ceased to be used as such. An elderly couple moved into it and made themselves very snug in there. Mr and Mrs Wintner were very lonely. They had no family at all. Their only daughter, son-in-law and grandchildren, whom they had never seen, lived in England. They had not heard from them for a long time. Mrs Wintner, a tall, thin woman with enormous bags under her eyes, was very quiet. Mr Wintner, a big, heavy man with a loud voice, held forth every evening on the political situation – giving his assessments and predictions. Everyone listened in rapt attention. I understood none of it, but I still liked to listen, if only to hear the strange names rolling off his tongue with which his discourse was thickly peppered. They, too, like everybody else, became quite adept at brush-making. Sometimes, Aunt Josephine came down accompanied by her teenage daughter, Irena. Lola and her daughter, also called Irena, who were the occupants of the other room (and Aunt Josephine's sister and niece) in Grandmother's flat, came every evening. They all made their contribution and the pile of 'finished' brushes grew.

Occasionally, the gathering was graced by Helcia – a cousin on Grandmother's side – a poor relation. She was in her late twenties – a pretty woman with large, green eyes and dark, curly hair. She was married to a watchmaker and had two children, a girl and a boy. She was in despair. They had not been able to find anywhere permanent to live and were being sent from pillar to post ever since they came to the Ghetto in December. She did not sit at the table. She stood with her back to the tall, tiled stove and sang to us. She had a lovely voice – warm and mellow – in which she sang old-fashioned, romantic ballads. A hush fell upon the room, as she took us to woods and fields, rivers and lakes, castles and peasant cottages.

One evening, in the early spring of 1942, crossing the entrance hall in Grandmother's flat I noticed just as I was about to turn right, that the door on the left, the door of what used to be the kitchen and now was the Wintners' room, was slightly ajar. It was strange; Mrs Wintner was most particular about locking her door. And their light was not on either. Quietly, I inched towards that door. Lightly, I pushed it inwards with the tips of my fingers. The room was dark, but by the light of the silvery moon, dribbling its sheen at the window, I was able to see an object. A cold stove. On the cold stove, a cold frying pan. In the cold frying pan a cold, nicely-browned mince-meat cutlet. I saw nothing else in that room. Softly, I walked up to the stove. Gingerly, I picked up the cutlet with my fingers. Joyously, I sank my teeth in it. Slowly, chewing well, savouring every bite, I ate it. I licked my fingers clean and left the room. I joined the usual brush-making gathering in Grandmother's room.

Later on in the evening, as the gathering started breaking up, Mr and Mrs Wintner said 'goodnight' and left. Within a minute or two of their departure, Mrs Wintner had lightly rapped on the door and opening it just enough to put her head in, said, 'Miss Sally, may I have a word with you, please?' Sally returned a few minutes later, scarlet in the face, and gave me a searching look. When the gathering had broken up, and as I was about to take Bartuś down, Sally asked us to remain. She said she wanted to ask me a question in the presence of Mr and Mrs Wintner, whom she fetched. They were already in their nightwear and dressing gowns. Sally was very angry indeed. Mamma and Bartuś, sensing a confrontation, placed themselves, like sentinels, on either side of me. 'Did you take the mince-meat cutlet?' asked Sally. 'Yes, I did.' 'I expect you have eaten it.' 'Yes, I have.'

Strangely enough, the Wintners did not appear angry. They said 'goodnight' again, and went back to their room. 'How could you disgrace us like that?' asked Sally. Mamma did not say one word in my defence, nor in my condemnation. All she said was, 'It is high time, as it is spring now, we started sleeping in our room.' She kissed her mother and sisters 'goodnight'. On the way down Bartuś asked, 'Are we all going to sleep together, Mamma? You, Yasia and I?' Mamma said, 'Yes, we are.' He started jumping for joy. Mamma and I hugged and kissed him.

10 · The Carpet

The long-awaited, fateful spring came at last. My twelfth birthday, in April, came and went like any other Ghetto day. It was only remarkable inasmuch as it was my one and only birthday in the Cracow Ghetto. I clearly remember waking up, squashed but warm, between Mamma and Bartuś, opening my eyes to the murkiness of the room and thinking, 'I am twelve years old today.'

In spring, the human heart fills with hope and its burden eases. One discards the heavy, restricting layers of winter clothing, one wears light, open shoes. The warm, soothing air reaches one's body. It bathes and caresses one's face, hands and feet. A warm breeze lifts one's hair and tangles it. Pale-green is the grass and nature is busy sprouting buds, shoots and leaves. Insects appear and buzz in the soft, fragrant air. A re-birth takes place. But we, in the Ghetto, felt none of the new season's manifestations – only the cold, the frost and the snow had gone. Our hearts were oppressed and heavy; our bodies undernourished and weary; our clothes and shoes worn and shabby.

The atmosphere in the Ghetto was becoming one of tremulous fear. Rumours were flying, thick and fast, in every direction. The importance of useful, solid labour, for the Occupier's benefit, could not be overstated. There were whispers in the air about registrations, selections, transportations which, in the light of subsequent events, we did not really understand. These simple words became swollen, enlarged with shades of meaning they did not originally possess.

Father, to our tremendous relief and joy, was assigned to a construction unit employing about twenty men and went outside daily with his group to a building site in one of Cracow's principal streets. He appeared to hold an advisory position rather than a practical one. He liked the job and his co-workers and they liked him. His gift for getting on with people and his genuine goodwill towards them stood him in good stead. The job boosted his morale, too. He

84

believed he was protecting his family and himself. His evenings were still his own, to spend as he wished.

Joseph, having inherited Mamma's 'Golden Hands', was attached to a tailoring workshop producing military uniforms – a much needed, no nonsense enterprise in which one had reason to feel useful and secure. He was nineteen years old and strong, healthy and handsome.

Uncle Dolek and his two children were in work as well, as was by now Sally. The wives and children, so it was said, came under the protection of the working husband's umbrella.

The three members of our immediate family whose safety exercised our minds were the two grandmothers and Regina. The latter, though her condition had greatly improved, was still an invalid. She still divided her days between the bed and the easy chair. Grandmother Heim, an old and frail lady, still pottered about the room unused to sitting down, unable to rest. Grandmother – seventy years old – on the other hand, was in good health and active.

We continued to trust and to believe. Nobody, that I knew, read or interpreted the multitude of signs and indications around us correctly. How could they? The enemy still took the trouble to maintain a facade. Of course, the day would come when he would tear off his mask and expose his hideous, blood-curdling visage, but not yet, not for a while.

In April, Mamma and I paid Frau Berger a visit. It was late afternoon, dusk was approaching. Walking along the street and only a few yards from her building we saw coming towards us, three abreast so that they occupied the whole pavement, two SS men flanking a civilian – a cripple. Cold with fear, we stepped into the gutter to let them pass; they did not so much as glance in our direction. I recognised the cripple instantly. It was our one-time grocer Mr Blochmann. His face mottled with purple patches, the sweat streaming down it, the thick, black veins standing out like knots on his temples. He, with his poor, mutilated body in a shabby suit, crumpled shirt and twisted tie, pushing his crutches energetically forward, was attempting to keep pace with those two most impressive physical specimens with their even, elastic gait.

Sally and the widower, Mr Richter, were planning to marry quietly in the summer. Life went on and people, believing that it would continue, made plans and preparations. But the screws were being tightened yet more, psychologically rather than physically, with the dreadful rumours gathering in strength and fanning our fears. The news from other ghettos reaching Cracow, however obliquely and disjointedly, was bad. Large numbers of people, whole families apparently, were being moved great distances to work. It was being put about that a vast network of labour camps to accommodate this new work force was being organised in the East . . . To my family, to me, it meant exactly what it said.

Grandmother, Sally and Regina were finding it hard to make ends meet. We were not able to help, as we once did, for we ourselves only just managed to keep body and soul together. Although Sally allowed herself little respite from the 'brush-making', her daily output amounted, at best, to the price of a loaf of bread. And Regina's medical prescriptions, always top priority, were expensive. Like everybody else, they were selling their household and personal possessions and, like everybody else, they dreaded the day when they would run out of articles to sell. We, ourselves, were already touching that point.

It was surprising what those two 'Ford Knox' wardrobes yielded up. They contained some fine household linen, which had never seen the light of day, had never been used. Many articles in Grandmother's house were reserved for special occasions, only the occasion was never quite special enough to vouchsafe their use. These fineries were now brought out to the accompaniment of deep, soul-stirring sighs. I was asked to sell them outside one by one, and buy food which was cheaper there than in the Ghetto. In a sense, I was now carrying the burden of two households, two families.

With the onset of spring, my 'Saturday job' came to an end, as did my 'Sunday job' when Hannah was released from prison in the spring. Some of the neighbours in our building made use of my 'services' to run errands for them on the 'Outside'. I would earn a little money, which I would promptly convert into food for us.

We were well into the spring when Grandmother received news from her married daughter, Anna, whom she had not seen for over two years, that she and her husband, David, were making plans to return to Cracow for good. On the one hand, we were overjoyed, on the other hand, very anxious because of the long, danger-fraught journey before them. Public transport, in any form, was no longer accessible to the Jews and whereas Anna, with her 'good' appearance might have risked a train journey, which would have brought her to Cracow in a matter of hours, it was completely out of the question for David. It was hardly possible to be endowed with a more Semitic physiognomy than David's. He knew it and his manner reflected that knowledge . . . They intended to travel by peasant cart from point to point, as and when they could, they wrote. It might mean several days and nights *en route*. We were very apprehensive about this means of journeying, but there appeared to be no alternative. The peasants' attitude towards the Jews was unpredictable; they were not infrequently ill-disposed. Motivated by greed, they were inclined to take advantage of the dire straits in which the Jews found themselves. Of course in David's case there was no pulling the wool over anyone's eyes. One look at him and even the simplest, the most unworldly peasant knew instantly who he was. Knowing that Anna and David were coming, that they would be in need of assistance, in every sense of the word, Grandmother decided to sell something 'substantial' in order to put an amount of ready cash at their disposal. She said, 'They may well arrive penniless.'

Mamma, when asked, fully endorsed Grandmother's and Sally's choice of the 'substantial' object. It was a sizeable wall-rug – a kilim. It had once hung above my grandparents' massive twin-beds covering the entire wall area behind them. I do not know what the kilim's provenance was, but, looking back, it was quite modern in concept for those days. Woven of fine quality, heavy wool, it had an attractive symmetrical pattern; row upon row of large, upright tulips – crimson, deep-pink, golden-yellow – on long, leafy, pale-green stems against a warm, oatmeal-coloured background. It was brought out, neatly rolled up and wrapped in threadbare sheets, from a corner between the wall and one of the two wardrobes. It was placed, for size, upon my shoulders like a yoke. The ends only just cleared the floor. I would be able to carry it a short distance.

Grandmother, who made no demands upon her family, did enjoy a cup of warm milk with a sprinkling of ersatz coffee in the late afternoon. Fresh milk, especially in the warm weather, was difficult to obtain and very dear in the Ghetto. I had, however, discovered in my peregrinations on the 'Outside' an Aryan woman who lived only a few yards away from our nearest pedestrian-gate and who traded in dairy produce. I bought Grandmother's daily litre of fresh milk from her. The milk was diluted with water so generously that no 'skin' formed on it when brought to the boil. But I did not know that at the time. I set, quietly, about finding what the lie of the land was as far as smuggling the carpet out and disposing of it went. I knew I could carry it only a short distance; it was heavy and cumbersome. Also, I did not want to attract attention to myself

'Outside' bent under its weight. The milkwoman, Mrs Szenc, lived so close to the Ghetto that in this respect, at least, she would be ideal to deal with. I had no reason to be suspicious of her. She was a young married woman with two children. She was rough, but by no means witless. I did realise that she was greedy and only interested in the people from behind the wall insofar as they were a source of profit to her. But that was not unusual. She appeared to have neither sympathy, nor ill-will towards them. I sounded her out about the carpet. She was interested. She said, the peasants who delivered her produce were buying all manner of fine things these days. She could easily sell it for me, and sell it well, she said. She would, of course, want a cut . . . She would not want the carpet for herself, she added and she made a round movement of the hand towards the interior of her flat as if to say 'What, a carpet, here?' Her home was, indeed, very modest.

I explained all this to Grandmother and Sally. They thought I was doing well . . . The next step was to speak to the policeman on duty at the pedestrian-gate, our nearest. I kept an eye on it from Grandmother's window. When 'Johnnie' took over, just after lunch, I went down to speak to him. He was the kindest, the most approachable of all the policemen guarding the Ghetto. He was very dark and not very tall for a policeman. He could almost have been a Jew. He wore a Charlie Chaplin moustache and had the bandiest legs I have ever seen. His name was not 'Johnnie', of course. It was a nickname I had made up for him in my mind. I positioned myself near the gate and in a moment of lull, when there was nobody going through, I approached him explaining what I had in mind. He said, if I was sure I could manage the carpet, then there was no difficulty, he would let me slip out. Discreetly, I placed the banknote that Grandmother had given me for him in his hand. It was all arranged. With luck, the transaction would go off without a hitch.

I did deliver the carpet to Mrs Szenc. It was a warm day and I felt it burning my neck and shoulders as I carried it. I was glad to put it down. She said I was to come back in a couple of days' time; she would probably have the money for me by then. I left the carpet, bought the usual litre of milk for Grandmother and returned to the Ghetto.

Two or three days went by and Mrs Szenc told me that one of her suppliers, a peasant woman, liked the carpet very much and wished to buy it. She had let her take it home to show it to the family. She was a regular supplier and an honest person, 'That's why I let her have it . . .' The money, she assured me would be there next week. I still bought Grandmother's milk from her every day and although over a week had gone by and there was no sign of payment or carpet, I had to tread very carefully, very delicately. I did not dare ask the question which was on the tip of my tongue and she, very busy and brusque of late, did not bring the subject up at all.

Grandmother and her daughters found the situation disquieting. After a fortnight or so had gone by and there was still no payment and no clarification, I broached the subject with Mrs Szenc – who had became very impatient with me, these last few days, muttering, 'All this fuss for one litre of milk' – as tentatively and politely as I knew how. She turned on me, in a fit of temper and literally barked out, 'If I had any news, I would give to you, wouldn't I? Stop badgering me, will you!'

Grandmother, the aunts, Mamma, the whole family, were extremely distressed by this incident. I let a few days go by. I entered Mrs Szenc's building and knocked on her door. She would not open it to me; she pretended not to be in. I let a few more days pass and I tried again. There was no answer. I gave up. I knew we had lost the carpet. Life went on and we were propelled forwards by it. It would bring me face to face with Mrs Szenc again.

11 • Trip to Tarnov

'Operation Carpet' having miserably failed, a sum of money was, nonetheless procured: I do not know how, but it may be, as I rather suspect, that Sally's husband-to-be, a generous, kindly man, came to the rescue. I am sure he was not asked, it was just not done in my family; one of Grandmother's tenets being, 'Neither a lender, nor a borrower be'. Mr Richter must have offered and insisted, off his own bat.

It occurred to Grandmother and the aunts that it would be helpful to Anna if she had a resourceful female companion on the journey. Also, there was no other way of sending her financial assistance, of which she was very much in need and being sure that it would reach her, except by messenger delivery. My parents agreed. I was to travel to Żabno – a small town, a backwater, some distance from the large city of Tarnov. It was a hot summer, the summer of 1942. Mamma prepared a small bundle for me with my things. She also put in it a few slices of bread and two apples. Round my neck was hung a small draw-string cotton bag containing a thin layer of banknotes.

I set off from the Ghetto on a fine May morning. I caught a tram outside it, which took me directly to Cracow's main railway station. There, I bought a one-way half-ticket for the express train to Tarnov. I felt scared. I was on my own; I was carrying a large amount of money; I was going a long way. The station was crawling with *Bahnschutzpolizei*, the black-uniformed German railway police – their reputation was none too good. I knew that. It was the first time, I think, that I was really frightened for myself. I was twelve years old now. A seasoned ghetto-dweller and smuggler. My illusions about kindness to children, having received some severe knocks, were wearing thin.

I found the right platform and climbed aboard the Tarnov Express. I entered an unoccupied compartment and sat down, further abashed by the silent emptiness of the train. The compart-

90

ment filled up – every seat was taken – minutes before the train was due to depart. That was how it was done. One hopped on at the last moment, minimising unwelcome attention to oneself. I did not know that. I would remember, though. Once the train had set in motion, I surveyed my travelling companions. They were all middle-aged, or elderly, well turned out and tight-lipped. Bland, non-committal expressions on faces marked by time and the strain of the Occupation. Oh, they did take stock of each other and of me, as I did of them, but nothing was given away.

The train was going at a tremendous speed. I had never been on an express train before. I liked it. The bright, sunlit scenery outside the window flew by. One no sooner caught sight of a thatched-roof cottage by a clump of trees in their summer greenery, than it was gone, left far behind. Not a word was said, everyone was keeping their own counsel. I wondered what dark secrets they had locked in their bosoms, but I was sure none was as frightful as mine.

It was hot. I felt tired and thirsty. I took out a slice of dry bread from my bundle and they all noted that it was dry – not a sandwich. I chewed it slowly, because my mouth, too, was dry. When I had finished it, I took out an apple. I broke its rosy skin with my teeth and took a big bite out of it. It was cool and sweet in my mouth and I crunched away. They all watched me from the corners of their eyes. I put the core, without a shred of flesh on it, in the palm of my left hand – holding the stalk in between my fingers – and proceeded to tease the black pips out of their pods. I cracked them, one by one, in between my teeth, swallowing the white seed and working the brown skin out with the tip of my tongue onto my lips, to remove it with my fingertips. In the end, I had the core and the pip skins in my palm and did not know what to do with them. They did not take their eyes off me, but followed my every gesture. Then I simply put them back in the newspaper wrapping with the rest of the bread and the other apple.

Overcome by the heat and fatigue, I started feeling drowsy. I closed my eyes. I do not know how long I slept, but I realised, on waking up, that my head had been resting against the sleeve of the elderly, rather aristocratic gentleman sitting next to me. I apologised. He smiled at me so kindly and said that 'it did not matter'. These were the only words exchanged during the entire journey.

The train reached Tarnov in the late afternoon. When it pulled into the station and stopped, my travelling companions just melted away. I had to to change at Tarnov onto the Branch Line for Żabno.

The station concourse, all grey concrete, seemed vast. I was on 'foreign' territory and did not know my way around. The dreaded black uniforms were everywhere. I felt alone, lost . . . But I knew I had to keep my head. I located the train for Żabno. It was only a short journey. It was still daylight when I came out of the station in the peaceful, provincial little town.

Anna's house was a brick bungalow not far from the station. Anna and David were out. The landlords, a young couple with a bevy of children, pushed the door of Anna's room open. I could wait in there. The room, except for the most essential items of furniture, was bare – and sad. It gave onto a rough, overgrown patch of garden. I sat there, in semi-darkness, for a little while. Then I heard the landlady saying, 'A surprise, yes, a surprise, there in your room.'

She walked in, my beautiful aunt and before I could utter a word, she was hugging and kissing me and asking a thousand questions. David, too, was overjoyed. As she struck a match to light the oil lamp, she kept repeating, 'You came, you came, all the way from Cracow, you came . . .'

They wanted to leave Żabno as soon as possible. A great concentration of Jews – a transit camp – was afoot in Tarnov into which all the provincial Jews would be drawn and whence they were to be despatched to the new labour camps, much vaunted by the Germans, out in the East. Anna and David wanted to return to Cracow. They had very few possessions, two bundles and a suitcase at most, said Anna.

I did not know exactly what I had expected, what I had imagined, but it came to me as a shock that they were living very close to subsistence level. We would leave as soon as possible – within the next two or three days.

Straightaway, I was struck by David's tenderness towards Anna. He loved her whole-heartedly. When he came out of his shell, when he felt surrounded by friends, he showed a lively sense of humour and greatly enjoyed a joke. He spoke Polish beautifully; he was witty. He was kind and gentle towards me and I liked to see him laugh – he had very white, truly rabbity teeth. Somehow it made me feel good inside to hear, to see him laugh. It was a boy's laughter, happy and free. But he was a different person when he was outside his own four walls. His appearance was a source of terrible fear to him. A form of fear I, personally, had never experienced, had never observed in anyone else. My own appearance, on the contrary, was a re-assuring factor to me. I neither fully understood, nor fully appreciated, when I first met him, what this fear did to him. How deeply it affected him. But it did not take long to see the light, the change between David at home and David outside; every pore of his skin exuded fear; every glance of his eyes betrayed anxiety.

They were ready to leave; the only sadness was that David was leaving his elderly mother and unmarried sister behind in Żabno. The next day was Friday and David's mother and sister, Mrs Rostal and her daughter, Bronia, came in the late afternoon to share a little bread and herring with us. They wished us 'Good Shabbat.' I do not think that I have ever met two human beings to whom my heart went out so instantly and so completely. I have a picture of Golda Meir, towards the end of her life, which reminds me of the mother, and the daughter was a younger edition of her. Nor have I ever come across such total, perfectly natural, abnegation of the self. A quiet, serene acceptance of all hardship and sorrow. The old lady was of the same breed as Grandmother Heim, only much more evolved, much more articulate, although she used language sparingly. Her daughter, a large, plain woman, was like her. The way they broke their bread and cut up their strip of herring, the measured delicacy of their gestures and the quiet enjoyment of God's gifts, turned the little meal into a feast. 'And isn't the water good? So fresh and cool.' And Bronia? She was of that new breed of daughters which emerged in the ghetto days, young and able-bodied themselves, who renounced the chance of survival offered to them and chose, instead, to accompany their elderly parent on that last journey; to share all things . . .

Mrs Rostal told me that she expected Bronia and herself to be transferred to the transit camp at Tarnov. 'We are still capable of a hard day's work. Aren't we, Bronia?' And Bronia, smiling: 'Yes, of course, we are, Mamma.'

Mrs Rostal had a married daughter, a son-in-law and a three-year old grandson in the Cracow Ghetto. Olek, the little boy, had been born in Palestine in 1939. His parents had returned to Poland, when he was a few months old, in the summer of 1939. They had found life out there unbearably harsh. She asked me if I knew them. Had I seen Olek? Yes, I knew her daughter and Olek. I did not see them often, but the Ghetto being small, one did bump into friends and relations from time to time. I told her, without being asked, for I sensed that was what she wanted to know, all I knew about Olek. In looks, he resembled his mummy, I said and always had his hand in hers when I met them. His mummy looked after him beautifully. He was always clean and neat and wore a warm, red coat in winter. He was a fine little boy – strong and sturdy and good-looking too, with his large brown eyes and black hair. They lived in a bright room with a large window. His mummy had told me that he liked to spread his toys on the window sill, pull up a chair to it, and play with them and talk to them. He was lively and inquisitive; he often wore her out, she said, he asked so many questions. Sometimes he was naughty; he would touch, just touch, the scissors and the knife which he knew he was not allowed to do. He slept in a big bed with his mummy and daddy. He loved a cuddle . . .

We said good-bye to Mrs Rostal and Bronia on Sunday afternoon, as we were leaving early on Monday morning. The old lady said that I had made her and Bronia very happy. Every night, before going to sleep they 'took out' my story about Olek, like a most precious gift, and told it to each other without changing, without losing a single word.

We set out on our return journey to Cracow in the early hours of Monday morning. The sun had already risen. It was going to be a scorching day. Our travelling was done in open peasant carts, lined with an armful of straw, bumping along country roads, the sun beating down mercilessly. The heat, the fatigue, the sun's blinding glare tended to induce a state of torpor in us, travellers. David never succumbed to it. Anna and I were less resilient.

We protected David between us. In the late afternoon, Anna would go in search of lodgings for the night, whilst I stayed with David. When she returned, I would set off in search of food, whilst she remained with him. I bought freshly-baked country bread and cool, sweet milk and, sometimes, a wedge of white, crumbly cottage cheese. These we shared sitting in the shade of a tree, looking forward to a wash and a night's rest. Another day's travelling was behind us.

It was a long and arduous journey, but on the whole, it went rather more smoothly than we had anticipated. We experienced no animosity, no ill-will. Nobody tried to rob us or take advantage of us. In fact, some of the peasants we came into contact with, on that long, sun-drenched trek through the beautiful, but wilted and tired-looking Polish countryside, were quietly helpful, looking the other way, pretending not to see . . .

We reached Cracow on the fifth day and joined a group of Jewish workmen returning after a day's work to the Ghetto. One of the Ghetto's nicest and handsomest policemen was on duty at the

Square of Peace pedestrian entrance. He did not even bother to count the group.

There was great joy as Grandmother and her four daughters were re-united – for the last time – for neither God, nor the world, would come to our aid in the days that followed.

12 • The May 1942 Registration

By the time Anna and David arrived in the Cracow Ghetto, in May 1942, the Ghetto was in turmoil. That same month, its inhabitants were commanded to submit to a 'registration' to be followed by the 're-settlement' of a number of them. Both words, innocent in themselves, nonetheless placed the Ghetto population in a grip of extreme anxiety.

Happy and delighted as we all were to have Anna and David with us, a big, black cloud cast its shadow over what, even in the straitened circumstances, might have been a joyous re-union. The four sisters and their mother spent three brief days together; there was so much to talk about. The conversation bounced from the present to the past then back to the present – only to bounce forward to the future. And although the future was discussed, as if everyone in the family had a good helping of it in front of them, the imminent registration and the possible re-settlement were not conducive to making plans. We were walking on shifting sands. Fear of the unknown was everywhere, on everyone's mind, in everyone's heart.

At that time in May and June 1942, there were still Jews living, and enjoying relative freedom, in the countryside within fairly easy reach of Cracow. They would continue to be permitted to live there till the early autumn of 1942, although they did not know this. Anna and David could not remain in the Ghetto. They had no papers, they were illegal. They could not appear before the Registration Board. On the other hand, we already knew that evading it was an offence punishable by death.

The four sisters had cousins, a farming family, living in a village, Kościelniki, east of Cracow. The family was on good terms with them. The cousins would help Anna and David to find lodgings in their village; they would not be friendless or isolated. The three days spent together passed in the blink of an eye. Anna and David, not

96

even having unpacked, were again picking up their bundles and setting off for the country, pursuing the tragically futile cat and mouse game.

The Registration, which was, in fact, an unambiguous weeding out process, was now in full swing. The entire Ghetto adult population was submitting meekly, heart in mouth, to a selection. One went before a panel of SS-judges to parade one's physical attributes or lack of them, one's age, one's infirmities, and above all one's anguish – holding in one's outstretched hand one's identity card. Some cards the judges stamped with an SS *Polizei* stamp; some they did not. Those who had received the stamp would remain in the Ghetto; those who had not would be re-settled next month.

Although the selection procedure was quite arbitrary, even capricious, three factors were believed to govern the judges' decision; youth, or lack of it; physical fitness, or lack of it; useful, solid employment, or lack of it. Everybody's dearest wish was to be part of a 'worthy' labour contingent. The equation was simple enough: 'To work was to be useful, to be useful was to be needed, here, in Cracow.' As there were not enough official labour contingents to absorb all the willing hands and as nobody wished to see or feel themselves useless – although many were in the work sense, for the human sense had ceased to apply – the number of cottage industries, which already existed in the Ghetto, had greatly risen in recent weeks. They were unrecognised officially and produced goods which could only be labelled as 'luxury' items. Aunt Sally was working for just such an industry – it produced a variety of brushes for domestic use. Young, fit and attractive as Sally was, a mere flicker of the eye at her identity card and she was classed as 'dispensable'. After all, who cared if we scrubbed our backs, our nails or our floors? What did it matter if we brushed our hair, our clothes or our shoes? Sally's identity card was not stamped. She would be 're-settled' in June . . .

Poor Sally, whose employer, the owner of the brush-manufacturing factory, was very sweet on her, was making timid wedding plans and did not want to be re-settled. It was so inconvenient . . . I remember a friend of the family saying to Grandmother, for, as it happened, the bridegroom-to-be was also given short shrift by the judges. 'They will just have to get married "out there".' 'Out there,' signified in those days the mysterious East to which we were being despatched and Grandmother, who was not exactly elated at the prospect of gaining a son, simply sighed in resigned assent.

Sally was the only family casualty of the May Registration. She was the only member of the family who expected and whom we expected to be re-settled. She was young, healthy and more than willing to work hard. And, after all, Mr Richter would be there as well. He would look after her. They would get married. That was how we reasoned.

Father presented his own identity card and Mamma's in which Bartuś and I figured as children under the age of fourteen years before the judges. They were stamped. He came home, after having queued for hours, physically and emotionally drained from the suspense, the trepidation, the anguish, but joyful. Joseph, an adult in his own right, had also received 'the stamp', coveted and prized beyond all else.

Uncle Dolek, Aunt Rose and their two teenage children were to be counted amongst fortune's darlings, their identity cards having been stamped as well. Regina's doctor obtained a 'temporary' bed for her in one of the Ghetto's hospitals 'until things returned to normal . . .' Grandmother Heim, again, through the offices of a kindly doctor, was 'temporarily' admitted into the Ghetto's 'Old People's Home' – 'until the storm blew over . . .'

We believed these institutions to be sacrosanct. We believed Regina and Grandmother Heim to be safe and well looked after. Everyone breathed a sigh of relief on their behalf. Grandmother remained the only one for whose safety provision still had to be made.

Uncle Izydor, his wife and baby daughter had, at the time of the creation of the Cracow Ghetto in March 1941, chosen to leave Cracow for the country where now, in May 1942, they were still living. A forty-minute train journey from Cracow, direction east, brought one to Grodkowice, a hamlet, rather than a village, boasting a railway station. Starting close to the station, on the left-hand side, as one walked downhill along the hamlet's main road, was a wall of green, almost impenetrable, forest. On the right hand side, in large gardens, fields and orchards stood simple peasant cottages. Uncle Izydor and his family lived, in bucolic tranquillity, in a little cottage at the bottom of the hill. It was difficult for me to reconcile the two facts during that summer of 1942. On the one hand, thousands of Jewish men, women and children were being despatched, under conditions of unimaginable suffering, to – I did not know the true destination of those 'trains' at the time . . . On the other hand, Jewish families lived what I, a hardened ghetto-dweller, regarded as an idyll.

It was to this earthly paradise, to her son's rustic abode, that I was to lead Grandmother. There was no alternative. She was an active, healthy, but aged lady. She had to be spirited out of the Ghetto to endure, as best she could, endless days and nights without news, without any sign of life from those she had left behind within the Ghetto walls. When Grandmother and I slipped out of the Ghetto, to make our way to Grodkowice, she knew that her youngest daughter, Sally, was marked for re-settlement, and that she herself, if she wanted to avoid it, had to take 'temporary leave of absence' until she ceased to be a liability to herself and to her family.

She said little. She was not accustomed to couching her thoughts and emotions in words. She put a few things in a grip as she possessed so little that was personal. She had never travelled. Nor had she ever left her home or her family before. She hardly knew how to take leave of either but did what was asked of her. Minds far greater than hers did just that and they believed, at that early stage, what they were told. She believed too.

An old lady and a child – two perfect Aryan specimens – squeezed into a tightly packed compartment of a slow, oft-stopping train travelling from Cracow's main railway station, direction east. A middle-aged man stood up and politely offered his seat to the grandmother. She accepted with a 'Thank you, Sir.' She drew her grandchild to her, made her perch on her knee, and put her arm round the child's body. Nobody gave them a second look. They alighted at Grodkowice, the child helping her grandmother to negotiate the train's high wooden steps. Within two hours of leaving the Ghetto we had arrived at Uncle Izydor's cottage.

I remember being woken up early the next morning by the cawing and churring of birds, an experience I had never had before and which I liked immensely. The cottage had a very long front garden whose outer edge reached the main road, on the other side of which stretched a thick belt of trees, the forest. I could see it from my bed by the window. It was alive with birds.

For breakfast we had scrambled eggs with freshly-gathered mushrooms and as much bread and butter as one wanted. It was a princely breakfast. The simple, plentiful, country fare, which appeared on the table three times a day, was delicious and satisfying beyond my wildest dreams. I stayed in Grodkowice for three days and met a bevy of Uncle Izydor's relations by marriage. They were all well-nourished, sun-tanned, physically 'in the pink' individuals. The countryside, in its full summer splendour, was beautiful and peaceful. The Jewish men worked in the fields and in the gardens. Their wives looked after the family and sat out in the sun in their bathing costumes podding peas, hulling strawberries, sewing. The children, as brown as berries, played games, read and did school-work set by their parents. Uncle Izydor was the maths teacher.

On Sunday, 31 May 1942 – my last day in Grodkowice – we had rabbit stew and new potatoes for lunch. Soon after, I said goodbye to Grandmother and the family and caught the early afternoon train to Cracow. But for an accident, a piece of well-meant advice, I would never again skip along a country lane or breathe fresh, clean air. I would share the fate, in the coming week, of the thousands of Cracow Ghetto Jews – where I belonged.

Three quarters of an hour later the train pulled into Cracow's main railway station; it was no place for a law-breaker to linger in, swarming as it was with the German railway police. I crossed the large concourse at a brisk pace, but without indecent haste so as not to draw attention to myself, and hopped on the tram which went directly to the Ghetto area and beyond.

It drove through streets as familiar and as much part of me, through daily usage, as the fingers of my hand, and just as dear, and just as taken for granted.

The city was somnolent and peaceful in the afternoon's mellow sunlight. There were few pedestrians about, mostly elderly people on their way to church, to vespers. My city was a city of churches and gentle, but sonorous, organ music rose towards Cracow's serene sky inhabited, so I believed, by a loving and merciful God.

The tram was already crossing the Third Bridge. The Vistula's grey-green waters flowing on and on, unmoved, unperturbed in peace and in war, as they had done for centuries.

I became more watchful, concentrating on the feat before me – entering the Ghetto. I was about to perform an oft-repeated act, but, nonetheless, hazardous.

We were approaching the first Ghetto traffic gate, at the bottom of Lvovska Street, to the right of which, at a little distance, was the pedestrian Square of Peace entrance. Lo and Behold! To my great astonishment the traffic gate had an SS guard standing on each side of it and at the pedestrian gate – I could see all this very clearly as the tram approached, and plunged into, the Ghetto – there were several SS officers standing next to the Polish policeman. This had never occurred before. The rug had been pulled from under my feet. I felt confused and frightened. I stayed on the tram as it emerged through the traffic gate, a single SS officer standing on one side of it, at the top of Lvovska Street.

The tram ground to a halt on the little Aryan island between the two parts of the Ghetto. Normally, I would have remained on the tram, ready to jump off as it straightened out immediately after entering the Ghetto at the Limanowskiego Street gate. But I was very much on my guard – wary. The SS, personally manning every gate, why? I hopped off the tram, the only passenger to do so on the Aryan island and pretended to be walking away from the Ghetto, towards Wielicka Street. But at the same time, my head turned to the right, I was sizing up the situation out of the corner of my eye at the traffic and pedestrian gates in Limanowskiego Street – my gates. Fifty paces away from which was our doorway. Both gates, but particularly the pedestrian one, were under heavy SS guard. The Ghetto was surrounded for the first time in its existence. I still did not understand what it signified. I had no experience of that kind to draw upon. I was at my wits' end and very frightened. The Ghetto was out of bounds to me.

There was not a soul about in the Aryan street where I was uncomfortably lurking, nor in the Ghetto, which I could see from my mobile vantage point, was there a living being to be seen, apart from the SS and the Polish police. I meandered back to the Aryan tram stop, as if waiting for a tram that would take me to central Cracow. The sun was setting and the Ghetto, always so grey, was now bathed in a rich orange glow. My heart swelled with longing and fear. I wanted to be inside the walls with my parents, my brothers, my family, my people . . .

The Lvovska Street traffic gate was right in front of me, about twenty paces, if that, from the tram stop. The tram, when it entered it, would drive past the left-hand side gate-wall. The SS guard was standing on the opposite side – the right-hand side. When the tram came and ground to a halt, I very casually, very unconcernedly placed myself, feet neatly together, at the edge of the pavement; there were only inches between the steel-rimmed, large-hubbed rear wheel of the tram and my feet. The tram shuddered and set in motion. I moved in step with it, my person shielded from view (the SS officer on duty at the traffic gate was the only one who could have seen me, there was no one else about) by the body of the tram, my feet by the large, round steel hub of the rear wheel.

Within seconds, before the tram had even started picking up speed, I had slid into the Ghetto in between the left-hand side traffic gate-wall and the tram. I was already tearing down Józefinska Street as if all the bats out of hell were pursuing me, charging across the Limanowskiego Street thoroughfare, hanging onto the rusty handle, which I could only just reach, of the old-fashioned door-bell – for the hefty, wooden twin-doors of No. 42 were already locked for the night – the bell jangling furiously, reverberating shrilly through the tall building. Like a demented soul I kept tugging at the handle. And then I heard someone, on the other side of the doors, fumbling with the keys, opening the door. Old Mr Krautwirt, the landlord, every drop of blood drained from his naturally rubicund face, opened the door – just a crack. Quick as lightning, I slipped inside.

'You've frightened us all out of our minds! What do you think you are doing? Ringing the bell, at this time of night, in that insane manner? You should be at home, not . . .' 'Oh, Mr Krautwirt . . .' I fell against his pot-bellied person, the tears streaming down my face. I stammered out: 'I have just returned from the country. I took Grandmother there . . . to stay with her son . . . for safety . . . The SS are guarding every gate . . .' 'Yes, I know. But how on earth did you manage to get through?' I told him. He looked at me, his eyes almost popping out of his head. 'Good God . . . You are a plucky child . . . Don't cry, now . . . Your parents and brothers are upstairs with your Aunt Sally. Yes, she is still with us . . . So is my daughter, Lola . . . God preserve us . . . Yes, we are surrounded . . . Yes, the re-settlement action is under way . . . Yes, the Square of Peace is going to be used as an *Umschlagplatz* . . .!' 'Excuse me, Mr Krautwirt, as a what?' '*Umschlagplatz* – assembly point. Don't cry . . . there now . . .' 'Good night, Mr Krautwirt.' 'Good night, my child.'

13 • *The Sailor Hat*

Just as a small pebble thrown into a pond will ripple and disturb its calm surface, so an incident, a word, an object will release a flood of memories which one had believed safely locked away in the innermost chambers of one's mind.

On a hot afternoon, a half-century after the events described below, an elderly woman was walking along the platform of one of London's main railway stations scanning the windows of a suburban train for a clean, quiet compartment. Having found what she wanted, she boarded the train and seated herself by the window. She was slight and simply dressed. Her short hair, once very dark, was now silver white – naturally so, for she chose not to stay nature's hand. She opened her handbag to take out her reading glasses and her hands, of which she was rather vain, were delicately shaped and well kept. She wore a number of rings, including a wedding ring. Next to her lay her book. She was about to pick it up, when another passenger entered the compartment. Discreetly, but with a woman's innate interest in another of her species, she surveyed the new-comer. The woman was young, attractive and nicely dressed. She looked cool and fresh in spite of the heat. A dainty, white sailor hat, with a daisy chain round its crown and silk-ribbon streamers, saucily perched on her thick black hair, caught the eye. The elderly woman's gaze riveted upon the hat, her mind leapt, in one wild somersault, across the abyss of fifty years. The young woman, except for her hat, which grew larger and larger till it obscured all else, became a misty outline blurred by tears.

A hot summer's day . . . A train – a long string of cattle trucks – waiting. An open lorry parked by the kerb . . . a frivolous brooch fastened to the lapel of a coat . . . A face framed by just such dark, wavy hair and my mother's youngest sister, Aunt Sally, steps out of the shadows of the past to live again in the bright London sunshine for the duration of a twenty minute train-journey, and takes me back, years and years, into my childhood. The handful of memories which I have of my aunt spreads itself out before my mind's eye. Images and emotions unrolling themselves and succeeding each other like motifs in a tapestry on which one had worked a long time ago, but had not seen for many years – for it had been tenderly folded and carefully put away for a more leisurely, more introspective time – yet remembering sharply and painfully the thoughts of the mind and the feelings of the heart which had accompanied the labour of the hands.

Cracow, Monday, 1 June 1942. I am a girl of twelve. I live in a Ghetto. Today is the first day of a re-settlement action which will last eight days. A week and a day . . .

The word 're-settlement' is a new one to me, it has been on everybody's lips these last few weeks . . . I like words and I collect them. Sometimes, in the darkness of the night, I take them out, like a handful of infinitely varied pebbles and turn them around in my mind, honing the back of my thumb on their sharp, jagged edges and ridged, bumpy surfaces. 'Re-settlement' – it conjures up a series of images.

I have travelled very little and always third class; my imagery, therefore, is very ordinary. Trains packed with people. Every seat taken. Luggage racks piled up high. Children fidgeting. Babies whimpering. Shabbily dressed men smoking hand-rolled cigarettes out in the corridor. The travellers, overcome by heat and fatigue, being rocked to sleep by the swaying motion of the train and the tinkling music of steel against steel. A dark, cool night, punctuated by myriads of distant, golden lights. A warm, bright day, the luscious greenery of the countryside gliding by. The wooden benches are hard. One's body and limbs ache from them. More nights . . . More days . . . The carriages are dirty and littered. The travellers sweaty with the heat, dazed with fatigue.

A boundless, desolate plain. A stunted, leafless tree. Tufts of scorched, yellowy grass. A thin ribbon of brown, sluggish water. A clump of scarlet dog-roses. The blue sky. The fiery sun. Sparsely scattered humble dwellings – kneaded in clay, woven in straw. And the postman. He dominates the landscape for me, his bag bulging with letters. My imagination wavers; the images fade. They are all figments of a child's imagination – all except one: the vast, treeless plain bathed in brilliant sunshine. There are no dwellings waiting for the travellers at the end of a journey of unimaginable suffering. The trail loses itself in a wood surrounding the plain.

This morning I saw an endless coffle of people – so many young

104

children, so many elderly people – so many strong, healthy, able-bodied men and women, swaddled in layer upon layer of clothing. The injunctions heard time and again ring in my ears: 'One should take all the clothing one can on oneself; pay no attention to the heat . . . Take all you can carry!' Bundles, suitcases, a white-faced little schoolboy – his satchel on his back – grips, travelling bags – a Moses basket with sturdy handles carried in between two young parents – holdalls, shopping bags, an old man with a rucksack on his back, a saucepan dangling from each shoulder strap. Grave faces. Silent mouths. A weary tread. A long, long procession, in ranks of five, of men, women and children – the human family – wends through the streets of the Ghetto. They are escorted by men in green uniforms, the green of a fernleaf, and black, heavy boots – men with hard, brutal faces – men with a strong, even stride.

This is the first quota of deportees to leave the Ghetto for the East. They are making for Plaszow, the nearest railway station – the nearest, but distant . . . As I watch them move on, standing by the window, half hidden by the curtain, what strikes me most about them is their air of total acceptance and resignation and a kind of stiff, mechanical obedience. Their gait is that of wound-up puppets whose short movement cycle is nearing the end. I am numb with pain. I feel cold in spite of the heat. It cannot be that I am cold. It is baking hot in the Ghetto. The roofs, the houses, the streets are flooded with warm, golden sunshine. The window in the room is sealed; there is not a breath of air. I shiver. I am afraid – terrified. Of what? I do not understand what it is that is taking place, here, today.

Up to this morning, the adults seemed most concerned with the practicalities of the re-settlement: 'What about housing? What about furniture? What about bedding? How will one cook? Will the family be able to send things on? Will there be a regular food allocation?' On seeing the reality – the re-settlement in progress – all concerns of a practical nature are pushed aside, except the heart-rending physical distress evinced by those moving on and on and on, down in the street, below our window . . . The pity that rises in one's heart and spreads through one's whole being is suffocating. The sight down in the street . . . And it goes on and on – they drag their tired feet, burdened by their bundles, lowering their heads under the broiling sun and our tears flow and flow . . .

At no stage of the re-settlement action did we have the slightest inkling of what awaited the deportees at the end of the journey. As the week unfolds we are filled with terrible dread and foreboding.

Something macabre, something very fearful is lurking behind the events we witness.

I did not know, nor did any one else in my circle, that a string of cattle-trucks, as hot as furnaces, was waiting for the deportees at Plaszow station. Nor did we know that these trucks were but coffins on wheels. The *Aktion* is a totally unknown phenomenon. The very uncommonness of the experience seems to rob people of their ability to think, to judge . . . Who could imagine, perceive, even most vaguely predict, what the events unrolling before our eyes signify? It would be years before I grasped that on that day, 1 June 1942, I was witnessing the preliminaries to annihilation. A new way of death was being implemented across the land and we, the Jews, were being sent to it. But no one, around me, possessed the gift of divination; no one was able to read the writing on the wall . . .

It is such a beautiful day. A splendid summer. The best we have had for many a year, the summer of 1942.

The Ghetto, now that the first wave of deportees has left, is like a plague-stricken city. Abandoned and silent. Stifling and oppressive. Closed. Not a sign of life to be seen anywhere, except at the windows, and even there not outright, but at some distance, safely in the room, yet catching a glimpse of the deserted, sun-blanched streets, of strained, pale faces at other windows, of the glorious June sky – the Cracow sky. Slowly and painfully the blazing afternoon drags on. At about six o'clock in the evening, still in broad daylight, as the heat is beginning to abate and the labour contingents are returning from the outside, its droning dullness is broken.

The curtain rises once more on the strange and terrible events of the day. The last act, a belated encore to the morning's performance, is about to take place.

I did not know that the deportees, who were marched out of the Ghetto in the morning, spent the whole of this sweltering June day, tightly packed in the sealed cattle-trucks, waiting . . .

Some brilliant individual, some most zealous officer of the SS, actively involved in the *Aktion*, must have had the commendable idea that a goodly handful more Jews could be squeezed into the waiting trucks. He ordered a fleet of lorries to return to the Ghetto to pluck them.

Deftly, smoothly, almost decorously, the final act of the day's drama is enacted. A fleet of open lorries arrives in Limanowskiego Street. They are stationed, evenly spaced out, along the full stretch of that long street, ready to receive the haul. Expertly, the SS cast

106

their nets into the old, cavernous houses – the mute chorus of the tragedy – and, in a matter of minutes, bring them out heavy with the catch – those whose documents do not bear the '*SS Polizei*' stamp. The tall tenements, the low houses lean and huddle against each other. They will remain, mute witnesses, when those of flesh and bone have gone, to bear their testimony.

We are standing in the hallway of our building, its twin wooden doors wide open, a lorry parked right outside it. My parents are holding in their outstretched hands their identity cards – bearing the life-saving stamp ready for inspection – with Bartuś and me wedged tightly between them. Joseph has not yet returned from work.

From the entrance of the drab, grey one-storey house opposite, emerges nineteen year old Adam Immerglück. He is tall and slender and has a habit of pushing his unruly, dark hair away from his eyes. He was unlucky – in spite of his youth and fine physique – his identity card was not stamped. He is carrying a small parcel containing a few items of clothing and a newspaper cornet full of carrots, the only food his mother had in the house. I have known him and his brother, Richard, and their parents ever since I can remember. It was Richard who taught me to read the time on his 'one-hand' wrist-watch beginning each time-problem with the words, 'Supposing the missing hand were on . . .' They have always been very poor. Their father is an artist. There was not an inch of wall in their flat which was not covered with the pictures for which there was no market; his source of inspiration being the Jewish people at work and at prayer . . . Following in Adam's wake is an old Jewish couple, the parents-in-law of the Ghetto's richest grocer, his shop, in The Square of Peace, is like Aladdin's Cave. There is nothing one cannot buy there for money. They are very old and frail. They are both dressed in their best Sabbath garments of heavy, fine quality, black silk. The old man, although bowed with age, towers above his tiny, shrivelled wife. His long, white beard is beautifully groomed and there is great dignity in his mien. They are carrying between them a large, leather suitcase. I cannot help thinking of the loving care with which their daughter has packed it. Of the riches contained in it. Of the delicious morsels to sustain them on the journey.

They are walking towards the waiting lorry dragging, rather than carrying, the suitcase along the pavement. From the opposite direction a young SS officer with the natural, easy grace of a thoroughbred horse is advancing towards them. Father tightens his grip on my hand. We stand very still, holding our breath. The officer is within three paces of the old couple . . . In the glimmer of an eye, with the sleight of hand of a magician, he raises a black object . . . The silent solemnity of the ritual is shattered. One discordant note in an otherwise flawless performance. The old man, like a gigantic blackbird, flaps his wings but once and falls to the ground. His wife abandons the suitcase and stands, irresolute, for a moment – torn between love and fear . . .

Aunt Sally is coming down the stairs suitably dressed and prepared for a journey. Sally, Mamma's youngest sister, did not receive 'the stamp' in the May registration. She is, thus, destined for annihilation, but neither she nor we know this.

Sally is in her thirties – in full bloom of womanhood. She is coming down the stairs wearing a light, grey coat of the kind that is worn in the late spring or early autumn. She has pinned a rather frivolous ornament to its lapel – a miniature sailor hat with a daisy-chain round its crown and gay, red streamers. She has slung a travelling rug over her arm and is carrying a neat suitcase. The SS-man standing on the landing checking documents, without having removed his exquisite pearl-grey gloves, looks up at the tap, tap sound of her high heels. For a brief moment he looks at her as a man looks at a lovely, desirable woman. Her fresh-complexioned, rosy face is framed by a mass of curly, blue-black hair. The cleverly-cut coat accentuates the lines of her supple, well-proportioned body. There is a glow about her – a glow of perfect health and scrupulous cleanliness. The SS-man's face registers surprise – a flicker of pity – but only for a fleeting moment. He raises his gloved hand in a curiously cruel gesture, half-chivalrous, half-mocking, inviting her, as it were, to pass on, his face a hard, arrogant mask once again.

She brushes Mamma's cheek with her lips as she passes by us – that is all she has time for. Neither of them knows that the eldest sister will survive the youngest by a week.

We watch her being herded, with others, into the waiting lorry. The engine revs up. The lorry, with its human cargo, disappears behind a bend in the road. The world will never see Sally again.

'East Croydon, Three Bridges, Gatwick . . .'
'Your ticket, please . . .'

14 • *The June 1942* Aktion

Grandmother's room is empty; Grandmother herself is in the country; Regina is in the Ghetto hospital; Sally is on her way to the East. The other room in the flat is empty too. Lola, its occupier, has also been taken. She left her twelve year old daughter, Irena, with the child's grandfather, Mr Krautwirt. It is a temporary arrangement until Lola finds her bearings out there – in the East. The Wintners remain in the kitchen. They were lucky to receive 'The Stamp' at their age. Suddenly, there is so much space in the Ghetto! Empty rooms, empty flats.

Mrs Wintner asked Mamma if we would come and live upstairs. She and her husband feel uneasy in the flat on their own. Regina, whom Mamma visits in hospital every day, has also asked if we would move in and keep an eye on things. Mamma says we are not going to move till life has stabilised again; we 'commute' between our basement room and the upstairs flat.

Father and Aunt Rose visit Grandmother Heim every evening in the Old People's Home. She is so happy to see them. She does not really appreciate the necessity for keeping out of harm's way and asks many times in the course of their visit when she will be able to return home. She enquires after everyone, but particularly after her five grandchildren.

My wings have been clipped. We are sealed off in the Ghetto. There is no strolling in and out. Only the Labour Contingents are allowed to come and go, and their papers and numbers are meticulously checked by the SS at the pedestrian gates.

The price of food is soaring by the hour. The Ghetto prices have never been within our reach. They are quite, quite outside it now. For the first time since the Ghetto came into being, it is suffering a food shortage. Until now, those who could pay the going rate were able to indulge themselves to their hearts' content. The bakeries, the shops, the restaurants received regular deliveries of whatever they required. Thanks to the Polish police, carts and trucks of food

109

entered the Ghetto as regular as clockwork, mostly under cover of darkness, and there was no shortage of anything. But now that the Ghetto is surrounded, all contact with the outside has been severed. Prudent people always put a little something by for a 'rainy day'. We have a bag of flour and a bag of semolina – about a kilo of each – and we found a few, very welcome, odds and ends of dry goods in Grandmother's cupboard upstairs.

We live on a knife-edge, not knowing what misfortune or misery is about to befall us. Only half the unfortunates who do not possess 'The Stamp' have so far been rounded up and despatched to the East. The remainder is awaiting further action on the part of the Germans in great suspense and anguish. The weather is overpoweringly hot and people's nerves are stretched to breaking point. Fear stalks the streets and the homes of the cordoned off Ghetto. Nobody leaves their building or room without dire necessity. We do not know what is taking place in other parts of the Ghetto; we are only familiar with the events in our immediate field of vision, the patch we can see from the window. The Square of Peace, which is at the other end of the Ghetto, has been turned into an arena. It is there that those to be deported are assembled; it is there that terror and brutality, unseen until now, are being unleashed. Nobody, who does not positively have to, goes near it. I did not see it once during the June *Aktion*. It is referred to as the '*Umschlagplatz*.'

The tension on this side of the wall is almost solid – palpable. The grown-ups whisper to each other. We, the children, are not supposed to hear, to know, to understand . . . But the grown-ups' faces, voices, movements, deliberately expressionless and void, low and indistinct, soft and self-obliterating, as if they had already ceased to exist – and, in truth, they have – fill me with dread . . . Father knows what is taking place in the Ghetto; he shares his knowledge with Mamma, but they both make a point of not letting us, Bartuś and me, in on it. They wish to protect us, as if it were possible.

We are isolated from the rest of the world. We are waiting . . . The day drags on pregnant with fear of the unknown, of what human beings can do to each other, of power cruelly used . . .

At lunch-time, Mamma gave me a saucerful of sunflower seeds to divide between Bartuś and myself. We took it down to the courtyard and sat down in our favourite spot on the horsehair sofa. The horsehair is coming out in handfuls, but whereas in winter the sofa was sopping wet, now in June, it is bone dry and still very comfortable to sit on. I share out the seeds. One for Bartuś, one for me, one for Bartuś . . . We sit on the sofa in a corner of the yard and play a game; which of us can spit the striped black and white skins the furthest.

Mrs Wintner told me on Wednesday morning that she and her husband have a friend, an old gentleman, a widower. He has not received 'The Stamp' and is waiting to be re-settled. In the meantime, he has nothing to eat. She was preparing lunch. They would share it with their friend, she said, if I would be kind enough to take it to him. Just one small pot . . . He lives in Rekawka, at the other end of the Ghetto. I was wary, like everybody else, of stepping out of our building, but she had appealed to my better self. I said I would. I set off for Rekawka at lunchtime walking on the shady side of the street, for the sun was very hot and the glare was hurting my eyes. The streets were deserted. No Jew is foolhardy enough to venture out. I was the only one. In Benedykta Street I came across a group of SS officers – about six or eight of them – tall, elegant men in high spirits, talking, laughing, brimming with vitality and energy even in this heat. They were on the sunny side of the street. I nearly sought refuge in the closest doorway, but as they did not even deign to glance in my direction, though I am sure they saw me, I pressed on.

The old gentleman has thick, white hair, kindly blue eyes and an inner equanimity, even joy, that I could not help but admire. He was so courteous, so pleased to have someone to talk to, if only for a little while, that he quite won me over. I do not regret going. I came back without any misadventure on the way. I repeated the 'Good Samaritan' gesture on Thursday, which was not wise, for the Ghetto was seething with activity – the second quota of deportees was being assembled in the '*Umschlagplatz*'. But I saw nothing to frighten me and met not a soul in the streets, for I went in the opposite direction to the Square of Peace where it is all happening. I found the door to the old gentleman's room open – the room itself empty. I stood there, taken aback, for a minute or two. As I was returning along the landing, a door creaked open and a woman, barely putting her head out, whispered: 'They took him early this morning.' I must have been really still quite childishly naive, for I asked myself, 'How could they take such a sweet, kind old gentleman?' I was so sorry.

Mamma made a small ball of dough which she rolled out and baked on either side, on the naked surface of the stove, as we had no oven, till it was golden brown. A kind of pitta bread. She let it cool and cut it into strips. Bartuś and I had one each for lunch.

Thursday must have been the hottest day of that whole torrid week. The sweat was trickling down people's faces and necks and there were big, dark stains of dampness round their armpits.

At about three o'clock in the afternoon the second quota of deportees was marched out of the Ghetto. They were led from the Square of Peace along Lvovska Street. Standing at the window, we saw them as they emerged from the Ghetto into Wielicka Street – the Plaszow railway station route – about a hundred paces from our vantage point. They were being driven under a sky white with the heat. But whereas the Monday morning procession was orderly and the ranks of five quite straight and serried, this afternoon's endless march, almost from the very first row, was disjointed and straggly. They were not marching in step, but each one shuffling along as best he could...We could not see their faces – it was too far away.We saw their backs and could only tell if they were men, women or children.

Many of them must have abandoned their bundles in The Square of Peace, for they were not carrying any luggage at all, their arms hanging limply by their sides, their bodies swaying back and forth, their heads lolling from side to side, the guards' long whips unwinding above their heads to keep them moving . . . We have never seen that before. We stood at the window frozen in horror and grief. They disappeared, row after endless row, into a golden shimmering haze . . . I did not dare look at Mamma's face. I saw Aunt Josephine's, who was standing next to me, and it was tumefied with tears. Mrs Wintner was sobbing, invoking God's pity. And the ranks of five tottered, lurched, stumbled – forward, forward, on and on . . . under Cracow's searing sky.

I went down to the basement and as I opened the door, a strange, unaccustomed sight met my eyes. Father, in the middle of the afternoon, sitting on a hard kitchen chair, his head bent forward, his face buried in his hands . . .

'Daddy . . .' Slowly he takes his hands away from his face, exposes it, grey and haggard. Father is crying. I have never seen Father cry before. It grieves me more than words can say, more so, because he cannot cry; he does not know how to cry properly, not as I would. His eyes are red and tiny droplets of moisture gather around the lower eyelids. 'They have taken Grandmother Heim . . . I went to see her this afternoon, but she was not there . . . They came and tumbled half the inmates of the Old People's Home into a lorry . . . They are putting them on the same train as this afternoon's deportees . . . She is so helpless, so frail . . . Without her family . . .'

112

Father has not seen this afternoon's procession and I say nothing. I want to spare him. The tiny droplets gather into two large tears which course down his cheeks. My father does not know that it is not a train, nor do I, but a string of burning-hot cattle-trucks waiting in Plaszow . . .

Although all the Ghetto inhabitants without 'The Stamp' have now been despatched to their final destination, the Ghetto has not returned to its everyday, vegetative existence, for it continues to be under siege, the SS guards remaining at their posts. A clammy terror is holding us in its grip. A rumour, at first barely articulated, but increasing in vocal strength by the hour, is beginning to circulate from street to street, from dwelling to dwelling, from mouth to mouth. The *Aktion*, just terminated, has not been a success in the eyes of the Germans. The harvest reaped was poor – the offerings sent out to the East were considered paltry in number.

On Friday afternoon, the heat being less fierce, Mamma, Bartuś and I set out for the nearest bakery to see if bread was being baked, if we could buy a loaf . . .

We crossed the Limanowskiego Street thoroughfare, Bartuś and I clinging to Mamma's hands like limpets. We turned slightly to the left of the Jewish Police Headquarters, towards the bill-board sunk into what must once have been a strip of grass and is now a scorched, weed-choked little patch. Glancing at the bill-board has become a reflex action. There is a new Proclamation upon it! Fat black print on a fresh white background. It was pasted on this very afternoon. There was nobody in front of it. No jostling, no elbowing, no pushing. We could take our time; read it at leisure and fully absorb its contents. I only read the first few lines; a second registration of the entire remaining Ghetto population – starting on Sunday morning 7 June 1942. I looked at Mamma. I have never seen her face this sad. The expression in her eyes made my very soul shiver with icy-cold fear. Her lips white, her voice barely audible, she said: 'Oh, another registration . . .' We abandoned the trip to the bakery and slowly, silently, weighed down by the paralysing knowledge we have just acquired, Bartuś and I holding onto Mamma for dear life, returned home.

We are still reeling from the cruel blows only just dealt us. Countless entire families gone and no one left to remember them or to grieve for them. Hardly a family which has not lost a loved one. Innumerable families depleted or dismembered by the events of this week. We are not permitted the luxury of sorrowing. Our exhausted bodies, our numbed minds, our riven souls already pitting their meagre resources against the latest, publicly-announced, calamity – a second weeding-out process and yet another, the third, re-settlement action.

By Saturday, the Sabbath, there was nobody in the Ghetto who was not aware of the impending third act to the week's tragedy. There were those, however, who chose to keep the Sabbath as of old; to spend the Holy Day in prayer and supplication, seeking the Almighty's counsel and guidance; meekly bowing their heads before His will; putting their well-being, and that of their loved ones, into His hands . . .

For most of us Ghetto Jews, however, it is despair. Having been eyewitnesses to the events of the last six days, we are now filled with dark foreboding and all-pervading fear. And still we did not know. And still our fears in no way approximated reality. People have ceased to be preoccupied with practical arrangements. They are less ready to say: 'One can live just as well out there, in the East; so it isn't Cracow . . .' We are confused and bewildered – 'The Stamp' having been refused to the elderly, to the infirm, to couples with large families, as well as to young people in less than solid employment – at whom can they be aiming this time, having already sieved through the 'undesirable' elements? A physical and mental torpor ensues. People are not able to think, to act, to swallow their food, to close their eyes, to rest . . . An apathy enfolds us which springs from helplessness and hopelessness. Planning presupposes a future. How can we plan? For what future?

Darkness comes. The Sabbath is over. Will the Lord answer the prayers of those closest to Him amongst us? The saints amongst us? They have spent the day in communion with Him, praising His infinite wisdom . . . Will He make a sign that He understands the urgency of their appeal?

On Sunday morning – the 7 June 1942, Father and Joseph, having made themselves as presentable as they could, went to join the registration queue. It is a pleasant, warm, Sunday morning. Father, as head of the family, has taken Mamma's *Kennkarte*. I have never before seen Mamma in such distress, so anxious as she has been this morning waiting for their return. After what seemed like an eternity, Joseph came back alone. Father has been detained. Mamma, Bartuś and I are going to join him later in the day. The registration this time is conducted along different lines. Joseph, having presented his *Kennkarte* before a German arbiter, had a

'Blauschein' (a blue docket) – giving explicit permission from the SS *Polizei* for the undersigned to remain in the Ghetto – stapled to it. 'The Stamp' is no longer valid. Only the *'Blauschein'*.

Father's and Mamma's *Kennkarten* were confiscated on the spot and added to a steadily mounting stack. Father was not permitted to leave the registration centre, but was immediately placed under SS guard. Father and son were, however, allowed to say good bye. I do not know what they said to each other. I have never had the courage to ask Joseph. He has never had the strength to describe that last good bye.

We know where we stand now. Mamma has very quietly started putting a few things together for the journey . . . We have so little left that is portable and nothing of value. Mamma is the only one who has two pairs of shoes and both have seen better days.

On the corner of Limanowskiego and Wegierska Streets, very close to where the new registration is being carried out, there stands 'Optima'. It is a large, old, dilapidated building – once a chocolate factory. It possesses another asset, apart from its proximity to the registration point. It stands in one corner of an enormous wall-encircled courtyard. It has just one large gate through which, once, distribution vans, packed with carton upon carton of sweetmeats, left the 'Optima' courtyard. But that was long ago . . . Today, groups of men, women and children are conducted, at frequent intervals, all through the day, under SS escort, from the registration point to the 'Optima' courtyard – which is so near, so handy, unlike the previous assembly point – The Square of Peace, much further away, at the other end of the Ghetto.

We already know that Father has been transferred to the court-yard. There, he is soon joined by his sister, Rose, and her husband, Dolek. They, too were parted from their two children who received the *'Blauschein'*, whereas the parents did not.

It is a long, very warm day. There is no shade in the 'Optima' courtyard. Those like Father, his sister and her husband, who were detained on the spot, have not so much as a slice of bread on them. On leaving home they did not for a moment envisage, whatever misfortune overtook them, not being permitted to return to it to gather together a few things for the journey, for the new life out in the East . . .

Mamma, having sorted out and gathered together what she thought we could, and should, take with us on the journey, came upon a dilemma. She spread out on the bed the two dresses, belong-

115

ing to Frau Berger, on which she was working at the time. Both still required a few hours' work before they could be returned to her ready to wear. I can still see very clearly today, those two dresses spread out on Sally's bed. One was a very simple short-sleeved shirt-waister in pale, yellow silk with a wide belt to accentuate Frau Berger's tiny waist. The other, also in silk, the colour of Parma violets, was a cocktail frock. Again, it was very simple, except for a lightly flared peplum, to go round her slender hips, encrusted with embroidery in the finest silver cord. Many considerations, still of a practical nature, in the belief that she will live and work, pass through Mamma's mind. If she could finish the two dresses, Joseph would somehow manage to deliver them to Frau Berger and collect payment in whatever commodity she chose to make it.

We are upstairs in Grandmother's room. There is a knock on the door and Mr and Mrs Wintner come in to say how very sorry they are about our situation and can they help in any way? They have, miraculously, received the *'Blauschein'* again.

They both notice the carefully spread out dresses and remark on how lovely they are. Mamma, her face so sad, so grave, explains to them the quandary she finds herself in. And then, Mr Wintner, as it were in reply, says: 'Have you at all considered, Mrs Fischler, leaving your daughter behind? You may, you know. Many people are leaving their children with relations. Just for the time being, till they have settled down. Yasia is such a sensible, resourceful girl. Joseph and she will look after each other and they will not be on their own – there is the family. And their grandmother will be back from the country soon. Yasia will find you, wherever you are. She will be a link between you and the family, and your interests, here, in Cracow.' Mamma looks at me and I look at her, the tears are streaming down our faces. And Bartuś cuddles up to me – his big sister – 'Aren't you coming?' 'Not today, Bartuś, I'll come later.' It is decided. I shall remain in the Ghetto. Mamma is putting her sewing implements into a cardboard box. She will take the dresses. We shall still hold onto Frau Berger – I shall be the intermediary.

Mamma's luggage consists of one small suitcase and a holdall. Nothing sizeable or cumbersome; this much we have learnt from the thousands we watched this week painfully pick their way towards Plaszow . . .

In the early afternoon, on that Sunday, already dressed for the journey in a navy-blue skirt and top, a silk square wound round her hair, Mamma went to the hospital to break the news to Regina that she, too, was being dispatched to the East with her husband and younger son, and to say good-bye to her sister . . .

The day was slipping away. The shadows were lengthening. In the early evening, still in broad daylight, Mamma said that she and Bartuś were ready to join Father in the 'Optima' courtyard. Bartuś, in short trousers, put on Mamma's navy-blue winter suit-jacket. The one from which we once unpicked the grey, Persian lamb collar and cuffs. The sleeves turned half way up his arms, the garment was pathetically big and long on him, hiding his thin legs and bony knees. Only his feet in heavy, worn lace-up boots were peeping out.

Joseph carried Mamma's luggage; the four of us walking slowly down Limanowskiego Street. Mamma and Joseph in front, Bartuś and I, holding hands, following them. We did not speak. We reached the corner of Wegierska Street and rounding it, we found ourselves in front of the 'Optima' gate. There was only one German sentry, fully-armed, on duty outside it. He took no interest in us whatever – obviously bored stiff by the many good-bye scenes he had witnessed that day – but was looking straight in front of him. We positioned ourselves a little to the side of the gate, Mamma and Bartuś with their backs to it, I facing Mamma, Joseph facing Bartuś. The sky above the old chocolate factory, I remember, seemed ablaze. The sun, like an enormous diseased eye, discharging pus, blood and tears. We looked at each other, the four of us, our eyes brimming with tears. We kissed and we hugged and Bartuś, not able to reach Joseph's cheek, got hold of his hand and was about to lift it to his lips, when Joseph tore it away saying: 'What are your doing, Bartuś?' And the big brother picked up the little one and they clung to each other and kissed each other's cheeks. Then they turned round, Mamma and Bartuś, and slowly entered the gate. They were gone. We had delivered our Mother and our eight year old brother into their hands.

Slowly, in silence, each with his burden of pain, the tears unashamedly streaking our cheeks, we returned home. Our parents, our brother will spend their last night in the Ghetto, their last night in Cracow, out in the open, in the 'Optima' courtyard.

Late that same Sunday evening, Aunt Josephine came to see me. She said:

'You know, people are being released from "Optima" – Even families . . . People with money, people with influential friends are being given the "*Blauschein*", and are returning home . . .'

117

'You know perfectly well, Aunt Josephine,' I said, 'that we have neither money nor influential friends.'

'Spitz! Have you thought of Spitz? Your Father knew him well. If anybody can help, he can. I think you ought to go and see him – beg him if need be . . . He can get your parents and brother released! I don't know anybody who does not like your father, whom he has not done a good turn. They'll march them out tomorrow, empty the courtyard, put them on the train . . . Try! Talk to Spitz! He won't refuse a child . . . I'll call you, early! He'll be at his mistress's flat. You know where it is?'

'Yes. I do. I'll go. Aunt Josephine, come down in the morning, please . . .'

Simon Spitz – a dark, ugly being existing on the fringes of humanity. A hollow being – devoid of conscience, unfamiliar with integrity. Despised, spurned, he used to hang around Cracow's Jewish cafés . . . Father knew him since they were both boys. Father always greeted him, exchanged the time of day with him, offered him a cigarette, sometimes stood him a drink, when others feigned not to see him, preferred not to be aware of his presence. That was before the war. Father's attitude towards him – Father was like that, he had a good word for everybody – brought out in Spitz some deeply buried, barely flickering spark of humanity: I cannot say decency, for decency he had none. He would have sold his grandmother, as the saying goes, had it been advantageous to him . . . But like all human beings he had feelings, albeit only for himself, and his atrophied spirit was not altogether unresponsive to kindness, of which little enough came his way.

With the Occupation, this tall, lanky man with a vulture's face and a predator's cunning, traded the only asset he possessed – and he would settle plenty of scores, having a long, long memory – the knowledge of his people for the Occupier's privileges. He offered his services to the Gestapo. They were accepted. Having risen in the world, so that people cowered at the very mention of his name, and bowed obsequiously from the waist down when they met him in the street, he still greeted Father, whenever they ran into each other and stopped to exchange a few words.

In the morning, Aunt Josephine came down to the basement and tapped on the window pane. I was already awake. In no time at all, in semi-darkness, I was crossing the Limanowskiego Street thoroughfare. Night was gathering her sombre cloak about her, the starless sky paling to receive a fresh summer's dawn. I wished, as condemned men must wish, the night would never end. I wished, as they must do, the new day would never rise . . .

I entered a tall building in Józefinska Street and climbed the stairs to the second floor. I had only just touched the doorbell and the front door was flung open. Aunt Josephine was right. Spitz was already at his morning toilette. He stood in the doorway naked from the waist up, his face covered in soap lather. Even so, even in the poor light, I could detect a hint of surprise in his dark, vulpine eyes as he looked down at me. 'I am Yasia F . . .' 'You don't need to tell me your name. I know who you are . . . Come in, come in . . .'

I would not enter the flat beyond the entrance hall and I apologised for disturbing him at such an early hour. He seemed to be in a good mood – jovial and friendly – maybe even a little amused. I explained that my Father was refused the *'Blauschein'* and that my Mother and younger Brother had joined him in the 'Optima' court-yard last night. 'I have come to beg you, Mr Spitz, to come to their rescue.' The dark, restless eyes fastening upon my face, he said: 'They'll be back this morning, I promise. Now, go home and don't worry.' 'Thank you, Mr Spitz.'

I went straight home and repeated what Spitz had said to Aunt Josephine. 'You see,' she said, 'I was right.'

I then sat down to write a letter to my parents and Bartuś. It was the first letter I have ever written to them and the last . . . I told them that I had been to see Spitz, that he had received me very cordially, and that he had promised to help . . . I sent them, all three, kisses and hugs . . . I put the note in an envelope and addressed it to Mamma. I left the building again. I suppose it was about breakfast time and there were people in the Ghetto sitting down to breakfast. The Ghetto was now fully awake. The sky, which earlier appeared pale, was purple – grey, ragged clouds floating across it – the air taut with despair and suffering.

I approached the sentry at the 'Optima' gate holding the white envelope in my left hand and said to him, pointing with my right hand towards the interior of the courtyard: 'Bitteschön, meine Mutter . . .' He nodded and took the envelope from me. I said 'Dankeschön' and walked away.

I sat at the window in Grandmother's room waiting . . . I would see them coming long before they entered the building. I did not take my eyes off our side of the pavement along which they would walk – Father, Mamma and Bartuś, if Spitz kept his promise . . .

Never again in my life would I look out of a window, await the arrival of a loved one with quite the same depth of yearning, with quite the same ardent prayer in my heart.

We knew that by mid-day the 'Optima' gate would be closed; that after that hour the thousands imprisoned behind it would be deported, every last one of them. Those of us in the Ghetto whose loved ones remained behind the closed gate as the clock struck mid-day, knew that they had lost them. But not yet with quite the certainty that leaves not a shred of hope. That would come later.

Aunt Josephine came into the room and I turned my head towards her. Her large, green eyes filled with pity, she said: 'Look, it's getting late.' 'Yes, it's getting late . . .' 'You must go and find Spitz – ask him, beg him.' 'Where shall I find him at this time of day?' 'Go to the Jewish Police Headquarters, they'll know his whereabouts; he may even be there.'

The Ghetto was silent and deserted, under the overcast sky, with the heavy, muggy air that precedes a storm.

Outside the headquarters a policeman was on duty. I asked him if he knew where I could find Mr Spitz at this time of day. He evinced no surprise at my enquiry and replied: 'He is right here, sitting in the back parlour.' 'Would you take me to him, please?' 'Yes, follow me.'

Inside the building, on the ground floor, he knocked on the second door on the right. He held it open for me. I entered the room. He came in behind me and remained by the door.

Spitz was sitting in a large easy chair smoking a cigarette. The dark eyes flashed with impatience at the sight of me. I approached him and knelt down before him, 'I beseech you, Mr Spitz . . .' Looking over my head, he said to the policeman. 'Take her away.' He came over, helped me rise and gently guided me out of the room, out of the building.

In mid-afternoon, on Monday 8 June 1942, the third quota of Cracow Ghetto deportees was led out, through the wide open gate of the 'Optima' courtyard, to wend its way along Limanowskiego Street – passing under the very windows of our building – towards Plaszow railway station. It was a sunless afternoon. The weather had broken. Black, ominous clouds were gathering in Cracow's mournful sky. The long, silent procession of totally submissive figures – men, women and children – marching in straight, orderly ranks of five had the solemnity, the gravity of a funeral cortege.

About half-way through the piteous coffle, there came a row of five – Father, Bartuś, Mamma, Aunt Rose, Uncle Dolek – both the image and the pain would remain with us, Joseph and me, for as long as we lived. Mamma raised her head to look up at the window of Grandmother's room to catch a last glimpse of her children, but Father, his head held high, looked straight in front of him.

Some time later, after the third quota of Cracow Jews had been marched out of the Ghetto – perhaps as they were reaching the long line of cattle-trucks – the skies started to weep. A fine drizzle set in.

15 · Anna and David

In the late afternoon of 8 June 1942, the first Cracow Ghetto re-settlement action, which had lasted eight days, was terminated. 20,000 people had been consigned to the East. The SS squad directing the action, having carried out the task allotted to them with singular speed, efficiency and frugality – wasting neither time, effort nor resources, for these were precious commodities, especially in time of war – was recalled to other, no doubt, equally onerous duties. The Ghetto returned to normal, as a man whose limbs had been amputated with a blunt instrument, in full consciousness, returns to the life he had led when he was a whole man. And still we had no inkling. And still we had not the faintest suspicion of the fate of that multitude despatched to the East.

The following day, Tuesday 9 June, Joseph and I were invited to an evening meal by Siggie and Sophie, our cousins, in their room at No. 4 The Square of Peace. They, too, had been dispossessed of their loved ones. Siggie was then eighteen years old, his sister, Sophie, two years his junior. The brother and sister, apart from each other, had nobody left, except us – their only cousins.

I remember Sophie had spread a clean check cloth on the table. Grandmother Heim's china. Grandmother Heim's pots and pans . . . She had cooked a large saucepan of thick vegetable soup and there was a whole, fresh loaf of bread on the table.

We felt, all four, so bruised, so scarred, so deeply conscious of the absence of our loved ones that we could not speak. The smell of the soup, the sight of the bread, brought such an overwhelming sense of loss and desolation that we, all four, wept. Every spoonful of soup, every morsel of bread made us think of them . . . And as we ate, our tears mingled with the soup, and were soaked up by the bread . . .

We did not offer each other solace; we did not even attempt to do so. We knew that there was nothing anybody could say, or do, that would lessen our sorrow, our yearning, but we felt closer to our cousins than ever before, because of the common bond of pain and loss. Aunt Rose's hairbrush on the bedside table, Uncle Dolek's slippers by the bed . . .

When we did talk, it was about the events of the last ten days. Siggie and Joseph, having some knowledge of Poland's eastern cities, provinces and the distances between them and Cracow, were saying that by the end of the following week, very likely, news from the East would start reaching the Ghetto.

That same week, we decided, Joseph and I, that I would go and stay for a while in Kościelniki with Anna and David and take the news to them. For whereas Grandmother and the relations at Grodkowice already knew what losses we had sustained as a family, Anna and David, being that much further away, that much more cut off, did not. I would be the harbinger of bad tidings.

Anna and David were renting a room in a peasant cottage inhabited by three generations of the same family. It stood on top of a small hillock. The large, well-kept garden surrounding it was on different levels, rather like terraces.

Our room was at the back; it was small, whitewashed and had a hard, dried mud floor. The bed, a straw-filled, sacking covered mattress, resting on a rough-hewn wooden base, occupied the far corner of the room. A wooden table and four chairs had been placed under the window. Against the wall, opposite the window, there stood a tall, gaudily painted linen chest on which I slept. The wall on the right-hand side of the door had a few wooden pegs driven into it on which garments were hung. A small suitcase was wedged into the corner of the other wall, on the left-hand side of the door. The suitcase, in which Anna kept her personal possessions, was always closed, for its lid served as a surface on which she kept her very modest hoard of china, cutlery and domestic utensils. It was the humblest, barest room, yet peaceful and filled with natural light – the window giving onto the pretty garden and a large panel of the tender, blue Polish sky. To this day I wish, with all my heart, that it had been given to Anna and David to pass the war years within its walls.

David went out very little. He felt it was wisest not to imperil his person by exposing his face. His dark, Jewish eyes, behind the thick, steel-rimmed lenses, had become larger, more protruding, it seemed to me, and filled with stark, naked terror.

He was clumsy and awkward with children. He had no experience of them; did not know how to befriend them; but he was innately kind and gentle; his heart went out to me in my trouble. He

123

remarked that I was very quiet – extinguished – was the word he used. I knew Anna loved me and now felt responsible for me.

I had only been with them for a couple of days – not even a week had elapsed since I had seen my parents and Bartuś being marched out of the Ghetto – when I felt, one afternoon, an extraordinarily deep sense of sadness, of solitude come over me. I went out in search of a spot to hide. I found it at the back of the barn. I sat down on the ground, in the oppressive afternoon heat, under a sallow sky, resting my back against the barn wall. Like my father, only a few days earlier, I buried my face in my hands and started to sob. It was like a deluge. The sobs made my whole body shudder. The grief was tearing me apart, suffocating me. And then I realised that someone was trying to put his arm round my shoulders, that a large, strong hand was gently smoothing my hair . . . And David was saying, 'Yasia, Yasia, come home. Anna is so worried . . . come . . . take my hand . . .'and he led me indoors.

Two days after the outburst by the barn, I had a dream, a vivid, technicolour dream. I remember as much of it today as I did on that morning, many, many years ago, when I woke up from it. I saw a fire in my dream. Somewhere, far away, maybe in the East . . . There was a clearing, but I could not tell where it was or what it was surrounded by, where it led from, or where it led to. There was nothing around the clearing to help me locate it – nothing familiar or recognizable, nothing solid or firmly rooted. Outside it there was a void in which all dissolved, turned into mist, drifted away. Whatever it was that encircled the clearing seemed to be floating away in wisps and tatters – grey and weightless – and melting into nothingness.

Only the bonfire, which was immense, had body and substance. It was piled up very high. Its base glowing, red hot, but burnt out, spread over the whole clearing. As it rose from its base, it was very tightly packed, its upper half burning vigorously, fiercely. The flames were brilliantly colourful, orange, blue, yellow, purple, merging, running into each other, twisting, twirling – dancing and leaping towards the very sky. I could see them shooting up, torn and ragged at the edges, their tips licking the sky, setting it ablaze, eating it up . . . But I could not tell why I was there, the only one, watching the fire.

A new phrase had crept into my vocabulary, 'Living on one's capital'. Although I had vaguely understood its meaning up to the time I went to stay with Anna and David, it was when I saw it in practice, day in, day out, with all its ramifications and implications; all the restraints and self-denials, that its true meaning was brought home to me in its full poignancy.

Anna and David practised the most stringent economies. He held the purse-strings and watched his meagre savings dwindle daily. He had a fine mind and he applied all his faculties to making his modest nest-egg last as long as possible. Cautious and abstemious by nature, he now had all the time in the world to devote to his obsession, for an obsession it had become. He spent hours, pencil and paper in hand, working on the four basic arithmetical equations.

Every few days he would introduce a change – an expenditure whittling attempt – to our diurnal diet. When I first arrived, we had a slice of bread each in the morning and in the evening, apart from the midday meal. After a few days the morning slice of bread was withdrawn and a windfall apple appeared in its place.

Our staple diet consisted of milk and boiled potatoes. The top of the milk was carefully skimmed by David into a little jug to be used as a sort of dressing on the potatoes. On one occasion, carrying the jug, I clumsily stumbled on a pot-hole in the floor – it was very uneven – the jug's precious contents spilling in a viscous, winding rivulet across the beaten mud floor. A bowl of freshly-boiled potatoes was standing in the centre of the table, a cloud of steam rising from it. There was a deathly hush in the room. I felt foolish and guilty, but before I had time to say how sorry I was, David exclaimed, 'We are not going to let the potatoes get cold, are we?' He pulled out a chair for me and as I sat down he passed his hand lightly over my hair.

One day, in the afternoon, David agreed to accompany us across the fields and meadows on a visit to the cousins' farm. I was keen to go, as we were always well received and offered plenty of refreshment. My appetite had not diminished.

Walking along a narrow path hemming a meadow, we saw a couple of gypsy caravans, their occupants, except for the children who were running about, a motley crew sitting on the grass talking in high, raucous voices. As they saw us approach, an old gypsy woman stood up and detached herself from the others, walking towards us. David, with his long stride, hastened ahead and was already some distance from us when the old gypsy woman approached Anna. She was old and as thin and flat as a stick, her richly gathered skirts and petticoats barely staying up upon her scrawny frame. A thin, pepper-and-salt pig-tail hung down her back. Her brown, wizened face was seamed with deep lines. She got hold of Anna's hand saying, 'Le'me tell ye yer fortune, lady . . .' and brought it close to her tired but knowing eyes. Peering at it, but stalling, as if to gain time, she said again, 'Le'me tell ye yer fortune, lady . . .' But Anna, for some reason, withdrew her hand and said, 'Read the girlie's hand instead.' One shrewd glance of the deep-sunk, tired eyes and she knew that talk of romance past, present or future would not do. 'A letter' she said – 'a long letter, much wished for, eagerly awaited, is on its way.' I do not remember what else she said, because she had uttered the one word I so desperately wanted to hear – 'A letter.' Anna put a coin in her hand and she shuffled back, the colourful skirts swirling round her ankles, impeding her movements.

'A letter', said Anna, 'Ah, if your mother could hear you call her, as I do, in the night, she wouldn't just write, she would come back to you . . .'

16 • No. 4 The Square of Peace

By the time I returned to the Ghetto, in July 1942, it was being whispered, where and how the whispering had originated I do not know, that the Jews living in the countryside – the last bastion of relative freedom – would be drawn into the Ghetto in the early autumn. There was nothing but sadness for us. I use the word 'sadness' advisedly, but with hindsight it seems a mild, poetic word. Yet, we still did not know. People like us, ordinary mortals, did not know; did not suspect, could not possibly imagine the tragic fate of their loved ones and, ultimately, of all European Jewry. We were living on credit, of course, but it took time to absorb, to make one's own that arcane knowledge with all its ramifications.

I said 'goodbye' to my aunt whom I loved dearly, and to David of whom I had become very fond. They were both extremely anxious about these latest rumours, for they feared, rightly, more than anything else having to enter the cauldron of the Ghetto.

When I returned to the Cracow Ghetto, I found that a great many changes had taken place in my absence.

There was no news from the deportees of the June action. No letter, no message, no word in any form or shape had arrived from a single one of the thousands despatched to the East. They had vanished leaving no trace, no mark, no ripple. But, at that time, it did not even vaguely occur to us that they might not be alive; that the labour camps in the East were but primitive death factories. We waited. We hoped . . .

The Jews are, I think, both inventive and optimistic people – these traits may stem from the unsurpassed suffering and hardship they have had to endure. Explanations, reasons, justifications galore were in circulation in the Ghetto. I have heard it said that we were gullible – possibly. But we did so want to believe and in what form was one to consider the alternative? I, at the age of twelve, was neither mentally nor emotionally equipped to look the truth in the face, even if it had been presented to me.

In my absence, the Ghetto had been diminished in size. A standard procedure after a re-settlement action, but new to us. Looking back – and I see the Ghetto so clearly, in every detail, to this day – I would say half the area originally allocated to us was clawed back. The even numbered side, our side, of Limanowskiego Street and the thoroughfare with the 'Aryan' trams formed part of the reclaimed portion. Our basement room, Grandmother's room, the whole building at No. 42, as well as 'Optima' with its courtyard, were no longer in the Ghetto. My family – Joseph, Grandmother (who had in the meantime returned home) and Regina – had moved in with our cousins at no. 4 the Square of Peace. Joseph and Grandmother, with the cousins' help, had transferred as much furniture and as many household goods as was possible, and as the room could accommodate. The room – drab, shadowy, overcrowded – was still an improvement on our basement, but a very considerable come-down on Grandmother's first abode in the Ghetto. It contained four beds and a sofa. Grandmother slept on the latter.

All Joseph managed to squeeze into no. 4 was one of our parents' twin beds, an oval-shaped mirror from Mamma's dressing table and the precious 'Singer' sewing machine; bedding, a few household utensils, a handful of personal belongings.

The same went for Grandmother and Regina, although they succeeded, no doubt with immense effort, in bringing one of their wardrobes in. It just fitted into a niche in the wall. What with transport difficulties, the speed with which they had to vacate their previous homes, and the general hurly-burly of the move, no sleeping provision was made for me in the room. But already a sense of transitoriness, of impermanence was making itself felt. One adapted, one made do.

I spotted, standing in the corner, the headboard of my parents' other twin bed. Joseph must have brought it in. In the evening, I placed it over two high-backed chairs – one at each end – tossed a blanket and a pillow onto it and I slept like that for well over three months, and do not remember ever being uncomfortable or cramped. I could curl up, in those days, on the bare floor and sleep soundly.

Grandmother, Regina, Joseph and I were now one family; we shared whatever little there was to share. If it had not been for Grandmother's enterprising spirit and courage, we would have found ourselves in truly desperate financial straits. Grandmother, at the age of seventy, found paid employment within the Ghetto walls. She was taken on by Mrs Nagler, the Chief Supervisor at the Ghetto Public Baths, as an attendant. She not only received a regular weekly wage, she also collected, daily, a certain amount in gratuities.

Joseph and I had almost nothing left to sell. Grandmother and Regina, who still had a few odds and ends tucked away, were both quite reluctant to part with personal possessions. They thought, I believe, that they would find it hard to set up home after the war without their bits and pieces. Grandmother's 'post' at the Baths was a godsend to us all.

Very soon after my return to the Ghetto, towards the end of July, Regina asked me if I could smuggle out her winter coat and place it for safekeeping with a trustworthy, reliable pre-war neighbour or acquaintance. I was rather taken aback at this request. Regina could not have physically, under any circumstances, walked out of the room and taken a few steps out of doors on her own. Although her condition had ameliorated, she was still greatly dependent on her mother and those close to her. She had not worn, she had not needed, her winter coat once since becoming ill.

Depositing property with Aryans was a delicate and, to some extent, hazardous undertaking. Not everybody wanted to guard Jewish property. Equally, those who undertook to guard it did not always want to return it on request, or at all. Jews who deposited personal property with Aryans were usually people of substance and the property itself, in whatever form, was valuable. One very ordinary winter coat? I did not question Regina's wish at the time. Perhaps it made her feel that her hold on life was less tenuous; that she would move again, walk again, free and freely, in the streets of Cracow; that after the war she would return to the life she had once led; that she would need her coat to go out in, in winter, as she once did. On the other hand, a winter coat in my family was a very precious garment – it had to last, if not a lifetime, then a good part of it.

I took the coat to a pre-war neighbour of ours, a middle-aged widow, whom Mamma had liked and trusted and who seemed genuinely well-disposed towards us. She not only accepted it, unconditionally, for safekeeping, but invited me to sit down at her kitchen table and put a slice of buttered bread and a glass of milk in front of me.

One evening, in August, a group of my brother's and cousins' friends, all teenagers, many of whom were on the threshold of death, gathered in our room at the Square of Peace for a 'social evening'. They all knew me as 'Joseph's little sister', and, although I was sitting quietly and inconspicuously in a dark corner of the room, everyone of them, boys as well as girls, came over to say 'Hullo', to give me a kiss and a hug.

Henio Birner – he and my cousin Sophie were sweethearts – was one of the guests. I liked him very much. He was tall with curly, coal-black hair and, like Sophie, only sixteen years old. He had a naturally sweet disposition and a quiet, gentle manner. He never came to see us without what we came to call 'his visiting card' – a loaf of freshly baked bread, still warm, from his uncle's bakery. Henio, at that time, had two months of life in front of him; Sophie, his sweetheart, had two years in front of her. They behaved as young people do at parties. They chatted, they laughed, they flirted mildly . . . The stack of buttered slices of bread disappeared. The jugs of raspberry cordial were emptied.

They were happy to be together, to momentarily forget, to briefly lock out the awesome reality of their lives. The pleasant interlude did not last long, for the 'question' was in the forefront of everybody's mind: it never stopped tormenting our souls. Why, why has not a single word been received from a single one of the deportees? Indeed, in no time at all the youngsters were pondering that unanswerable question, which was consuming everyone of us in wakefulness as in sleep: Why, why is there no sign of life from a single one of them? Days have turned into weeks; weeks have turned into months and still no news . . . Various theories were put forward, and I do remember that in the light of what we eventually learnt of the fate of the deportees, not one of the theories advanced contained so much as a grain of reality. Racked by anguish and longing, we talked about what was closest to our hearts – the desperate anxiety with which we lived.

And then one of the young ladies, a girl of about sixteen, tossed her head, her rich mane of black, silken hair falling over her round, childish face like a dark curtain, and raising her voice she spoke clearly and emphatically: 'I would find a way, I know I would, to get in touch with my family, to let them know where I was . . .' The strength and conviction with which she uttered those words made everyone look at her in wonder. She was wrong. How could she know how wrong she was? The answer was so simple it was staring us in the face: 'The dead do not write letters. They remain silent.'

No. 4 The Square of Peace

Sometime in August 1942, shortly before an official edict would have obliged them to do so, Anna and David left the country and returned to Cracow. Briefly, they went into hiding. Anna turned to a close Aryan friend for help in their desperation not to be swallowed up by the Ghetto. The friend, true to her promise of help, took them in and harboured them for a few weeks. She must have been a person of great loyalty and courage for the risk she took – the certain death penalty for herself and her family – was terrifying. Anna, with her perfectly Aryan face and manner, stood a fair chance of survival on the Aryan side, but David was doomed from the start.

After a few weeks, the friend asked if they could move on, find somewhere else to stay. There was nowhere else – not for David. All routes of escape were closed. The day came, in September 1942, when the inevitable step had to be taken – the dragnet had reached them. They entered the Ghetto and moved in with David's sister, little Olek's mother, at No. 11 Lvovska Street.

That same month, September 1942, a couple with a child entered our room at the Square of Peace. The woman, waving an official looking piece of paper announced: 'The Housing Committee has allocated us to this room.' Whilst we, dumbfounded, were sizing them up, they were critically inspecting the room. 'We are Mr and Mrs Kalfus. And this is our daughter, Irene. Irene is eight years old. Aren't you darling?' The little girl, very shy, nodded her head. 'You'll have to make room for our things. We haven't got much, though. We are moving in right away.'

Fenia, for that was Mrs Kalfus's first name, her husband and daughter were strangers to Cracow. They had only just arrived in the Ghetto from the Bielsko cloth-manufacturing region – a sort of Polish Lancashire. They were provincial, small-town Jews. The husband, a fine figure of a man, very well turned out, alert and confident, already looked out of place in that bleak, dingy room. Space was made for them. Their double bed, bedside cabinet and cupboard were accommodated. Having settled in his wife and daughter, and having speedily, but accurately, assessed the existing inhabitants of the room. Kalfus went out, not to return till late in the evening.

Fenia made herself at home. She made up the bed and arranged her cupboards. She took Irene by the hand and they left the room to find out where the 'facilities' were. When they returned from the inspection, they carefully washed their hands, with proper soap, in a bowl of water. Fenia then set about preparing their evening meal.

131

We watched, with unbelieving eyes, as bread, butter, hard-boiled eggs and cheese appeared on the table – and fruit, apples, pears, plums. The Kalfuses are rich was one's immediate mental conclusion, although one would never have guessed it from Fenia's or Irene's appearance. The husband's wardrobe, the fine bed-linen, the soap and, above all, the comestibles spread on the table were clear indications and spoke for themselves.

17 • Daily Life

The tenement at No. 4 the Square of Peace was an old, dilapidated one-storey building. Normally, it would have been considered unfit for family habitation.

On the ground floor, where we lived, there were two large rooms facing each other across a dingy hallway. On the first floor there were three rooms. At one time, they had all been workshops where small groups of artisans worked at their different crafts. Ours had been a bookbinder's workshop.

There was no water or internal sanitation in the building which, now in the autumn of 1942, resembled an antheap. Three or four families packed to each room and only too glad to have a 'solid' roof over their heads. The only toilet – a primitive one – was outside and became a source of endless friction and misery. It was nearly always occupied. In the morning, there was a mad scramble for the relief and privacy behind its closed doors. A great deal of squabbling and arguing went on outside it. Its fortunate occupier, who had probably got up extra early to enjoy its privileges unmolested, was harried and hurried in very strong language indeed. But it was in the evenings that the ugliest, the most demeaning quarrels broke out for the possession of the coarse-grained wooden seat. The tenants, at that time of day, were after a longish, peaceful session. Some were impervious enough or had the stamina to withstand the abuse and the threats of those impatiently waiting their turn, desperately hopping from one foot to the other, and took their time. But, on the whole, the chivvying had the desired effect and one expedited one's business as smartly as one could. Also, it was no place to linger in; the stench, the cold, the dark were forbidding. The toilet, it so happened, was contiguous with our room, so that we had the full benefit, through the flimsy partition wall, of its inside and outside activities.

The inner courtyard, which our room gave onto, was quite large in area and as bleak as the tenement itself. There was an arid, desolate harshness about it that, even then, offended the eye. There was a hovel right at the back of it in which 'the caretaker' lived. A haggard, cantankerous little woman, not unlike a brutalised, over-burdened little mare. I am not sure what her functions were, but I never saw her wield a broom or a mop of any kind. She was perma-nently angry and quite unapproachable. Surrounded by a brood of skinny, scruffy children, she shouted and distributed cuffs quite liberally. That courtyard, the caretaker's domain, already had the semblance of the 'ghost town' that the Ghetto would, one day, become.

The only communal water tap poked its verdigris encrusted head out of the courtyard wall. The tap, too, was a bone of contention, but to a lesser degree than the toilet, for the need, the urgency, was within one's control, could be contained. Water had become a very precious commodity – every drop had to be fetched and the slops had to be disposed of. One learnt to be frugal; to conserve, to measure out, to re-cycle. Fetching water in the summer was no hard-ship, even though a bucketful was heavy. But in winter, when the icy water splashed over one's hands and feet and clothing and the patch of ground around the tap was like a cobbled skating rink, then tempers would become frayed. Sometimes tenants would douse each other with the contents of a freshly filled bucket, or worse still – a basinful of slops, as well as, for good measure, a verbal shower of scurrilous expletive.

On a good day, however, these toilet and water queues, when there was no particular rush or pent-up aggression, could also be a source of information and instruction; of gossip and rumour. One could while away the time whilst waiting one's turn and improve one's mind, learn, bring oneself up to date on Ghetto matters, from the interpretation of the latest SS edict to the day's price of gold and, of course, on the progress of the war. 'Hm . . . hm . . . the Russian front . . . They are getting the drubbing of their lives . . . Things are going badly for them . . . Thanks be to God!' I close my eyes and the room at No. 4 and its inhabitants swim into view quite vividly.

It was a large room. One entered it straight from the hallway. It had one biggish window at the near end so that, as the room was deep, its far end was permanently plunged in cold, clotted gloom. Against the dank, stained walls there stood all manner of wardrobe, cupboard and chest, all tightly wedged against each other, to fully utilise every inch of space. Enclosed by this garland of upright furniture, were beds, sofas, couches, pallets – all bulging with square, lumpy pillows and plump goose-down comforters. The focal point of the room was a solid wooden table and an assortment of chairs. I no longer remember to whom it belonged, we all used it; we all felt we had a right to it. I do not recall its ownership ever being in dispute, unlike many other objects over which we squabbled and bickered and took each other to task.

One corner of the room, at the near end, was occupied by an iron cooking-range which we fed with wood from chopped up furniture and lumps of coal smuggled in our bags, even pockets, by those who worked outside. The stove, too, was a source of bitter arguments and recriminations – at times even direct accusations. There were sometimes as many as a dozen saucepans sitting on it, and everybody wanted theirs centrally placed where the heat was most effective. They were being constantly shifted and shuttled. One only had to turn one's back to find that one's soup was teetering dangerously on the edge of the stove; or that it contained five potatoes, whereas seconds earlier it had contained six; and worst crime of all, that the top layer – the one containing all the goodness – had been skimmed off.

Most of the rows and fights broke out in the evening, after people had returned from work, tired and hungry and when the pressure on 'the amenities' was greatest. Even then, there were those who managed to preserve their dignity and decency and those who ranted and raved at every opportunity lashing out indiscriminately. Just as there were those who washed themselves and their smalls every day and managed to look clean and neat, though the effort these operations required, after a day's backbreaking work, was gigantic.

Opposite the stove, by the window, stood two buckets – one with clean water, one with slops. They, too, were a source of arguments, for nobody liked emptying the slops down the communal toilet.

The room was crammed to bursting with everyday personal objects; crockery, cutlery, clothing, shoes, spare bedding. Under each bed there was a veritable market-stall in second-hand merchandise.

Then, there was the matter of eating one's food. There was something almost shameful in eating one's fill, so that one became secretive and underhand. One developed a manner of eating in which one shut oneself off, isolated oneself from the rest of the room, so as not to feel, not to see the need, the want, the mute appeal in the eyes of those who had no food.

In the evening, in the dim light of a naked electric bulb swinging to and fro from the ceiling to the rhythm of our comings and goings, the room really did become like a toiling antheap.

Grandmother would be erecting a screen made of sheets and blankets round her confined territory behind which to wash herself and her incapacitated daughter, whilst Regina would be resting on her bed shading her eyes from the bulb's crude glare. Siggie, on all fours, would be rummaging under his bed for some object he had hidden with such cunning ingenuity that he, himself could not find it. Sophie, his sister, would be straining her eyes, in that meagre light, to darn her virtually disintegrating stockings. Fenia would be sitting on the edge of her bed, her hands folded in her lap, gazing at her peacefully sleeping child. There was always washing being done; water bubbling, water gurgling, water hissing on the stove; water squelching and splashing in the basin; water being poured in, water being poured out, smalls being washed, rinsed and wrung out. The room was permanently festooned with washing lines. Basins and saucepans were being strategically and ingeniously placed all over it to catch the drips. Even so, one often felt a cold trickle slither down one's neck or found oneself sleeping on a wringing wet pillow.

But all these activities were manifestations of life and to some degree of hope – they bore out the belief that there was a tomorrow, maybe many tomorrows . . . People were always saying, 'so long as one washed oneself, ate, slept, looked after oneself – keeping one's body healthy and one's mind sane one might outlive the nightmare!'

Although by now nothing belonged to us, not even our bodies, not even our souls – ourselves, and whatever we still possessed, was the undisputed property of the Third Reich. But as old habits die hard, the proud sense of ownership still lurked and manifested itself here and there. Our cousin, Siggie, a tall, handsome youth, had it to an acute degree. He and his sister were the original and longest-standing occupants of the room. They had lived in it with their parents and grandmother ever since the winter of 1941. They had lost their family in the June re-settlement, and when the Ghetto was diminished in size, as a result of it, the present inhabitants of the room, the new-comers, were 'billeted' upon them, as it were. Siggie, thus, saw himself as something of a landlord and expected, as such, a degree of deference and consideration from us, his lodgers, but of course nobody paid any heed to his expectations.

Siggie and Sophie both belonged to 'solid' labour contingents and went daily to work outside the Ghetto. As children and adolescents they had been inordinately pampered, spoilt and waited upon hand and foot. Yet, Sophie, a tall, slim girl with magnificent 'Titian' hair and sparkling white teeth, turned out to be a practical, resourceful girl. She was also sweet-natured and singularly unselfish. She shared with us whatever scraps of food she managed to glean in the course of the day. I remember she never went anywhere, in those days, without her capacious canvas shoulder-bag. When she came home in the evening, she would empty its pitiable contents, but at the time the most coveted treasures, onto her bed; tiny little potatoes, a handful of beans, an onion or two, some carrots, perhaps a hunk of bread. She would peel the vegetables very finely and make a thick nourishing soup, which was a meal in itself . . .

Fenia, whose husband was out every evening either philandering or entertaining his cronies, and being entertained by them, spent the evenings sitting on the edge of her bed watching, like a benign Cerberus, over her sleeping child. She would sit there for hours – inert and quite oblivious to her surroundings – her gaze riveted upon the child's sleep-suffused face. Who knew what went through Fenia's mind? Who could have divined her mental processes? What she wished to remember? What she wished to forget? Who could have unravelled the tangled web of her thoughts? Except that they were all concentrated on her child . . . Everything she did – was a hope, a prayer, a wish to protect her child. Torn between fear and hope, she wanted to guard her child with her own large, strong body against the evil forces lurking, she knew not exactly where, but outside this bed, outside this room, in the great beyond . . .

The Kalfus family had only recently come to share what Kalfus tersely termed as 'Siggie's grace and favour residence'. They were new to Cracow, new to its Ghetto. But whereas her highly enterprising and convivial husband had quickly 'found his feet' and already had a circle of buddies, as well as a daily solace – a very attractive mistress – Fenia, who was totally devoid of social graces and, I believe, social aspirations, was all alone. Like her own little girl she, too, had been an only child, a gauche, plain, lonely child. She understood, I think, that there were things in life, good things, to do with the mind, with the senses, with social relations, which had passed her by. She could not have named them – it was more of a presentiment than knowledge – she could not have fleshed out her thoughts and feelings on the subject, but she sensed, rather than knew, that there was more to life than had been her share. She wanted 'it', whatever it was, for her own child. She wanted her child to live and to experience that which made life rich. Those were the thoughts, I believe, that went spinning round and round in her head, nebulous and shapeless, and yet containing the essential truth however dimly perceived, as she sat on the bed.

Apart from dodging the daily possibility of extinction, which by now had become a reflex action, eating one's fill was uppermost in everybody's mind. On this score, the Kalfuses were much envied. Half a century after the events described in this book, I would meet my millionaire cousin, Siggie, in London, and he would say remembering those dark, far off days: 'The Kalfuses were not short of a bob or two . . .' Indeed, they were not short of money. They were not short of food. Fenia was the only able-bodied adult in that room who did not go out to work. She stayed 'at home' and looked after her child. That, in itself, constituted a luxury. She was, also, in our eyes, to be envied on yet another count. She still had her parents when so many much younger people, children, like myself, had been parted from theirs . . .

Fenia's parents, elderly and both frail, lived just a short walk from the Square of Peace. Although they were people of means, because of their age, physical dependence on others and the living conditions prevailing in the Ghetto, they felt totally bewildered and exposed; they felt they had been transplanted into a jungle – which they had. Fenia saw them daily. Mostly she went to them, but sometimes they came 'to call' on her. I could not help staring at them. They seemed to me more like winter garments that had been stuffed with fine tissue paper and sprinkled with moth-balls taken out to be aired than people. The last representatives of an accursed, doomed civilisation. They were so prim and proper. So Jewish in appearance, dress and mannerisms. They sat stiffly round the table – she in black silk, he in black alpaca – and spoke in Yiddish to their daughter. They always brought a little gift for their grand-daughter, a sweetmeat wrapped in crisp white paper, tied with coloured ribbon. Their rheumy eyes darted about uneasily, their arthritis-riddled hands shook visibly – they were so suspicious and so frightened.

Fenia, who could not turn to her husband for understanding on a daily basis or comfort and companionship – for there was almost no dialogue between them – oscillated, emotionally, between her child and her parents. They filled, it seemed, the gap created by her husband's infidelities and total scorn of her. They were the only people she could unburden herself to; verbalise her worries and her fears to. Or so it appeared. Yet, when one came to know her better, one realised that this was not so. She cheated. She pretended. She put on a brave front. She never told them how much her heart ached for them. She protected them as much as she protected her little girl. She was very tender with them. She feared for them. Her fears were very real and well founded. They did not stand the slenderest chance of survival. They were, as we would fully realise after October, the staple diet of the extermination camps. Before October, all we could see was their tenderness and love, their devotion and attachment to their daughter and, of course, their money. In fact, when one had penetrated Fenia's external carapace, she was not to be envied on any count.

Then there were the four of us; Grandmother, Regina, Joseph and I. We still formed, at this stage, a proper family nucleus and we still did not know – certainly not Grandmother, Regina or I – what fate had befallen our loved ones, those deported in June . . .

Our grandparents had had nine children – five sons and four daughters. The first-born, a son, had perished in Auschwitz as early as 1941, but Grandmother did not know this – the family had, advisedly, kept it from her. The three youngest sons had found themselves, soon after the partition of Poland, in Russian occupied territory. Later, in the summer of 1941, when the Russian Army started retreating, they were swept on the gigantic wave of men and equipment and driven into the interior of that boundless, enigmatic land; no news had been received from them, or of them, for over two years. The fifth son, his wife and small daughter were now living in the Bochnia Ghetto.

Of the four daughters, two were in the Ghetto now: Regina with her mother at No. 4 the Square of Peace, and Anna with her husband, David, at No. 11 Lvovska Street, just round the corner from us. Grandmother's eldest and youngest daughters, Eva and Sally, the former, my mother, with her husband and eight year old son, had been despatched to the East in the June action.

The June re-settlement took place fifteen months after the Ghetto came into being. Nothing in its existence had prepared us for the June action. It was an entirely new phenomenon and although the elaborate preliminaries to the action served to allay our fears, the action itself, carried out in three stages over eight days, whipped them up again and filled us with a sense of dark foreboding and stark dread, but nothing we envisaged or feared did, even remotely, approximate the naked truth.

The fate of her children must have exercised Grandmother's mind day and night. Yet, she said very little on the subject; partly, because she did did not possess the facility of couching her thoughts and emotions in words and, partly, because it did not do to complain. She often said, 'One only has to look around to see people much worse off than oneself.' This was hardly true in her case, but she was not given to self-pity. Looking back, she was a stoical old lady and very much a doer. She accepted, unquestioningly and, it seemed, unresentfully, all misfortunes and hardships of life.

18 • Regina's Coat

In the summer of 1942 my relationship with Aunt Regina began to deteriorate. She could not move freely; she was not independent. During her entire stay in the Ghetto, which was only four months short of two years, she did not once set foot outside the building, outside the room in which she lived. She found it hard to accept being an invalid, as would any woman, not yet forty years old, who had always been active, always very much a doer. She had to rely on me for many small, but regular daily services. I was a difficult child, wilful and independent – too much so – and, once I had lost my parents, very much a law unto myself. I irritated Regina who was, by nature, thoroughly reliable in her dealings with people. I was now inclined to suit myself. She felt that her world was disintegrating around her which, indeed, it was, only she did not realise to what extent. She was using a personal, pre-war yardstick in her evaluations and judgments – a yardstick which had no application whatsoever to our present plight . . . She clutched at straws in her brave, but, in the circumstances, meaningless attempts to hold her world together.

She had always been a scrupulously clean, fastidious person. And she liked things. Cleanliness and inanimate objects were a form of religion with some members of my family. They were equated with security and respectability. Living as we now did, water became a most precious commodity. I was fortunate in that I could take myself off to the Ghetto Public Baths and have a jolly good scrub as often as I wished . . . In Regina's case, every drop of water had to be fetched in a pail from the communal water tap in the courtyard. It had to be heated in a large saucepan, which was heavy and which she, herself, could not lift. Then, when she had finished her ablutions, and had re-cycled the precious liquid by washing her smalls, the much-used water had to be poured down the communal toilet. Naturally, she liked to carry out these operations when the room was not crowded, when most of its inhabitants were out at

141

work. But she was not able to tackle any of these tasks single-handedly – she needed my assistance. I was often not there when she needed me. I did not always keep my promises; I did not show the consideration and thoughtfulness which she, my aunt, merited. Albeit unconsciously, I was already taking short-cuts, morally, in preparation for the greatest feat of my life – outlasting the nightmare.

Things came to a head quite unexpectedly. Regina had taken to counting her cutlery pieces. On one occasion, after counting and re-counting her soup spoons, she found one of them to be missing. It meant she no longer possessed a full set – another loose brick in the crumbling edifice of her world – and she was greatly upset. She re-traced her steps meticulously. She was positive that the previous day her cutlery set had been complete, but today it was minus a soup spoon. She remembered that I had done the washing-up the previous night, after our evening meal of a bowl of soup and a slice of bread. She was quite right. I had done the washing-up and I had disposed of the slops in the usual manner. I must have, also, quite inadvertently, disposed of the soup spoon. I did not mean to do so and it was, certainly, beyond retrieving. Regina became very agitated indeed, and took me to task with great vigour enumerating all my faults and shortcomings loudly and woefully. I was the last straw . . . I was not paying attention to what I was doing . . . God only knew what my mind was on . . .

I, too, felt very upset and shaken. I felt very much a child. Very much alone. The bravado evaporated. The stiff upper lip was trembling. I started to cry. All I wanted to do was to cuddle up to Mamma, to feel the warmth of her body against mine, to feel her arms around me . . . It was already over three months since I had last seen Mamma and Father and Bartuś, and in all that time not a word from them or anyone else . . .

Now that Anna and David were in the Ghetto, Anna would drop in on us every day, sometimes in the afternoon, sometimes in the evening. It was a great solace and, in every way, a help to have her around. It did us good to look at her; to be with her. Her presence was like a healing balm to our wounds – for we all had deep, raw, bleeding wounds. As soon as she and David arrived in the Ghetto, they started looking for work. They were both young, fit and more than capable of a day's work. They understood, only too well, how vital it was to be assigned to a solid, weighty labour contingent . . . David was the luckier of the two – though 'luck' seems a totally inappropriate word in this context, yet it was used a great deal by us, Ghetto Jews. He found himself, within days of entering the Ghetto, in a Luftwaffe factory producing spare parts for aircraft – a very good and prestigious assignment. Anna, on the other hand, although she left no stone unturned in her attempts to find work, was still waiting to be allocated to a work detail. She was, thus, free and available to bind wounds, to explain, to soothe – to maintain peace within the family.

The day after my confrontation with Regina, still feeling extremely aggrieved, I mentioned it to Anna. I added, 'I know that when Mamma comes back she will make it up to her.' I looked up at Anna expecting confirmation, but instead I caught an expression of frozen horror on her face. My mind had only just registered it, because it was gone before I could be absolutely sure that I had seen, not imagined it . . . It was coming up to four months since the June re-settlement and the extermination camps in the East had been working at full-throttle for months now, but I had no inkling of their existence . . . If the grown-ups had any knowledge about the true destination of those trains, they were very much on their guard with me. Anna managed to smooth things over, to pacify Regina.

Anna now had access to her 'bottom drawer' – the contents of which Grandmother had carefully guarded and preserved. Every week she would ask me to sell an item or two for her on 'The Outside'. She and David lived, as modestly as before, off the proceeds of her trousseau, but helped us unstintingly.

Very little home-baking was done in the Ghetto. We had no oven at all. In any case, an oven required fuel and that, if one had some, was most sparingly used. The Ghetto bakeries now accepted individual baking and cooking. Now and then, I took a large pot of meat and vegetable stew, which Grandmother had prepared, and left it at the bakery to simmer gently for a time. When I collected it, the meat was deliciously tender and the vegetables soft and permeated by the meat juices. It would feed the whole family, usually on the Sabbath, and it amounted to a feast. We had never eaten a cake in my family that was not home-baked. Regina had been a dab hand at knocking up a cake in no time at all and it would be light, fluffy and delicious. She had found of late that she could again make and knead dough; her hands, her fingers were again supple enough. And it gave her great pleasure to exercise that homely skill. A cupful of flour, a knob of yeast, an egg, a blob of margarine, a little sugar, a cupful of water and she would fill the baking-tin with her fine dough. She would place an immaculate tea-towel over it and ask me to take it to the Ghetto bakery.

I took Regina's cake, one of the few she had made since her illness, to the bakery and removing the tea-towel I placed it on the counter. A woman in a white overall came over and tore two tickets, bearing the same number, off a pad. One she stuck to the cake, the other was to be produced when claiming it. I went back to our room and handed the numbered ticket to Regina to look after. She took it, but she continued to hold out her hand. 'Well . . .' she asked, 'where is the tea towel?' 'I . . . I don't know; I must have left it at the bakery . . . Shall I . . .?' 'You'd better go straight back. It's a good tea towel, as new, freshly washed and ironed.'

I went back immediately, but there was no sign of it at the bakery, nor in the streets along which I had walked. It had disappeared.

I was in the doghouse again. Regina was very cross with me. 'A fine tea towel like that, of course, someone would pick it up. For God's sake, can't you keep your mind on what you're doing?'

Although officially there were nine persons living in our room, unofficially there were, more often than not, twelve. This included Helcia, the cousin with the lovely singing voice, only she did not sing any more, and she had still not found anywhere permanent to live for herself, her husband and their two children. They were still being shunted, with their little ones, from pillar to post.

Helcia was a shy, gentle person, but independent and proud. She found it hard to ask for favours. But she had no choice. She had to swallow her pride for the children's sake. She would appear, after a few days' absence, and approach Regina. Using the tenderest diminutive of her name, she would quietly say: 'Resia, the children and I have nowhere to sleep, may we stay with you?' Regina, without a moment's hesitation, would reply, 'Indeed, you may! And if you want to do any washing or cooking, it's best to do it in the day-time, when most of them are out at work.'

Helcia's husband, the watchmaker, had a pallet somewhere, for he never joined his family in our room. He belonged to a work detail, but he also made a little money on the side buying, selling and repairing clocks and watches – that was how she was able to feed her children. I do not know how she managed it, but they looked well fed, clean and tidy, though very passive, very quiet. They were good-looking children. Halina, who was about seven, was big for her age, with thick ash-blonde hair and large brown eyes. She wore a red bow in her hair. Jack, who was about four, was a lovable little boy. Gentle, affectionate and as quiet as a mouse. He had his mummy's large green eyes and straight coppery hair, fine as silk, cut into a short fringe above his eyebrows. To this day, the tears fill my eyes when I remember Helcia and her children.

September was nearing its end; autumn was upon us again. I used to be sharply aware of the seasons before becoming a Ghetto-dweller. Within the Ghetto walls, nature did not exchange one set of splendid robes for another, as the seasons subtly merged into each other. There were no trees – those perennial reminders of the seasons' identities and inner lives. The Ghetto remained colourless and drab . . . Yet, the autumn of 1942 was one of the loveliest and warmest Poland could remember. A true Indian summer. We, too, benefited from the sun's golden rays, from its mellow warmth. It did not discriminate. It distributed its gracious gifts of light and warmth upon all Cracow in equal measure.

Regina was, nonetheless, aware that winter was not far off and that one should prepare for it in good time. She asked me to bring back from the 'Outside' her winter coat, the one I had deposited, on her behalf, for safekeeping with a pre-war neighbour of ours.

I had not seen Mrs Kopiec since leaving the coat in her custody back in July. Nor had I given the coat any thought. I was, originally, under the impression that Regina meant to leave it 'in storage' until after the war. But her condition having improved, she was considerably more active and able to perform various little tasks which, even a few months earlier, were quite outside her physical strength and agility. But she still had a long way to go before she could put on her coat and walk out of the building accompanied; even though she already saw herself strolling about unaccompanied . . .

The world had greatly changed since she first became ill – both the German-ruled Aryan world and the German-overseen Ghetto world. Regina and Grandmother had both lost touch with the world, as it was in 1942, on either side of the wall. Grandmother, even though she said very little, was, I think, the more realistic of the two. Regina still entertained certain illusions, although there was direct, solid and convincing evidence that they were no more than a will-o'-the-wisp. She believed the family would again sit round the kitchen table at Wielopole, as it did before the summer of 1939, as if nothing much had happened in between and that she would wait on them, fully recovered, sprightly and energetic, as she once did . . .

I slipped out through the Square of Peace pedestrian gate, almost on my doorstep, and crossed the Third Bridge towards central

Cracow. There was no point in catching a tram – Mrs Kopiec lived within easy reach of the Ghetto. In any case, in those days, I was not easily daunted by distance. My feet, it seemed, were the surest, the most reliable means of transport. I did not give my mission much thought – my mind was not so much dwelling on fetching the coat, as on the possibility of being offered a slice of bread and butter and a glass of milk by Mrs Kopiec.

I found Mrs Kopiec at home and she invited me to come in. Having exchanged the usual pleasantries, she looked at me as if to say: 'What brings you here?'. 'I wonder', I said, 'could I have my Aunt's winter coat back, please. She feels she may need it soon.' Mrs Kopiec opened her eyes wide. 'Your Aunt's coat? What coat?' 'My Aunt's winter coat.' 'Your Aunt's winter coat?' 'Yes, the navy-blue one.' 'The navy-blue one?' 'Yes, the one I left with you last July.' Mrs Kopiec gave me a close, searching look. 'You left no coat with me, my child.' 'I . . . did . . . last July . . .' 'You left no coat with me, my child. You must be mistaken. Of course, you may have left one with someone else, but not with me . . .'

I knew I was in no position to insist, but I tried, cautiously, one more time.

'I am sure . . .' 'No wonder your brain has become addled, hearing what they do to you, poor people . . .' Pleasantly, we bade each other 'goodbye.'

I really was in a cleft stick now – how to face Regina? How to explain to her? I sauntered back. I was in no hurry to face the music. I knew that nothing I could say would lessen Regina's anger, her sense of loss. My aunt took it very hard indeed. She, a person of true integrity, could not conceive, could not comprehend how anyone could appropriate what was not rightfully theirs. I was the instrument through which she had been dealt a shattering blow. And I was deeply sorry.

I asked Anna to explain to Regina how it was 'Outside' nowadays, how powerless one was, how entirely at the mercy of others . . . how delicately one had to tread . . . But she was not able to understand how greatly times had changed and that those changes brought out the best in some people and the worst in others . . .

19 • *The Grandfather Clock*

On 28 October 1942, the Cracow Ghetto, cordoned off by the SS, was undergoing its second re-settlement action – it was brief, lasting not even twenty-four hours, but inordinately brutal. In Józefinska Street, outside the Ghetto Public Baths, a dark seething mass of people – composed of different Labour Contingents – was being subjected to a selection process by the SS. Some would be marched out to work and live, if only for a short time – others would be pushed into the day's transport to 'The East . . .'

From my vantage point inside the Public Baths – where my Grandmother worked and where, in all innocence, she had reported for duty early that morning bringing me with her – glancing across this dense crowd of men and women, I spotted a black-clad figure – my Aunt Josephine, a woman in her forties who had never worked outside the home. She was first and foremost a wife and a mother. She was, also, an exceptionally capable and accomplished house-wife. Her husband, her family, her home had once been her life; she had never been trained to do anything else. She was now working long hours of strenuous toil in a factory, giving her all to the Third Reich war effort in the hope of surviving it.

Aunt Josephine had been a comely woman in her day with her shapely, compact figure and pleasant, open face. I looked at her now, as she stood there, in the very first row of a group of women, and it struck me how much she had changed. Her hair, once very dark, fashionably bobbed and elegantly waved, had turned white, and she wore it scraped back in a straggly little bun. Her face was mottled with dark, beetrooty patches, as if she were running a high temperature; she kept her lips pressed together hard, almost sucked in, no doubt, to choke back the scream rising in her throat. But it was the eyes, above all else, that bore testimony to the changes in her life. They had been large, sparkling green eyes. Their sparkle had long been extinguished; they were sunken deep into their sockets and hooded by yellow, withered eye-lids – they had become mere slits.

She stood there, in her tightly buttoned winter coat consumed by anxiety.

I had some idea of what was going through her mind; what had brought the unhealthy flush to her cheeks, the tautness to her mien. Aunt Josephine, who had been married to my mother's eldest brother, was a widow and the mother of three children.

Scraps of conversations, not meant for my ears, which I had carefully pieced together, came to me now as I looked at my aunt who, today, in October 1942, bore very little resemblance to the woman she had once been. The last three years had taken an enormous toll of her, as would the next two, but all in vain . . . But I was not to know this, as she stood there, in the bright October sunshine, her heart thumping. Although physically my aunt was with her Labour group, I knew that her heart, her mind, her entire being were with her three children. Her two teenage children – a girl and a boy – were, like herself, part of labour groups and she believed them, quite erroneously as it turned out, to be as safe as it was possible to be in those dark, fearful days. Her thoughts and her prayers were wholly concentrated on her youngest son, Stefan, the apple of her eye. Stefan was only eleven years old, an intelligent, handsome boy. He had taken after his father; he was very Semitic in appearance with his smouldering dark eyes, jet-black hair and long aquiline nose.

When I approached my aunt, that October morning, to ask her where Stefan was, if she had hidden him well, I received no reply – just a pale glimmer of her tired eyes. I asked her if she wanted me to go to her flat to stay with Stefan. I assumed, rightly, that he was on his own. Her lips barely parted in response to the second question, but she delivered the one word, one syllable answer – 'No' with such positive vehemence, such forbidding insistence, that I skipped off nonchalantly pretending indifference, whereas in reality I was quite hurt, for I felt I did not merit the blame for what had happened; that I had not mishandled the mission with which she had entrusted me some days earlier . . .

A few days before the October re-settlement action, rumours began circulating in the Ghetto – rumours to which I was not privy – I was only a child, that there was trouble just round the corner, that an action was imminent. Aunt Josephine must have obtained this intelligence from a very reliable source, for she lost no time in acting upon it. Her instant reaction was to protect Stefan, the most vulnerable of her children, to get him out of the Ghetto and place him with an Aryan family, cost what may, until 'the storm blew over'. She had no friends or acquaintances outside the Ghetto, having always lived and moved among her own people, the Jewish community, and she was at her wits' end with fear and anxiety to find a solution. Improbable as it may sound, she appealed to me, a twelve year old child, for help. She knew that I moved quite freely between the Ghetto and the outside world; that I had 'business' contacts on the other side; that I kept in touch with my parents' Aryan acquaintances and pre-war neighbours. She asked me to find a family willing to shelter Stefan for a few days. She said I could stay with him. She would pay for both of us. 'Anything – Just to have him out of harm's way . . .' she said. She wanted to pay in kind. She said: 'You know I have no money, nothing of any value left. It's all gone, one way or another, gone . . . But my sister has some lovely things; she says I can have anything I want. For pity's sake find someone to take hin in, just for a few days till it blows over . . .'

The commission I was being charged with was not an easy one. The penalty for harbouring a Jew was death – and it was no empty threat; it was stark reality. People – kind, generous, feeling people – were afraid to take the risk; to jeopardise their life and above all, the lives of their family. To place a male child, especially one with such unmistakably Semitic features, was pretty nigh impossible. But I managed to find a family who showed some interest in my proposition. They had lived next door to us before the war and had since moved to a quiet, sparsely populated suburb not far, as it happened, from the Ghetto. They were a middle-aged couple with a teenage daughter. They allowed greed to override their common sense. It was simply and purely a business transaction. No noble, no humane motives attached to it.

I, the middle-man, trotted back and forth between the Ghetto and Mr and Mrs Drega's suburban abode, conducting very difficult and delicate negotiations with, I think, reasonable skill. Although I had to play down the danger element and highlight the profit 'margin', I was fully conscious of the enormous risk they were taking and knew that nothing we could offer them was adequate compensation for it. I had to reel off, time and again, the list of 'goodies' which my aunt could offer in exchange for this priceless service. It was altogether a very tall order indeed, for I had to spread out, as temptingly as possible, and to their best advantage, invisible and intangible wares. My aunt made the transaction a little smoother, a little easier for me to carry out by a far-sighted gesture on her part right at the outset of the negotiations. She sent a gift – a gold trinket. It oiled the wheels; it made the running smoother . . .

Mr and Mrs Drega very pleased with the gift, omitted to ask what my cousin looked like assuming, perhaps, that like me he had a 'cast iron' Aryan appearance – and I, bent on a happy conclusion to the 'deal' did not take it upon myself to disabuse them. I realised that had they known the truth, these preliminary negotiations would break down irremediably.

For several days I carried the Dregas' instructions for extreme prudence and caution, and my aunt's pleas, offers and assurances back and forth. In the end, they agreed to take us in for three or four days, no more, in exchange for a particularly fine nineteenth century German grandfather clock. I had the full run-down on the clock, including its antecedents, off by heart. My aunt, in whose family it had always been, had primed me well. I described the clock to the Dregas in the minutest detail dwelling on what I found most pleasing about it, its very pretty face, depicting a pastoral scene, hand-painted in soft pastel shades and its grave, sonorous chimes. I must have described it quite graphically and convincingly, for in the end they set their hearts on the grandfather clock. My aunt promptly and eagerly agreed to hand it over. But it was a heavy, cumbersome object – it would require two adults to transport it from the Ghetto to the Dregas' home. We now proceeded to work out the finer details of the transaction. It was finally agreed that Stefan and I should arrive at the Dregas' on the evening of 25 October.

We set out from the Ghetto, having slipped the Polish policeman on duty at the gate, that late afternoon, a banknote and under the cover of darkness walked all the way. We could have caught the tram, but I felt – and my aunt had left 'the travelling arrangements' up to me, telling me to use my common sense, my judgment – that attention was more likely to focus on us in a lit-up public transport conveyance than in the blacked-out, deserted suburban streets. We walked briskly and purposefully saying hardly a word, but holding hands for cheer and companionship. We were both frightened.

The Dregas must have been watching out for us, for we had no sooner reached their front door in the quiet, sleepy street, than it soundlessly opened and we were admitted into their tiny entrance hall. Mr Drega, a small, weasel-like man, was doing the honours. Stefan politely doffed his cap in the brightly lit hall and Mr Drega seeing him thus bareheaded uttered, albeit involuntarily, a groan of

1. Eva Weinreb (my Mother) as a young girl.

2. (*left to right*): My Aunt Regina, Cousin Rosie and my Mother in the Cracow national costumes.

3. (*left to right*): My Aunt Sally, Aunt Anna and Erna Zelinger (a friend).

4. Mme Henia Wiktor, Aunt Anna and Aunt Sally (Mme Wiktor, a Christian, sheltered Aunt Anna and her husband David, at tremendous risk to herself, in late Summer 1942).

5. My Aunt Sally, 1941.

6. My Grandmother, Helena
Weinreb, 1941.

7. My Parents – Henryk and Eva Fischler– on the occasion of their wedding, 12 March 1922.

8. My Brother Joseph, aged 17 years.

9. Me, Janina, aged 14 years.

10. The flat where my paternal Grandmother Heim lived, 15 Sebastian Road, Cracow.

11. The window by which my Aunt Regina, Aunt Anna and I sat on 27 October 1942, hours before the October *Aktion* on 28 October. Aunt Regina died next to that window. Flowers were placed by me in 1996.

12. A fragment of the Cracow Ghetto wall, 1941–1943. Flower placed by me.

13. Manhole through which Joseph and I escaped on 13 March 1943, at the final liquidation of the Cracow Ghetto. I conducted a group of Israeli students around the Ghetto area.

14. The window to our basement room at 42 Limanowskiego Street, Cracow Ghetto, 1941–1942. Flower placed by me in 1995.

15. Entrance and window to our basement room in the Cracow Ghetto.

16. 42 Limanowskiego Street, Cracow Ghetto. It was from the far right window on the second floor that we saw our Parents and 8-year-old Brother being led away.

17. Me in the doorway of 38 Dluga Street, Cracow, where Joseph and I were re-united in August 1945.

deep horror. There was no mistaking Stefan's identity, and Mr Drega fully realised it. He also realised, there and then, that he had placed himself and his family in very great danger indeed. Mrs Drega, in response to her husband's anguished cry, emerged from the kitchen and at the sight of Stefan her florid face turned chalk-white.

None of this was lost on Stefan. He was a sensitive, observant boy. Also, it was the first time he had ever been separated from his mother. A dark-red stain gradually suffused his entire face; his eyes glistened with tears. But he controlled himself. Rather tremulously, he said 'Good evening' – like the well-brought up boy that he was.

Somehow that diffident, but courteous, greeting broke the ice. The Dregas', who were not unkind people, felt sorry for us. Mrs Drega took us in tow and led us to a room where a bed, with clean, fresh linen, had been made up for us. She told us to remove our coats and we took it as a sign that she was letting us stay. After a while she brought us a mug of hot milk each. We sat on edge of the bed and sipped it slowly, savouring its rich warmth. I took the empty mugs back to the kitchen, but she would not allow me to rinse them. I understood that apart from 'our' room, the flat was out of bounds to us. She said. 'You must be tired, try and get a good night's sleep . . .' We both felt downcast and alone – cut off from the family, from the Ghetto . . .

We lay down and after a minute or two I knew that Stefan was sobbing, and desperately trying to stifle the sound in the pillow. I had had a younger brother. I had loved him dearly. I had looked after him. We had slept in the same bed. I had lost him and my parents, only five months earlier . . . I put my arms around Stefan and tried to soothe him, to comfort him, saying, 'Don't cry, Stefek, don't cry. It will be allright, you will see, it will be allright . . .' Soon we drifted off to sleep.

The next day, 26 October, we spent sitting on the edge of the bed and not going anywhere near the curtained window. Mrs Drega made us promise we wouldn't, although she did not need to. We knew perfectly well we had to 'lie low'. She brought us our food, and it was tasty and the helpings were generous. Stefan only picked at it, but I ate with my usual unimpaired appetite. I could not feel guilty about eating; I never knew when or where my next meal was coming from, and so I would eat my fill, and more, whenever the opportunity presented itself.

The hours dragged on. It seemed a very long day. We were bored

151

and tense. Stefan was sorely missing his mother, although he did not say so. Some time after lunch, he picked up the bag in which she had put a few things for him and after rummaging in it for a while, he brought out what he had been looking for – a set of the smoothest, roundest, most beautifully polished marbles. He tossed them onto the bed and seeing my delight, smiled shyly. 'Let's have a game . . .' I was only too happy to oblige; it was a game I loved. Both my brothers, big and little, had been keen players and I had had plenty of practice. We got quite absorbed in it and the sense of oppression, which had gripped us earlier, lifted.

Now the agreement between Aunt Josephine and the Dregas' was that they would be waiting at a pre-arranged meeting spot and time on the evening of the 26th on the Aryan side of the barbed-wire, whilst Aunt Josephine would be there, on the Jewish side, ready to push the clock, wrapped in sacking, through the gap between the lowest strand of wire and the pavement. The Dregas were then going to carry the clock to the nearest tram stop, haul it onto the tram and bring it home. As soon as dusk fell, Mrs Drega came to tell us that she and her husband were setting out on their errand.

When the Dregas arrived at the appointed spot, Aunt Josephine was waiting for them, but minus the clock. Almost distraught with anxiety at not being able to keep her side of the bargain, she tried to explain, through the barbed-wire tracery, to the very disappointed and angry couple that her sister had changed her mind at the last moment, that she felt the clock was the one object she could not bear to part with.

The husband and wife returned home empty-handed and very angry indeed. They told Stefan and me to leave there and then. It was dark; it was late; it would soon be curfew time. Dismayed and very frightened we found our way back to the Ghetto – home . . . I made straight for the spot where I knew the barbed-wire was cut. Gingerly, I parted the strands and let Stefan, who was totally inexperienced in these operations, whereas I was a dab hand at them, slip through first. I followed. Once on the Jewish side, I neatly pulled the wires to. There was not a flicker of life or light anywhere. Fear was stalking the silent, dark streets. The Ghetto was waiting for a cataclysm. I saw Stefan into the block of flats in which Aunt Josephine lived and then made straight for our room in the Square of Peace.

Within twenty-four hours of our return, the Ghetto was surrounded and sealed off by the SS. A re-settlement action, in which children like Stefan and I stood more than a fair chance of losing their lives, was in progress. Aunt Josephine managed, with the aid of her family, to wedge a bedroom wardrobe into a niche in the wall. Stefan spent the day of the 28th flattened out behind it. When his mother returned from work in the evening, Stefan emerged from behind the wardrobe safe and sound. But like so many Ghetto mothers, she paid a heavy price that day. She lost her eldest child – her sixteen-year old daughter and her beloved sister whose clock continued to tick and chime long after its owner had perished.

Neither my aunt nor I knew, that October morning, that the death factories of Europe would claim both her and her youngest son, Stefan who, like his father, perished in Auschwitz aged thirteen years as late as May 1944. Aunt Josephine – of whom the last three years had taken an enormous toll, as would the next two, but all in vain – would not survive the war.

In the winter of 1944, she was an inmate of a women's concentration camp in Germany. With the Allied Armies advancing, the camp guards gathered up the handful of starved, sick women and took them on what was becoming a regular occurrence – a death march. With the Russian Army in hot pursuit on their heels, they drove these emaciated, ragged spectres for mile after mile across the frozen German plain. Aunt Josephine did not survive the death march. But she was not to know this, as she stood there in the bright October sunshine shivering with fear for her youngest son's safety.

20 • The 28th of October 1942 Aktion

Although sadly depleted by the series of misfortunes which had befallen the Jewish people since the invasion of Poland, on 27 October 1942, we were still very much a family; a family which consisted of my maternal grandmother, my elder brother, Joseph, my aunts – Regina and Anna – the latter's husband, David, and myself, a girl of twelve. We all lived together in a room which we shared with two other families at No. 4 the Square of Peace, except Anna and David.

The 27th started like any other Ghetto day. Joseph and David went to work, outside the Ghetto, with their separate labour contingents. Grandmother, who was in her seventies, but strong, healthy and active, spent the day working at the Ghetto Public Baths. She divided her time between the Baths and her employer's household. At the Baths, she helped with the scouring and cleaning of tubs and cubicles, dispensed small cakes of gritty soap and fresh, threadbare towels, and saw to it, generally, that everything was kept spick and span. At the house – her employer had four children – she cooked, washed, ironed and mended. She had a nice motherly touch about her and was well liked by both her employer and the Baths' clientéle.

The 27th was a fine, sunny day; Regina, Anna and I, after a very frugal midday meal of soup and bread, were sitting by the wide open window enjoying the autumnal sun. It gave onto a squalid, cluttered backyard which had become an open-air furniture storehouse. Regina, who knew a good thing when she saw one, surveying it, would always sigh and say: 'Such lovely things going to rack and ruin.' Summer and winter, in all weathers, bleached by the sun, washed by the rain, the tenants' furniture stood out in the yard, for there was no room for it in our very cramped accommodation.

Stunted, but daring blades of yellowy grass sprouted around table and chair legs. A clump of robust stinging-nettles had pushed up next to a bedside table. The communal water tap dripped onto a slimy stone-grating. It was warm and peaceful.

We said little. None of us would broach the subject which was closest to our hearts – that no sign of life had been received from a single one of the thousands of Ghetto inhabitants 're-settled' nearly five months earlier in June, for fear of adding to the anguish and uncertainty with which we lived. I would look at my aunts searching, surreptitiously – for I would not own up how much I missed Mamma – for some feature or outline, the roundness of the cheek, the setting of the eyes, the curve of the lips – that reminded me of her . . .

Regina, having suffered her stroke two years earlier, was now on the mend under her mother's tender and scrupulous care. Although still an invalid, she could get about the room, wash and dress herself and plait her long, dark hair.

Anna, on the other hand, was in the prime of womanhood. Nature had been very generous to her; she was good-looking, intelligent and vivacious. By temperament she was optimistic and high-spirited. She was, also, something of a rebel and a non-conformist. She was desperately keen to be assigned to a labour contingent, since we all believed in the efficacy of work and its power to save us from extinction, and knocked daily on the door of the Ghetto Labour Exchange ready to accept any job, however menial.

Grandmother's earnings, our only income, were not nearly enough to keep us all, body and soul together. Every week we parted with an article or two of clothing or household linen, or a family 'heirloom' in the shape of a china or crystal ornament, to supplement our meagre income.

Anna touched upon the subject of this week's sale, suggesting a brand new tablecloth – one of her wedding presents; she had only been married three years. It was a beautiful tablecloth. Made of the strongest, yet gossamer fine, white lawn, it had a border of appliqué, shaggy-headed sun flowers in varying sizes and stages of blossoming; their long, leafy stems twining round each other to form an unbroken chain. It seemed, to me, splendid enough to grace a royal table. Since I carried out all the family business transactions, we discussed the asking and the selling price. I was then immediately to convert the money into items of modest daily fare and we made out a list of the provisions I was to bring back.

The afternoon was drawing to a close. Anna stood up and gave Regina and me a light peck on the cheek saying she would come round in the morning and bring the tablecloth. She exuded cheerfulness and hope. She seemed to be saying; 'Tomorrow is another day . . .' She put her hand on the door-knob, but instead of going out she turned round and smiled at us. Standing in the doorway, her arm outstretched, her fingers curved round the knob, she looked very graceful and feminine in her well cut navy-skirt and gaily striped blouse, her whole face lit up by her charming smile. Although it is now half a century since I last saw her, I only have to close my eyes and there she stands, except that another picture superimposes itself upon the one I wish to remember . . .

By the time Joseph, Grandmother and the other inhabitants of the room came home from work, it was being whispered that something was afoot, that something was in the air . . . There was a general disquiet and a kind of throbbing nervousness, but not panic, not yet . . . Invisibly and inaudibly, on paws of velvet, fear was beginning to steal upon us and, with insidious cunning, bury its deadly claws in our flesh. And it festered, and it spread, and it swelled up like a fully-ripened tumour about to burst and spill its poisonous contents. But the cat-and-mouse game had not even begun . . .

It had been a very fine summer in Poland – the summer of 1942. We were now, at the end of October, enjoying a spell of unusually warm and sunny weather; a touch of magic – an Indian summer. The sky above the Ghetto was clear and perfectly blue; not a flaw, not a blemish stained its serene purity. The Square of Peace, on our very doorstep, dappled with the molten gold of the setting sun, was the only large, open space in the Ghetto. In the event of a 're-settlement' action it would serve as an assembly point and a marshalling yard. Right now, one could see knots of people, here and there, huddled closely together, their mouths working feverishly, their hands going up in gestures of hopeless supplication. With the deepening of twilight the volcano, which had started by gently simmering, reached boiling point and erupted. The Ghetto was surrounded; a 're-settlement' action was in progress. The SS-men took up their posts quietly and efficiently. They formed a pretty, green ring-a-ring o' roses round the Ghetto. They were tall and slender and ramrod straight, only their bellies bulged with tightly packed holsters which they would finger and fondle, now and then, lovingly.

The usual, simple 're-settlement' action procedure formula was adopted. The Chief of the Jewish Police, Spira, received an order from the SS-*Polizei* to have 4,000 people assembled in the square ready for deportation on the morning of 28 October. The task of compiling the list of the future deportees, with directives from the SS, fell to Spira and his subordinates. But the Chief and his trusties had failed miserably in their assignment. They had carried out the duties allotted to them with the utmost laxity and incompetence – in some cases because they were moved by pity and acceded to the pleading and entreaty of their brothers; in some, because they were unable to resist the bribes offered.

We thought we had learnt our lesson in June. We thought we knew the pattern now. The aged, the infirm, the unemployed and the orphans would form the target.

Nobody in our room went to bed that night. We sat up, fully dressed, waiting for the sound of footsteps in the entrance passage. They would be plainly heard on the concrete floor. We, as a family, had much to fear, for we represented every one of the vulnerable categories. Grandmother was old; Regina was an invalid; Anna was unemployed; I was . . .? I did not know. One of the men suggested that Grandmother should 'hide'. The idea found immediate support. We were all urging her to hide. She knew, as well as we all did, that there was only one place – the dark, communal, outside toilet. She was neither cowardly, nor heroic. She was an old woman who had lived her life and who wanted nothing for herself. She was very simple in her ways; very unworldly in her desires. Her allegiances, too, were simple. Her husband, whilst he was alive, her children, of whom she had borne nine, her home, her people. Being an old woman and a widow she thought about death. Before all this had happened, she hoped, I knew, to die in her bed, her family around her, and to lie, alongside her husband, in the Cracow Jewish Cemetery. What were her thoughts, out there, in the dark, alone?

I must have dozed off . . . I was wakened by the sound of firm, purposeful footsteps out in the passage. We all kept so still that the very life within us seemed suspended. We heard knocking; creaking of floor-boards; squeaking of doors; voices – but not agitated; perhaps it was the distance and the thick walls that muffled the sound of hysteria . . . After a time the footsteps walked away. The tenement was peaceful again. We fetched Grandmother. They had not even stopped by our door. We were not on the list! We continued the vigil till dawn. It came slowly. The sky was a symphony in grey. It changed from one shade of grey to another; after each

157

mutation, the hue becoming softer, paler. Someone said it would be a lovely day . . . We looked from one ashen mask to another. It was not quite daylight yet, but one could already distinguish the outlines of objects and creased, tired faces.

I was soon to realise that my brother had spent the night racking his brains for a means to ensure my safety. He believed he, himself, was well protected. He would join his labour contingent; they would be marched out of the Ghetto; they would do a day's work; they would come back in the evening. But who could tell what fate had in store for those left behind, in the sealed-off Ghetto?

We had a distant relative in the Jewish police. He, and his family, lived just round the corner from us. The Ghetto was so small and confined that everybody lived 'just round the corner' from everybody else. Joseph had made up his mind to take me to him to ask if I could stay with his family till he came back from work. They knew me well for my 'business acumen' and had often made use of my ability to slip in and out of the Ghetto to run errands for them.

We left the room and groped our way out of the house. Night was yielding to day. I cast a terrified glance at the square already under heavy SS-guard. It had become an assembly point in the night. Shrouded in loosely-woven grey mist, it was filled with phantom-like figures lying on the bare cobblestones, their heads resting on homely little bundles . . . It was all so quiet and motionless that it looked like a huge canvas depicting a macabre dream, conceived and executed by a visionary or a madman. In the Cracow Ghetto, the green-uniformed men did not work at night. They confined their activities to broad daylight. At night, they stood back and watched, sardonically, the Jewish police botch up what could have been a work of art.

It took us about five minutes to reach Blotek's door. We slid along the walls, in the penumbra that was no longer night and not yet day, like two soundless spectres holding hands. We knocked gently. Blotek himself opened the door. He was tall and burly and well-nourished. In his full, sleepy face the upper lip curled away from the teeth in a permanent snarl. Humbly, cap in hand, his voice tremulous, Joseph asked Blotek if his sister . . . In one brief, cold, unequivocal sentence Blotek refused and closed the door in our faces. In no time at all we were back in the room. The whole escapade had only taken about ten minutes. 'No, he would not,' said Joseph in reply to Grandmother's raised eyebrows.

The sky was now becoming suffused with a pale, pearly pink – as delicate and translucent as the inner lining of a sea shell.

Grandmother scooped up a jugful of water from the bucket and poured it into a small basin. She washed her face and hands. Her long, white hair had come undone in the night; very thick and fluffy it reached below her waist. With nimble, expert fingers she combed it all up, holding the back in position with her left hand, while twisting it, with her right, into a long, heavy rope. She then coiled the rope round and round on top of her head securing it in place with sturdy, black hairpins. The *coiffure* completed, it looked like an extravagantly iced Belgian bun with the blackcurrants peeping out at the sides.

It was broad daylight by now; it was going to be a beautiful day. The inhabitants of the room were leaving one by one. David, Anna's husband, dropped in, on his way to work, to say that he had hidden her well, just in case . . . Grandmother said to Joseph that he was not to worry; she would take me to the Baths with her; I could easily pass for an apprentice. Regina, it was decided, could safely be left in the room, since we were not on the list, but I was too restless, too inquisitive, too unpredictable.

The Baths, which was situated right at the other end of the Ghetto, but barely a five minute walk from our room, was opened on time. The cashier, a man punctilious in speech, dress and manner to the point of exasperation, was already at his post behind the glass pane. He smiled and greeted us most courteously. We went straight in and got down to cleaning the perfectly clean cubicles. Not a single customer came that day, nor did any of the other attendants turn up. Grandmother and the cashier held the fort between them.

The Baths was an old, rambling, one-storey building with a large inner courtyard. It occupied a rather strategic position. Its twin-leaved, heavy door – now wide open – faced, bang on, the Ghetto's main entrance and exit; main, because its gates, when open full width, admitted cars and lorries, as well as vast concourses of people. The Baths' door was only about a hundred yards away from this gate immediately behind which lay the land of our dreams, still somnolent and silent – the Aryan world. To the right of the Baths, on the opposite side of the road, stood a red brick building, one of the Ghetto's two hospitals.

Every so often I would leave Grandmother to get 'news'. We were all alone and had no idea what was taking place outside the Baths. I, for one, was being devoured by curiosity and quite enjoyed my 'news foraging expeditions'. I would creep as close as I dared, to the Baths' street door, stand on tiptoe, crane my neck and look out. There were the strangest goings on that I ever did see. A few feet away from the Baths, labour contingents were being counted or checked, I was not sure which, by a stern, impassive SS-man with a calm, impersonal voice. He was going through them with quiet efficiency, with the aid of a riding crop, directing one person to the right, one to the left. Right, left, right, left . . . I understood nothing of this segregation process. I believed, in any case, like everybody else, that the labour contingents were sacrosanct. Still, I reported, in detail, what I had seen to Grandmother. She was eager for news, but no wiser than I.

The sun was beating down on the Baths' roof and it was very close and humid inside the cubicles, but Grandmother did not think it prudent to open a window. Every so often I would say to her: 'They won't take us, will they, Grandmother, if they find us hard at work?' And she, bent over a tub which already shone like a mirror, would reply calmly and reassuringly that: 'They wouldn't.'

It was a torrid day. There was not a breath of air in the cubicle. I went out again. Every time I walked past the cashier's office, and I did many times that day, he nodded pleasantly and smiled. It was past noon. There was no sign of the labour contingents any more, but there was a different kind of activity taking place before my very eyes.

A big, tarpaulin-covered lorry stood parked, right outside the hospital entrance. The tailboard was down. The hospital staff, in white overalls, were bringing out patients on stretchers and depositing them, on the bare boards, in the lorry. In no time at all, they were piling them up, higgledy-piggledy, on top of each other. They were working speedily, in and out, in and out, whilst the men in green stood back, smoked and chatted easily, yet not a gesture, not a step escaped their well-trained, watchful eye. They would not let the pace flag and kept barking out orders which I could not hear distinctly and would not, in any case have understood. I could not see the patients' faces, nor the extent or nature of their incapacity, but I knew that they were very ill – they had to be carried . . . I realised that I was witnessing an act of infinite cruelty, of callous inhumanity and I was terribly frightened. I turned round to go back to Grandmother, wiping my face dry with my sleeve, so that she would not know I had been crying. I told her that the hospital patients were being deported, but, instinctively, withheld the details. She sighed deeply, 'Poor souls, fancy re-settling the sick . . .'

We continued to work and I kept posing the same question, just to hear her comforting reply. It was unbearably stifling and oppressive inside the cubicles, but Grandmother did not seem to feel the heat and the closeness. I used the need of 'a breath of fresh air' for yet another sortie. I was becoming bolder. I had crept right up to the end of the passage and was as good as standing in the middle of the street-doorway taking a good look outside. There was not a soul to be seen in whichever direction I looked. And then my gaze wandered right across to the Ghetto entrance and exit gate. It was heavily beleaguered by SS-officers lost in, what seemed to be, animated discussion . . . Suddenly, I could not move. I seemed rooted to the spot. My gaze had strayed beyond the gate and the barbed wire. There it was again, only a hundred yards away – almost in the palm of my hand – the other side; streets, houses, people, just like us, but not like us, not caged, not Jews . . . Illuminated by the dazzling sunlight, this very mundane scene assumed, for me, paradise-like proportions. I felt a wave of such indomitable, such passionate desire to live sweep over me that I closed my eyes and leaned against the door for support.

Soon, I became conscious of a sound like a giant's laboured breathing. A huge military lorry was rolling down the thoroughfare in front of the Baths. It had come from the direction of the Square of Peace and was making for the exit and the embarkation point – the cattle trucks at Plaszow railway station. It was an open lorry, crammed to overspilling with men and women, and it was going at a snail's pace. There was a green guard, a rifle slung over his shoulder, in each corner of the vehicle. As it took the bend, immediately opposite the Baths, I could see, perfectly clearly, the people pressed against the tailboard facing out. They must have been the chronically and the terminally ill from the Ghetto's second hospital, or else they would have been marched on foot to the Square to join the mass already gathered there. Their drawn, etiolated faces were contorted with fear.

A very tall man, swaying over the tailboard because of his height and the pressure from behind, caught my eye and his face, a cast in fear, has stayed with me. He was young – in his late teens? He was handsome, with nobly proportioned head and features. His eyes and hair were very dark. A dark stubble was beginning to stain his chin and cheeks. He looked delirious – a man whose illness had

161

reached its peak and must now either advance and cast its lot with the dead, or retreat and join the living. His skin was yellow – a mellow, fully-ripened yellow – of the same waxy, lifeless hue as an old, carefully preserved manuscript. His face was bathed in sweat which trickled onto his light, summer coat. It must have blinded him at times, so dense was it. His lips were open, as if he had difficulty in breathing, and so parched as to have cracked. There were thin, thread-like, black rivulets along the lower lip where the blood had dried up. The eyes which he fastened on me, for he, too, had caught sight of me, were large and lustrous and encircled by enormous violet shadows. The pupils, dilated by fear, shone brilliantly. But it was the mute appeal for pity in those eyes, the cry for help choked back in his throat that bored into my very soul. I knew he wanted to live as fiercely as I did, and I stared after him mesmerised ... When the lorry disappeared from view I felt a very old, a very tired woman of twelve.

I was beginning to have more and more inkling of what was taking place in the Ghetto ...

We were well into the afternoon. I was going back to Grand-mother, when the cashier coughed discreetly to attract my attention and beckoned delicately for me to come over. I put my face against the aperture in the glass pane. He said: 'Cracow is being made *"Judenrein"*.' I had never heard the expression before, but I knew, instantly, what it meant. He added: 'Since we are all being resettled, I feel justified to leave my post and join my family, so that we can all go together. Nobody will hold it against me, surely, or consider me irresponsible. Not under these exceptional circumstances ... Yes, I must be on my way! My kindest regards to your grandmother.' He bowed politely. Just as I was saying: 'Thank you, goodbye,' a young woman stopped outside the Baths' door – putting down a large suit-case – for a rest. She caught sight of me and called out: 'Did you know that Cracow is being made "Judenrein"?' I went up to her and said, 'Yes, I know.' 'I am going to The Square to join the transport' she said. 'May as well, instead of waiting for them to come and get me. Weighs a ton' – indicating the suitcase – 'but you should see the contents!' She was wearing a heavy, maroon winter coat of superb quality and cut. Even at twelve I could appreciate a good bit of cloth when I saw one, and I could only just restrain myself from taking hold of the lapel between my finger and thumb. She was quick to realise my appreciation and stroking the coat said: 'Isn't it beautiful? And look how it fits me – could have been made to measure and there it was hanging in a wardrobe, and I just slipped it on! And look at the lining! Silk . . .' she said softly. 'Yes' I replied, 'a top quality garment if ever I saw one, and it suits you.' She was pleased and hastened to add: 'I shall be in clover for a long time to come. There are whole houses abandoned there,' pointing in the direction from which she had come – 'You can pick and choose to your heart's content. Yes, I have really rigged myself out this time, I have. I shall look a lady. I have always wanted to look a lady! Why don't you do the same, I mean, help yourself, there is plenty there!' She was a tall, strapping girl, but even so the suitcase was much too heavy for her. I pointed out that she would have to carry it from the square all the way to the embarkation point at Plaszow, which was a goodish distance. 'I'll cope . . .' she replied, picking up the suitcase and tottering towards the square.

Now, I was a very practical little girl, and so I found myself in a dilemma. I knew only too well, the value of good clothing, nice bedding, leather goods, maybe even jewellery. I knew that one could eat and live for a long time off the proceeds of such merchandise. The temptation was so strong to follow in the girl's footsteps and 'kit myself out' that I stood there for a while racked by indecision, weighing up the pros and cons . . . No, I decided, I would not leave the Baths – it seemed a safe place.

I went back to Grandmother and told her about Cracow being made 'Judenrein'. But whereas I had immediately seized the full import of the word, she looked to me, her trusting old eyes on my face, for an explanation. I explained – I tried to do it softly and mildly, only I could not find the words – that the Ghetto was being liquidated. The blood drained from her face, but she did not lose her composure. Slowly she took off her apron and hung it on a peg. Automatically, in a gesture so natural to a woman, her hands went up to her hair and she quickly checked, with the tips of her fingers, whether the hairpins were firmly in place. She then smoothed out the folds of her skirt, with hands made pink and puffy through being constantly in water, and pulled down her cardigan. Her blue eyes, caught in a net of fine criss-cross wrinkles, were full of tears. She said she must go to Regina. She wanted to be taken with Regina. They would join the transport together. The tears were now rolling freely down her cheeks, as they were rolling down mine. I said that I would not join the transport, not of my own free-will. She did not say one word to make me change my mind. She held me close to her and kissed my hair and cheeks. I took hold of her hands and pressed my lips to them. She was my mother's mother, and as far back as I could remember into my childhood she had always been there – simple and honourable, hard-working and kind. She took a beauti-fully laundered handkerchief from her skirt pocket, shook it out and gently dried my tears, then her own. She folded it up again and gave it to me to keep. We knew, I think, that we would never see each other again.

After Grandmother had gone I felt very frightened and lonely. The Baths was so quiet that every little sound was magnified a hun-dredfold. An insect or a worm of some kind was working away most assiduously in the skirting of the cubicle. It was gnawing at the wood with a scraping, rasping sound rather like a giftless child doing his violin practice. I sat on the chair, my feet on the rung, hugging my knees with my arms and resting my chin on them. I wanted to shrink, to become invisible; yet, I remained alert to the sounds of the jungle in which I lived, my ears cocked, I listened. I listened for the thud of footsteps and for the sound of the imperious voices of the men in green. I could not bring myself to pretend to work any more. I turned, as if under a spell, into what I really was – a child of twelve numb with fear. I was half sorry I had not gone with Grandmother and yet, deep down in my heart, I knew that I would not surrender my most treasured possession – my life – just like that. Only if they come and get me. Then I shall go quietly and meekly, but not before. I did not pray. I knew it was useless. I knew that God had turned his face away from us. I heard so many people, clever people, say just that. I found the phrase evocative, grown-up. I liked the images it conjured up. It came to me now. There was nobody to turn to. I felt forsaken. Bereft. Only Mamma would understand my wretchedness, my loneliness, my heartache . . . But I also knew, I think, that I would never see Mamma again . . . And the incident which implanted the first seed of doubt came back to me yet again, as it had done so many times already and I turned it over in my mind. It had revealed something to me – I could not exactly phrase what – something that made me weak with grief.

Before the June 're-settlement' I had belonged to a children's library in the Ghetto. It was run by a middle-aged couple with two teenage daughters. They had moved at the end of June, when the Ghetto was diminished in size after the 're-settlement' action. It took a lot of doing, but I tracked them down. They had given up running the library, but they were genuinely glad to see me, just the same, greeting me like a long-lost friend. They were a delightful family, just to see them, to talk to them left a sweet taste in one's mouth, like dipping one's finger in a pot of honey to slowly lick it clean. The girls' mother was a gentle, softly-spoken woman. She said I could still borrow books from them. I was the girls' friend, wasn't I? I was so pleased to hear her say that because her daughters were so pretty, so fine. She invited me to choose a book. I did. I chose a travel book. She said it was a good choice. I would enjoy it – it was to be enjoyed by anyone, at any age. She added, 'Your mother will enjoy it, too.' Suddenly all the joy had gone out of the meeting. I was cut to the quick by this innocent, kindly-meant remark. I was unable to hide my pain. I stammered out, 'My mother? My parents and little brother were re-settled in June . . .'

The expression on her face changed. The most profound pity, infinite compassion were so plainly written upon it, that I could not fail but read them. I was aghast. I did not like being the recipient of such overt, naked sympathy. Why was I eliciting it? I felt chilled to the very marrow of my bone. I was choking with grief. It was all I could do to keep back my tears . . . People knew something that I did not . . . Grown-ups knew things which were not meant for children's ears . . . But the seed had been planted once and for all. In no time at all it started to germinate. The incident had sharpened my senses. I paid more heed to people's reactions – I became more aware . . . With time, the central inference of the pity my condition provoked began to emerge in my mind – I would never see my parents and little brother again . . . The incident came back to me now, as I sat in the cubicle, cornered, like a little animal wild with fear.

I do not know how long I stayed in the cubicle – I did not have a watch – but it seemed a long time and I could stand the suspense no longer. I crept out, on tiptoe, into the courtyard. There was a narrow, wooden staircase right in the middle of it, it led to the boiler-room. There, at the bottom of the stairs stood Fenia Kalfus, holding her little daughter, Irene, by the hand. Mother and daughter had spent the day hiding in the boiler-room and were now talking to a young Jewish policeman, the husband's friend, who had come to give them 'the all clear'. I cried out, 'Fenia, Fenia,' and rushed towards her. She gathered me to her and spoke to me soothingly, kindly – 'There, there,' she kept saying, 'it's all over, it's all over . . . We can go home now.' 'How?' I asked. 'Don't you know that Cracow has been declared "Judenrein"?' The policeman interposed. 'That was only a ruse, a rumour spread to inveigle as many people as possible to join the transport of their own accord.' My grandmother . . . He kept

165

talking loudly, quickly, incoherently as if he desperately needed to unburden his heart and ease his mind. He kept producing a grubby, sweat-soaked handkerchief and moping his brow, his face, his neck, his balding head and putting it away, only to take it out again.

And as he gabbled on, like one possessed, the very ground seemed to be giving way beneath our feet to a chasm of endless, boundless pain waiting to receive us. He went on to describe the indescribable. 'Yes,' he said, 'they have gleaned a rich harvest today. Mostly women and children, and the old, and the sick. The labour contingents will be coming home soon.' A sort of dry, tearless sob, that was not at all a human sound, escaped him. 'They will find their wives and children, their mothers and fathers, their sisters . . . gone . . . It was like a lottery! They went through some streets with a fine toothcomb and left not a soul behind. They combed the houses from top to bottom and ferreted them out, however well they believed themselves hidden. They winkled them out from lofts and cellars, from under beds, from inside wardrobes, from the most naive to the most unlikely nooks and crannies. Yes – from behind the most ingenious false walls and trap doors . . . One has got to hand it to them! They have the know-how!' A spine-chilling laugh. 'And the children made not a sound, only clutched tighter onto their mothers' skirts . . . Some streets they did not touch at all. As I said, the luck of the draw . . . The square was packed jam-tight! Solid!' I remembered the thin scattering first thing this morning. 'And the unassailable, the inviolate labour contingents were split in half.' I now understood the selection procedure outside the Baths – my brother – I was gripped by such cold terror that everything I had ever felt before paled into insignificance. 'Yes, one half was made to join the transport, the other half was marched out to work. In some cases they did not even trouble to carry out a selection. Whole contingents – our pride, the pick of our youth were marched to the square. The boys – young, strong, vigorous; the girls – tender, graceful, on the threshold of womanhood . . .' Again, the choking, gurgling sob, the filthy handkerchief . . .

I asked him in a voice that was not mine – mine was clear and firm; this one shook and stuttered – if he could tell me whether contingent *Standartenverwattung* had got through because my brother was in it. The man was coarse, and dissipation had already wrought its sad imprint upon his bloated, but still young, face, but he was not unfeeling. There was nothing but kindness in his red-rimmed eyes as he looked down at me. As far as he knew, he said, they had got through. He put his clammy hand on my shoulder and held me close to his side, adjusting his step to mine. But I was a true child of the Ghetto – the wool was not to be pulled over my eyes that easily . . . I knew all the rules of the game of 'Hope' – I was a consummate player myself. I knew the penalty – the lacerating pain which awaited those who practised self-deception . . .

We had reached the house, No. 4 the Square of Peace, and Fenia was about to thank him for accompanying us, when he produced a small, flat flask from his hip pocket, unscrewed the top, and tilting his head well back, took a long swig from it. 'It's kept me going, it has, these last twenty-four hours. Mind you, I have had to refill it a few times . . .' He winked broadly. 'Yes, I am going home, going to get stock – drunk, plastered, sozzled – going to forget it all . . .' He made a vague gesture of raising his fingers to the peak of his cap and sauntered off, muttering under his breath, perfectly steady on his feet.

Fenia, Irene and I walked silently along the long, cool passage to our door. Fenia turned the door-knob. Nobody used keys any more. We went in. The room was empty, shadowy and silent like a freshly dug grave. No sign of Grandmother, no sign of Regina. At the sound of our voices the door of the solid mahogany wardrobe was being slowly pushed open from within by a weak and cautious hand. Clumsily, Regina clambered out. She had spent the day hiding inside the wardrobe. Nobody had come. We could all have stayed in the room and no harm would have come to us. Anyway, not this time. 'Where is Grandmother?' I blurted out. She looked at me with the wide uncomprehending stare of an ill-used child. We stood there, in the middle of the room, two women and two children clinging to each other as if we were the last inhabitants on earth. Fenia put her arm round Regina's shoulders and was supporting her physically, for she was already crumpling up, when the door suddenly opened quickly and energetically. An SS-officer appeared in the doorway. We froze. A man in his thirties, tanned, clear-eyed, immaculately groomed, except for his knee-high boots which were grey with dust. He stood there, in the doorway, and looked his fill. Nothing escaped his grave, intelligent gaze as it travelled round the room. Finally, it came back to rest on the four of us; it expressed extreme weariness and sadness. He turned round and, not having uttered a word, gently closed the door and walked away.

Grandmother did not see her daughter again. She was swept on the tide of zeal and ardour with which the men in green performed their duties. She was stopped on her way. There were sedulous guards posted on every street corner waiting to gather up 'stray' victims such as she. When they had collected a handful, they would escort their trophies to the square. Almost within seconds of leaving me, she was caught in the dragnet. I was the last person to see her alive.

Regina was crying soundlessly. Fenia, whilst helping her to sit down, was speaking to her softly, comfortingly, as if to a child in pain. I drew back her blankets and plumped up her pillows. We had to drag her from the chair to the bed. She could not take a step. She felt very heavy. She was shivering violently and her teeth chattered. We made her as comfortable and warm as we could. The tears were coursing down her face; colourless, fragile tears of mute grief. I held her hand, averting my face, and stroked and caressed it. Her pillow was becoming soaked. I raised her head gently and put a towel under it. Barely audibly, she whispered; 'Yasia, fetch Anna.' 'Yes, Regina, yes, right away . . .' Fenia, holding a glass of water, took my place by the bed. What I did not realize, perhaps because I was too young and too inexperienced, and Fenia did not say anything, was that Regina had suffered a fatal stroke, either there and then, or within hours of receiving the news of her mother's fate – a stroke from which she would not recover.

I came out of the house to see the square empty – the men, the women, the children who had filled it, only a couple of hours ago, had been marched away to the cattle-trucks at Plaszow – except for a handful of SS-men busy about their weapons stacked up in tripods. I walked along the pavement on the right side of the square, keeping so close to the walls of the tenements that my frock was brushing against them. I kept my eyes cast down because of the men in green, in the square. I stopped, thrown, when I reached a patch of the pavement covered in a thick layer of glass fragments. The window pane and the glass doors of a greengrocer's shop had been smashed in the course of the day. Mingled with the sharp, jagged pieces of glass were potatoes, turnips, tomatoes, apples. I suddenly felt famished – I had not eaten all day – and I was about to stoop down to pick up an apple, when I thought better of it. The men in green, in the square, made me shrink back.

I turned the corner into Lvovska Street. I entered the one storey building in which Anna and David lived. Although I did not know it at the time, I was one of the first to witness the aftermath of a very large-scale, broad daylight man-hunt. It was the unaccustomed quiet, the eerie stillness of the house at No. 11 Lvovska Street that instantly filled me with foreboding . . . Normally, it was a busy, noisy tenement teeming with the hurly-burly of daily life. Now it was like a house of the dead. Heavy, awesome silence was all I was at first conscious of. I did not come upon any corpses. There were none. Yet the house was drained of all human activity and life. Nothing stirred in it. Not the faintest tinkle reached the ear.

Slowly, cautiously I climbed the worn, wooden steps to the first floor. One entered the flat straight from the landing. It was a mean little place consisting of a kitchen and a bedroom. The kitchen was inhabited by a family of three, the bedroom by Anna and David. One had to cross the kitchen to get to the bedroom. The door to the kitchen stood wide open; it was in a state of indescribable disorder, as if a viciously destructive force had gone through it – sacking, pillaging, looting with gusto and glee – leaving a wasteland in its wake. The bedroom door was also open, as was the window facing it. I entered my aunt's room. From the open window a shaft of multi-coloured sunlight, like a broad, shimmering silk-sash, with fine particles of dust gaily dancing in it, was streaming into the room – its beauty and warmth contrasting sadly with the garbage heap into which it had been reduced. The bed had been stripped and the bedclothes, trailing on the floor, trampled upon. The table and chairs overturned. The wardrobe gaped wide open – Anna's and David's clothes lying on the floor in a mangled pile. Saucepans, cutlery, broken china were strewn all over the room. Anna's hand-mirror, in which she had so often gazed at the reflection of her lovely face, lay, perfectly intact, on the floor. But there was no sign of Anna herself. I started calling out 'Anna, Anna, Anna . . .' I called out time and again 'Anna, Anna, Anna . . .' There was no reply . . . I went up to the window and leaned out directing my voice at the courtyard. I called her name again and again . . . There was no reply. My voice was the voice of a total stranger. Hoarse, trembling, swollen with pain and terror. I kept calling out to her till I could call no more. My throat ached so. The sobs were choking me. All I could produce was a whisper – 'Anna, Anna, Anna . . .' I left the flat and crawled down the stairs holding onto the banister. I dragged myself along the passage to the back door, the door which led to the cellars. It, too, stood wide open and there, at the bottom of a short flight of steps, yawned the cold blackness of the cellars. I kept croaking out my aunt's name towards that blackness, but there was no reply. Not a living soul had been left in that house, or any other house in Lvovska Street. As the Jewish policeman had said, only this afternoon, only a while ago: 'They went through some streets with a fine toothcomb and left not a soul behind . . .'

I meandered back to our room and Regina. At the sound of my footsteps, only mine, Regina opened her eyes, saw my face, and without asking a question, for she would never speak again, closed them.

But life must go on . . . Fenia was preparing an evening meal. The labour contingents, those that got through, would be back soon . . . Even though it was about six o'clock, it was still bright daylight. Regina was lying on her bed perfectly still; she was not crying any more; only her face had assumed sharp, rigid contours and in the shadowy, ill-lit room it looked the palest, the most delicate green. It made me think, incongruously, of a green, chiffon evening dress my mother had had; all transparent lightness and live, bouncy flounces – I used to secretly bury my face in it because I liked the feel and the smell of it.

Just after six o'clock Kalfus returned from work. Although there was no love lost between him and his wife, they kissed and embraced and he locked his treasure, his little daughter, in his arms and would not let go of her. They had the delicacy, all three, not to manifest their joy too openly because of Regina and me. They talked very low and moved about quietly, as one would at a wake. Regina seemed to be asleep. Her breathing had become so laboured that it was the only sound I was conscious of for a while. I asked Kalfus if he knew anything about my brother's contingent. He said he did not.

Fenia was busy setting the table for the evening meal and adding final touches to the contents of her saucepans. She then made a gesture of supreme magnanimity and kindness. She asked me if Regina and I would like to share their meal. Such gestures were rarely made in the Ghetto and never declined. I thanked her, but did not accept her kind offer. She understood.

Whilst the Kalfuses were eating, the door was flung open and David strode into the room. 'Anna, Anna, where is Anna?' Gone forever was the bespectacled, scholarly barrister. He already had the gestures, the voice, the stance of a madman. He took off his thick lenses – they kept becoming misted up – and looked around with unseeing eyes. His eyes were huge, brown and so prominent that they seemed to be straining to take leave of their sockets. Regina opened her eyes and looked at him, as if she had never seen him before. He stalked out . . .

I went out again. By now all the contingents that got through in the morning had returned. My brother had not come back . . .

The Ghetto presented a blood-curdling picture. Its entire population appeared to be out in the streets. Those who had come back and found their homes empty were out searching. And those, like myself, who had come out of hiding and whose dear ones had not returned were out searching. The Ghetto, on the evening of 28 October 1942 was like a battlefield after a great carnage. Those who still had a flicker of life left in them, for that was all we, the living, had left – wounded, stricken, howling with pain and despair – were groping around, quite disorientated, in the gathering dusk, as if in a thick, swirling fog, mumbling names, endearments, supplications . . . Names, names, litanies of names . . . We were calling out to our loved ones, gesticulating, pleading, stopping total strangers to ask: 'Have you seen my wife . . . my son . . . my father . . .?' In the Ghetto's main thoroughfare I came face to face with our pre-Ghetto days' neighbours. They had been a family of four; the father, a tall, athletically built man in his forties, was shuffling along like a feeble old man leaning heavily on his daughter's arm – 'We don't seem to be able to find my wife and son anywhere, have you seen them?' he stammered out. 'I . . . I am looking for my brother. He is only nineteen . . .' I added irrelevantly.

But my mind was still functioning. There was one more card left to play. I would go and find out if Joseph's friend, from the same contingent, had returned. I entered yet another tenement, this time in Targova Street, and knocked on yet another door. A strong, masculine voice bid me enter. Joseph's friend, his wife and two children were at dinner. The sight of him, his physical presence there, before my very eyes, had the effect on me of an injection of hope, energy, life . . . The numbness was dissipating. My mind was clicking away. It registered the graciously set table. The snow-white damask cloth. The gleaming silver, the sparkling crystal. The crusty rolls in an oval basket. The butter in a dainty dish. An array of condiments in beautifully fashioned containers. The exquisite porcelain tureen standing in front of his wife. The wisp of steam rising from it. His wife's hand closed round a silver ladle. And then he spoke. And his voice was harsh and impatient. He gave me to understand that my intrusion was most untimely; he could not tell me anything about the contingent; he was not a fool; he knew how to protect himself and his family; he had not joined his group in the morning; he and his family had spent the day in hiding; it was his children's first hot meal of the day . . . The children's clean, rosy faces; the wife's obvious displeasure at this interruption; the man's hostile, sullen scowl . . .

I then went straight to the Jewish Police Headquarters. It was being besieged by a wailing, sobbing, grief-overwhelmed throng of people. I tore my way through it and approached one of the Jewish policemen on duty outside. He took pity on me, perhaps because I was a child with a face swollen from crying, and listened to me patiently and attentively. By way of an answer, he spread out his hands, palms up, in a gesture of human impotence, and said not a word. I made my way again through that writhing, swaying human mass and started walking in the direction of our room, but my legs refused to carry me. I sat down on the kerb and buried my face in my hands. I sat there for a while. I heard a voice say; 'Yasia, is it you?' I looked up. A young woman – my aunts' friend. She said; 'Oh, you clever little girl, you have given them the slip again . . .' She smiled. Then her face grew grave. 'I saw your Aunt Anna being marched to the Square; yes, I was standing at the window of our flat; they never came near our house, and we could see the square as plainly as I can see you now. She must have resisted them or something; her face was so bruised . . .'

I sat there and I listened . . . For just as the eye retains an image, so the ear retains a sound. And mine has retained a heart-rending lament which drowned all else – the Ghetto's lament for its loved ones – a thin, piteous wail which spiralled round and round in the autumnal darkness.

21 · The Death Train

The October *Aktion* was one of the most tragic and the most cruel. Joseph was at that time attached to a large tailoring workshop – the SS-Strandartenverwaltung – in Straszewskiego Street. The following minor detail proves, if proof were needed, how cynically determined the masters were on extracting every last ounce of strength and energy from their slaves before consigning them to the East . . .

On 26 October, the Jewish workers at the SS-Standarten-verwaltung workshop were told that they would not be returning to the Ghetto for the night, as the batch of military uniforms they were working on was an urgent priority. They would spend that night and the following day, 27 October, at the workshop, applying themselves, with speed and industry, to the job in hand.

When Joseph returned to our room on the evening of the 27th, totally exhausted after the 36-hour stint at the workshop, the atmosphere in the Ghetto was thick with anxiety and fear – the characteristic preliminaries to an *Aktion*. That night, from the 27th to the 28th, with the Ghetto sealed off and the *Aktion* gathering momentum, Joseph, like everybody else in our room, may have snatched a little fitful sleep, but no rest. And he was worried about his little sister. Children, he well knew, were particularly vulnerable in a resettlement *Aktion*. I have already described the attempt he made, in the early morning of the 28th, to provide protection for me. It did not succeed. He left me in Grandmother's care. I was to accompany her to work at the Public Baths.

When Joseph left the room to join his Labour Group, the sun was already up and the promise of yet another beautiful October day was in the air, in the sky. Nonetheless, he put on his heavy, winter coat – just in case . . . A good winter coat, and his was a very good one, was a greatly prized possession; it bestowed social status upon its wearer; it kept him warm; he could sleep on it or under it; and finally, it was a valuable bartering token. In the street, he mingled

173

with the mass of people, the Ghetto's working population, converging on the Labour Groups' assembly point, the corner of Józefinska and Wegierska Streets. Although the crush was already terrible, still more and more people were flowing from every corner of the Ghetto towards this point expecting to join their Labour Group and march out to work.

In this immense, seething mass – composed of men and women of all ages and social backgrounds – the Labour Groups were the Ghetto's equalising melting-pot – some were trying to sort themselves out into proper Labour Groups. Others, unable to move, trapped in and by the crowd, helpless, were gazing vacantly around. Still others, already apathetic, overcome by the chaos and panic, seemed to have lost their bearings altogether. One was rooted to the spot – it was impossible to move, to locate one's group. It was only when the SS, the *Sonderdienst* and the Jewish Police started to tackle the frenzied throng, sifting it ruthlessly and indiscriminately – a large group of young, strong, able-bodied men and women to the square for deportation; another group, composed *ad hoc*, marched out to work; the next group to the square, yet another out of the Ghetto to work – that the crowd started thinning out and 'order' was established . . . But there was no rhyme or reason to the selection – only numbers seemed to matter . . .

By about 10 o'clock the fearful, but to Cracow as yet unknown, phrase – 'Krakau ist Judenrein' was being shouted and screamed at the dazed, disorientated men and women. Once the purport of those words was absorbed by their bewildered minds, those on the fringes of the crowd started turning round, changing their minds and direction, walking of their own volition to the square. 'If Cracow is being made "Judenrein" I may as well . . .'

The *Aktion* was assuming the desired verve and proportions – speed and numbers. The masters' top priority – to fill the square to bursting and beyond – was being implemented, was becoming reality. Hard work and devotion to duty were bearing fruit . . .

'If Cracow is being made "Judenrein," if we are all going . . .?' And men and women were turning around in handfuls, confused, numbed, facilitating the masters' task, to hobble towards the Square. And the jinxed phrase was on all lips – 'Cracow is "Judenrein" it's the end . . . we are all being despatched to the East . . .' Many were turning around desperate to return home to the wife and the children, to the elderly parents, to the younger brothers and sisters; to tell them to stuff a few things into a bag and make for the square

together, as a family; to stay together, as a family, whatever the fate
. . . But they soon found, as they detached themselves from the fear-
driven, floundering throng, that all routes were closed to them –
except one – that to the square . . .

They would not see their family again – maybe their loved
ones were themselves already in the Square, maybe they would be
escorted into it, later on in the day . . . How does one look for anyone
in a tightly-wedged multitude of 6,000 people? They would, later on
in the day, march in the same long procession to Plaszow railway
station, but not together. They would be pushed into the cattle-
trucks of the same waiting train, but not together . . . Not even
the solace of holding a dear one's hand, on that last journey, was
accorded.

Joseph, who was caught right in the middle of this churning,
pulsating human mass, never found his Labour Group. It was about
11 o'clock, on this bright, very warm October morning, when he was
driven, by the SS and the Auxiliaries, with a detail of men, none of
whom he knew, into the courtyard of a building at No. 14 Wegierska
Street. All exits from it were instantly blocked and a young SS-man
lithely mounted the flight of steps to the first floor, from where, feet
turned out, gloved-hands closed round the ends of his riding crop,
eyes upon the defenceless, cowering handful of Jews, he proceeded,
like a producer directing a play, to issue orders into the courtyard.
The men, already half-unhinged by uncertainty and fear, were
subjected to unbridled brutality. Joseph managed to evade the
violence. He had been in the courtyard for about half-an-hour, when
he noticed that a narrow side-entrance to the building was being
guarded by a single Polish policeman looking very bored. He inched
towards it holding a 20 złoty banknote – the price of a loaf of bread –
across the man's field of vision. The policeman stepped aside, just
enough for Joseph to slip out, and pocketed the 20 złoty note.

Once out, Joseph decided to walk back to our tenement at No. 4,
and hide there, maybe in the cellar. As he proceeded along
Józefinska and Targova Streets hot, thirsty, tired, in the rising heat of
noon, he saw people wandering in the streets – all lost, like souls on
the periphery of hell, in bewilderment and confusion. To join those
assembled in the square? To look for a hiding-place? Women with
children huddling in doorways overcome by the rising tide of panic,
by the wild screams of 'Judenrein . . .'

Joseph was about ten steps away from our tenement, when he
came face to face with a young German soldier, a lad about his own

175

age. He barred Joseph's way – his finger on the trigger of his rifle – and pointed at the square – already packed solid. Joseph walked in front of him and the soldier only turned away when Joseph had merged into the vast sea of people in the cordoned off square. Thousands, tightly compressed, were already gathered there under the broiling sun. One could not move forward or sideways and at the back, not many paces away from Joseph, was the SS rifle-bristling cordon encircling the Square. The deportees – silent and resigned – sat or stood around. Joseph sat down on a bundle next to him. Nobody objected. Heads down against the blazing sun, they waited quietly and patiently in helpless stupor.

After a time, Joseph spotted the Order family – husband, wife and their three year old son, Olek (they were David's sister, brother-in-law and little nephew – old Mrs Rostal's, from Żabno, beloved grandson). He jostled his way towards them. They nodded to each other in recognition, but they had nothing to say to him, nor he to them, except that Mrs Order, who was holding a bag of provisions in her hand, said, 'I have a large slab of butter in the bag, 'I am worried that it will melt in this heat . . .', and they vanished, swallowed up by the crowd.

The longer they waited, the more overcome and listless they became; yet each soul shivered in anguish and each heart beat in fear.

After hours of anxious, but passive waiting, round about 3 o'clock in the afternoon, when the Square was truly splitting at the seams and spilling over with the day's rich catch, the SS and the Auxiliaries started to form the long, long file of men and women, of old, frail people, of little children – all mute and submissive – to drive them along Lvovska and Wielicka Streets to the cattle-trucks at Plaszow. As Joseph was at the back of the square, he found himself in the end-section of the procession. Many left their luggage behind, already too exhausted to carry it . . . They trudged, they shuffled, they dragged themselves along in total silence till they reached the cattle-trucks.

A strange incident occurred, which provoked an extraordinary reaction, as Joseph was standing by the truck's door, pulled wide open, waiting his turn to climb in. A German military lorry carrying a handful of Jews pulled up at the loading ramp. The Jews jumped down. As they were being herded along to be pushed into the crowd of deportees scrambling into the trucks, the man standing next to Joseph, a man in his forties who, like Joseph, was on his own, looked at the newly arrived human cargo and made a comment: 'Good God

176

– are you telling me that this rabble, these criminals – they are Jewish prisoners from the *Kriminalpolizei* Headquarters at the Szlak. The *Kriminalpolizei* have been investigating them, and putting them through their paces, black-market, you know . . . That this scum is being put on the same train as people like ourselves – decent, respectable, law-abiding citizens . . .?' The man's sense of social injustice was positively outraged. Among the prisoners brought from the Szlak to the death-train, and whose presence on it the man standing next to Joseph so bitterly resented, was sixteen year old Henio Birner – our cousin Sophie's sweetheart. He had been involved in smuggling flour for his uncle's bakery in the Ghetto.

The moment Joseph found himself inside the truck, and whilst it was being filled, his gaze wandered over the truck's two windows, one at each end. He would say to me one day, in all humility, 'I was lucky, only one of the windows had steel bars across it . . .' One had steel bars across it; the other was covered with a barbed-wire mesh. It was on this second window that Joseph, who already knew that he would attempt to leave the death-train – for he was convinced that its final destination was death – was pinning his hopes. And when a hundred souls had been counted off, they started to roll forward the truck's door shutting out light and air. Shutting out life itself. And the heavy, metallic clanging of bolts and chains, as the truck was being sealed from the outside made one's heart stand still and the sweat of cold terror pour down one's body . . .

The word 'death' had not been uttered once within Joseph's hearing; neither in the square, nor during the march to Plaszow, nor in the truck itself, and yet, he knew . . . The window was, he decided, long enough and wide enough to admit his head and shoulders. It was late afternoon. The loaded, sealed train was standing still, ready to depart. It was late autumn. Twilight was setting in. Soon the truck would be submerged in total darkness. At the moment, in the meagre light entering through the two small windows, Joseph could see its interior and its one hundred souls. Some, totally overcome by fatigue were lying prone on the truck's floor; others were sitting or squatting against its walls; yet others, mostly men, were standing. It was hot in the truck and the women were tearing off their frocks, their blouses, their pale flesh, their burning eyes gleaming in the semi-darkness. No one was talking – a rustle, a murmur, a whimper and faintly, almost inaudibly, he heard the word 'water' whispered . . .

Joseph looked around for familiar face. The little caretaker from our tenement was there with her brood of children. So was fair-haired twenty year old Basia Reich. The Reichs were neighbours of ours. They lived just across the passage from us. Basia was the eldest of three children. Basia, too, saw Joseph and they looked at each other in mute understanding. And then he saw Rose standing not far from him . . . leaning against her father who had his arms round her. Sixteen year old Rose was our cousin Sophie's friend. Rose and Joseph knew each other well. They looked at each other, now, in recognition, and Joseph would remember, for as long as he lived, the look of utter despair in her wide-open, dark eyes. Rose was aptly named. She was, indeed, a rose in the first innocent freshness and dazzling beauty of womanhood.

The shadows in the truck were merging into a black, tangled mass. The darkness was deepening. Time stood still. Someone said: 'A woman here is dead . . . An old woman . . .' Was it an hour, was it a lifetime away since the truck was sealed up? He heard Rose, near him say, 'I am thirsty . . .' and her father reply, 'Once we get there, there will be water . . . We will be able to drink . . . To have a wash . . .'

It was about seven o'clock in the evening when the train heaved, shuddered and set in motion – gathering speed, gathering speed . . . There was a certain loosening of tension and suspense in the truck. 'On the whole,' Joseph will say to this day, 'they were hopeful'. Not far from Joseph a man was smoking a cigarette, the red-burning tip glowing in the darkness. Joseph, who was a smoker and who had not had a cigarette all day, suddenly felt that he would give his soul for a puff. He remembered the quarter-loaf of bread in his coat pocket. He had not thought of it, he had not felt like biting into it, all day. He now said to the man smoking, 'I have a hunk of bread here, will you swap it for a fag?' The man produced a cigarette and lit it for Joseph. He pocketed the bread. Joseph drew on his cigarette deeply once, twice, and said evenly and audibly, 'Ladies and Gentlemen, does anybody intend to disembark? Because I do! Two men, both close to to the window – one sitting, one standing, said they did. Nobody else evinced any interest in Joseph's proposition.

Then he heard Basia Reich's voice: 'Are you, really, going to jump, Józek, from the running train?' 'I am going to try . . . Do you want to try, too? We will help you . . .' 'Oh no, I would be too scared. I might break my legs and arms. I could cripple myself for life. Besides, I couldn't leave my friend, I mean my best friend,' pointing to a young woman, cuddling a baby in her arms, sitting next to her. 'The baby is only a year old – we'll stay together . . .'

Joseph shook off his coat with the Star of David armband on the sleeve, and his *Kennkarte* in the breast pocket; it would hamper his movements. A woman's voice rose in the darkness, 'You shouldn't leave the truck. They may count us on arrival.' Her warning received no support. Not another word was spoken. The boy standing – tall and slender – that was all Joseph could tell about him in the darkness, moved right up to the window, as did Joseph stumbling over legs, arms, bodies. The man sitting down never plucked up courage. He did not even change his position. He remained sitting.

The tall boy stood up straight against the window wall. He let his knees sag and slowly raised his hands, palms out. His hands, his arms, his head were outside the window seeking purchase along the truck roof's overhanging ledge. When he found it and had established a firm grip on it, gradually, with measured, even movements, his shoulders, his torso, his legs swung out of the truck. Joseph had not missed the tall boy's single movement, single gesture. The boy's body was now blocking the small window from the outside. It excluded, for a brief moment, the sole witness, forever silent, of the two teenage boys' deed of extraordinary daring and courage – the pale silver moon sailing sedately in a purple evening sky.

It flashed through Joseph's mind, as he tensed up for the greatest physical feat of his life – 'He is a sportsman, an athlete . . .' The tall boy had moved forward along the ledge, away from the window . . . Joseph's hands were now gripping the jutting roof ledge. From hand-grip to hand-grip – his body, his legs, his feet dangling in the void – only inches away from the black, fast-turning wheels of the cattle-truck – the chilly October breeze cooling his burning, sweat-soaked body, whipping up the back of his jacket. His hands moved along the ledge, the turned out toes of his right foot sensitively poised, delicately seeking purchase on a patch of terra firma. His foot found the little wooden platform in front of the truck, his right hand grabbed the long metal hand-rail – the tall boy, already standing on the platform, stretched out his arm and wound it round Joseph's waist.

They were huddling on the wooden platform, the train speeding on, speeding on; the wind swishing plaintively through the dark countryside; the moon floating unconcernedly in the sky.

'We stood, shivering, on the platform for a good while,' he later told me. 'Why didn't you jump down straightaway?' I asked. 'Silly,' replied Joseph. 'The train was rolling in the midst of live track; we had to wait till it had reached a clean grass verge.' When it had, the tall boy suddenly said: 'I am jumping . . .' and bouncing off the platform, soared up into the air to touch down gently and, as Joseph later told me – 'Without so much as a graze . . .' Joseph plunged down after him and was thrown, with immense force, beyond the grass verge, down a steep, gravel-covered embankment, ploughing, face down, against the gravelled surface. His face and hands were scratched and bruised; his front teeth were chipped; a large, sharp-edged pebble cut his forehead open, just under the hair-line. Sweet and thick, the blood trickled down his face from the gash.

The death-train had long disappeared from sight; there was nothing around except the pitch-black autumn night.

Joseph lay on the grass at the foot of the embankment in a state of mental and physical torpor. So overcome, so stunned was he by all he had seen, heard and experienced in the last twelve hours that he just wanted to remain lying there, in the clement darkness of the night. Not to have to open his eyes, not to have to raise himself and start moving, not to have to think . . . The blood was trickling down his face. He felt weak, sick, shaken to the very core of his being. He had a handkerchief in his pocket. He applied it to the gash to staunch the flow. It was soon soaked and his fingers, his hand were smeared with the thick, sticky fluid. He heard the tall boy's voice, 'Are you all right?' Dazed, his lips bruised and torn, he answered with a voice which seemed to come from far away: 'I think so . . .' He picked himself up. He was cold. He shivered. He would have been glad of the coat he had left on the death-train. 'My coat will get there . . .'

'We must find out where we are and look for somewhere to spend the night,' said the tall boy. 'Yes, that's right,' replied Joseph. Just to open his eyes – the eyelids seemed sealed with blood – was a great effort. There were lights twinkling not far away from the field in which they were standing. 'Must be a village. Maybe we can find somewhere to turn in for the night . . . Wash this blood off, get a drink of water . . .' 'Let's go' said the tall boy and he led the way. Joseph followed, his legs stiff, wooden.

Soon, they reached a low village cottage. The door was already locked for the night. They knocked and stood there for a while, but the inhabitants made no sign of life. The next house, a bungalow, was nearby. Again, they knocked on the door. A middle-aged woman answered and motioned to them to come in. They found themselves in a dimly-lit room. Even so, the woman gasped at the sight of Joseph's face. He explained that he had fallen off the steps of an overcrowded train in motion. She accepted the explanation. It was perfectly plausible. Trains were greatly overcrowded in those days and men often travelled on the outside of a carriage. The woman left the room to return with a basinful of cold water. She placed it on a stool before Joseph. He plunged his head in the cold, clear water. It turned red. The woman gave him a strip of white cotton – perhaps torn out of an old sheet and told him to bind his head with it. Her husband came into the room; he was already acquainted with the boys' story.

He said, 'You'll want to bed down for the night; I'll fetch some straw.' He brought in the straw and spread it out on the floor in a corner of the room. Joseph asked him, 'Where are we?' 'You are in Podłęże . . .' 'How far is it from here to Cracow?' 'Oh, about half-an-hour's journey by train,' replied the man. 'I work in Cracow – at Zieleniewski's Armaments Factory in Grzegórzki. I commute daily. There is a number of us, here, in the village, who catch the morning train to Cracow. You two can walk with me to the station in the morning. We catch the early train. We start at Zieleniewski's at eight.'

The woman brought them a couple of old blankets and a mug of milk each. They drank it and lay down on the straw.

The death-train was speeding through the dark, autumn night – handfuls of golden sparks flying and scattering in the wind . . .

Joseph and the tall boy were awake as soon as they heard sounds of movement in the house. It was early morning – 29 October. The woman brought them milk again. She said to Joseph, who had removed 'the bandage', 'Your head doesn't look good. Keep it covered.' He had a deep, raw gash in his forehead, as if a piece of flesh and bone had been gouged out. The tall boy was stirring beside him.

With the bright morning light entering the room, Joseph saw, for the first time, the tall boy's face. His heart lurched within him and he felt weak with fear. It was a perfect Semitic face – unmistakable! Fear was gripping him hard – every nerve in his body raw and exposed. 'I, with a smashed-up face and a blood-stained rag . . . the tall boy with his face . . . the Poles can smell a Jew a mile away . . . people . . . German station officials . . . the train . . . the Cracow streets . . . if we get that far . . . they'll catch us . . . was it all for nothing . . .?'

The man came into the room. 'Let's go.' Joseph and the tall boy thanked the woman and slipped her a few złotys . . .

They walked to the station, which was nearby, the tall boy instinctively keeping his head down, shielding his face from view. Joseph stayed close to the man. At the station, the man joined a small group of workmen – from Zieleniewski's – on the platform. The train was due in five minutes. 'All the travellers were regulars. They all seemed to know each other. We stood out like two sore thumbs in any case . . . The black-uniformed Bahnschutz-polizei – a vicious and sadistic lot if ever there was one – were weaving about. I tried to stand as close as was decently possible to the man and his mates, to appear one of the group. My heart wasn't beating, it was exploding . . . The tall boy was standing behind me . . . but a little apart from the friendly group . . . Suddenly one of the chaps, his eye on the tall boy, asked, 'What's that Jew doing here?' 'I have never known such fear; such all-pervading paralysing terror . . . It was the longest five minutes of my life . . .' To this day, Joseph will say, 'Waiting for that train, on 29 October, 1942, at Podłęże station, was the longest five minutes of my life . . .'

'The train pulled in and we all scrambled aboard. There was no incident. But my heart was racing . . . My insides were in one tight knot . . . I wanted to be sick, violently sick . . .'

Joseph and the tall boy spent a good while, each, in the train toilet or standing in the corridor pressing their faces against the window-pane – that way they could only be seen from the back. The tall boy had very black, wavy, rather oily hair – that in itself was an indication . . . Joseph, in a state of cold terror, was assailed by very bleak, very dismal thoughts, though wholly realistic. 'What if the Ghetto has been disbanded? What if there are no more Jews in Cracow? Where can I go? What can I do?' And in some little cubby-hole of his brain was the question, 'What's happened to my little sister? Was she in the square? Was she on the death-train?' He felt totally alone, utterly helpless and, above all, terrified of falling into their hands again . . .

The short journey was over in no time at all. The train had already entered Cracow. The travellers were preparing to alight, taking their bags down, buttoning their coats, adjusting their hats. It was not yet eight o'clock in the morning, but the sun was already in the sky, warm and golden; it was going to be a beautiful day.

Joseph asked the tall boy, 'Where will you go?' 'Oh,' he replied, 'I am going to the Aleje'. 'The Aleje' were Cracow's most elegant avenues bearing the names of Poland's greatest poets and writers – always an exclusive, patrician area, it was now, of course, 'Nur Für Deutsche . . .' A Jew would not have dared set foot in 'the Aleje' –

not many Polish males, for that matter, would have dared venture into the area, but a Jew with that appearance. Joseph's astonishment was boundless! He had been aware for the last few minutes that the train was slowing down. It was about to roll along 'The Blich' – a few minutes' walk from Cracow's main railway station. One side of 'The Blich' was a long grass covered railway embankment closed at the very bottom by a fairly high, but easily negotiable wall. Now, as the train entered the Blich embankment, at a leisurely pace, carriage doors were flying open and travellers, in numbers, were hopping out and skipping down the embankment. It was much more convenient for the workers at Zieleniewski's to leave the train at this point – the factory was just round the corner – only a few steps from the Blich. On the other hand, there were many smugglers on the train laden with precious contraband. They certainly did not wish to disembark at the main station – swarming as it would be with the Bahnschutzpolizei. They, too, tumbled out in the Blich. And there were yet others, in this fourth year of war, for whom discretion was the better part of valour – they, too, slipped gently down the Blich embankment.

Joseph and the tall boy went their different ways. It was not yet eight o'clock in the morning. As soon as Joseph set foot on the Blich pavement he saw a group of Jewish workmen marching along. 'A Labour Group! Can it be? They are going to work for eight o'clock,' he thought.

There was a familiar face in the group, Mr Liebling. Joseph and he knew each other well. The Lieblings used to live at No. 42 Limanowskiego Street, in the courtyard, in what was once a storeroom. Liebling, too, had seen Joseph and did not fail to notice his pitiful condition. He made room, as it were, for Joseph to slide into the Group.

'Mr Liebling, does the Ghetto still exist?' 'Yes, it does . . .' 'Are there any Jews left in the Ghetto?' 'Yes, a few thousand.' 'You haven't seen my little sister?' 'No, I haven't . . . But what's happened to you?' 'I jumped from the train last night. I want to get to the Ghetto, Mr Liebling. I left my coat, with the armband on the sleeve, in the cattle-truck. I need an armband. I am too scared to move around without it.' 'Our workshop is just down the road, come along, I'll get you an armband . . .' replied Liebling.

Hugging the walls of the houses, Joseph scurried through the back streets as fast as he could. It was a fine, sunlit day – 29 October. Once in Limanowskiego Street, he started treading very warily, for he was approaching the Wegierska Street Ghetto entrance, when he saw a strange equipage – a wooden platform drawn by a lean, brown horse with three Jewish policemen aboard. Joseph knew one of them. 'Mr Landauer, has something happened? Is there trouble in the Ghetto again?' 'We are driving to Plaszow, to the train, to rescue a few people taken in yesterday's *Aktion* . . . The train is still in Plaszow, you see . . .' 'To the train? To Plaszow? There is no train in Plaszow, Mr Landauer . . . The train left last night at about seven o'clock . . .' 'No train? What can you mean?' And Landauer touched the horse's flank with the whip to urge it on.

It was shortly after eight o'clock in the morning when Joseph entered the tenement at No. 4 the Square of Peace. He pushed the door to our room open. The Kalfuses, Siggie and Sophie, Regina – they were struck dumb at the sight of him! He looked around – 'Is my little sister . . .?' They answered in a chorus, their powers of speech restored, 'Yes, she is here, she is here . . .' Joseph fell upon his bed.

22 • The Aftermath

But life goes on. There were Jews in the Ghetto, on the evening of 28 October, who had not lost anyone in the day's heavy toll; some – like our cousins – because their loved ones had already been placed on the sacrificial altar. Some – like the Kalfus family, including Fenia's ageing parents – because after every action a handful of families would emerge unscathed. I understood, after the October action, that we were being dehumanised and destroyed. One did not feel or share someone else's grief. Nor did one feel or share someone else's joy. Both our cousins returned from work that evening. No doubt, they had feared brother for sister – sister for brother and were, now, happy to find each other safe and sound, but I must say that my consciousness only just registered the fact of their presence. I was not able to rejoice for them, nor do I remember receiving from them a word or a gesture of understanding or comfort. But then, the immensity, the depth of grief exceeded all such words and all such gestures. And yet my numbed consciousness did register that evening, when I was making my calls at Targova Street and the Jewish Police Headquarters, that looting was taking place in the Ghetto.

The Jews who had survived the day and who were not prostrated by grief and despair were crossing and re-crossing the square, that sacred ground where only this afternoon, only a few hours earlier, their brethren had been gathered like an enormous herd of cattle and thence driven, under Cracow's golden, autumnal sky, to be loaded onto the cattle-trucks awaiting them at Plaszow station. The blood and tears spilt by their brethren, that very afternoon, in the square, had not yet dried, but the survivors were already tramping across it laden with their still warm clothing and bedding, their possessions, their estate . . .

Lvovska Street and the turnings off it had been truly cleaned out – gutted – their inhabitants constituting the morning's fine catch, the afternoon's rich pickings, the solid backbone of the day's transport . . .

I saw my cousin, Sophie, dragging a large suitcase across the square. I did not stop. I did not speak to her. But I understood, in a flash, what she and the others were doing. Had I not been overwhelmed, frozen in body and soul by the day's events which had robbed me of the remainder of my family, I, too, would have been there, among the looters, helping myself as others were. The Jews were in situ; they were, thus, able to to lay their hands on the deportees' property before the German vans and lorries arrived to plunder and carry it off the following day. It was fairer this way . . .

When I returned to our room, late that evening, it was silent and dark; everyone, including Regina, was sleeping. I did not even bother to undress, but fell upon my headboard pallet like an exhausted animal that had spent the day evading the hunter – only to find, on reaching his lair, that in his absence his family had fallen prey to him. I felt no hunger, no thirst – only exhaustion . . . I slept.

I was woken at the crack of dawn the next morning, 29 October. The day's first, pale light was only just filtering into the room. I heard someone calling my name: 'Yasia, Yasia' with great urgency. I opened my eyes to see David bending over me. I was instantly awake, the last twenty-four hours engraved on my mind. He was whispering hoarsely, excitedly: 'Yasia, Yasia, the train is still in Plaszow . . . it hasn't left yet . . . the Jewish Police are driving out to Plaszow . . . it hasn't left yet . . . they will rescue a handful of people . . . bring them back . . . to the Ghetto . . . Come, come with me . . . we are going to beg them to bring Anna back . . .' I hopped off my pallet and together we left the room.

I do not know how David had spent the night from 28 to 29 October, but he cannot have closed his eyes or lain down. He looked demented – exhausted, sweaty, unshaven, unwashed. He had either spent the night pacing the Ghetto streets thronging with people as hurt, as desperate as himself, or else he had stayed in his room howling like a stricken animal.

The 29th, too, was going to be a beautiful day. A fresh, tender dawn had broken over Cracow – its inhabitants were waking to a new day. A day like yesterday, a day like tomorrow. An everyday, ordinary day of toil, of family life, of hardship and care, of hope and smiles.

We approached the Jewish Police Headquarters. The building was there, in the same spot, and against its facade, which had become a wailing wall, sobbing, swaying, knocking their heads against its stone hardness, the same lamenting crowd. As dense, as closely packed as last night they were clinging to the walls, doors, windows pleading for help, begging for pity. David and I added our voices to the imploring chorus.

But our ears soon became attuned to the tragic chorus's chant, 'They have gone; they are on their way; they will rescue whom they can . . .' This final message of hope travelled from one chanting, begging, pleading mouth to another. We understood, David and I, that we had come too late. That we had only just missed the Jewish policemen – the saviours. That they had already departed on their sacred mission to Plaszow. That it was useless to continue calling our loved ones' names. David called that of his wife; I, that of my brother – for blood ties, affections, loyalties sorted themselves out quite naturally, quite independently of oneself – for the saviours, already on their way to the cattle-trucks at Plaszow would not hear them, no matter how loudly we bellowed, no matter how beseechingly we prayed. But the conveyance, whatever it was, which they were driving to Plaszow and which we, the dispossessed, tricked so cruelly only yesterday, lied to so often, hoodwinked time without number believed would return to the Ghetto filled with deportees miraculously winkled out of the trucks of the waiting train, waiting in Plaszow . . .

We had not seen the conveyance, nor the gullible, trusting men driving it – David and I. We had just missed it. So it must be travelling down Józefinska Street, turning left into Wegierska Street, driving out through the exit and entrance gate of the latter, turning left to proceed along the Limanowskiego Street thoroughfare (which had ceased to be part of the Ghetto after the June 1942 *Aktion*) towards Plaszow railway station and towards the cattle-trucks waiting there . . .

The early morning sun has already appeared in the sky, but the air still has the sharpness left in it by the long, cold October night – for it is late autumn – which its warmth will soon dispel.

David, wild-eyed, looks at me and says. 'They have gone to Plaszow, they have gone to bring them back, but I didn't give them Anna's name . . . I was too late . . .' He whimpers. Large tears roll down his face. How is it possible for a man to change so in twenty-four hours?

The uneven-numbered side of Limanowskiego Street, the one that is still part of the Ghetto, and will remain in it to the end of its existence, has a fence, a barbed-wire screen running along the pavement. Its meshes are large. Every time the Ghetto is diminished temporary, shoe-string measures are taken to define its new boundaries. No more solid, brick walls with fancy crenellations. For it is only a matter of time before the Ghetto's feeble spark of life is extinguished.

The desperate, helpless throng besieging the Jewish Police Head-quarters, having somehow absorbed the message that it is futile to plead and sob, to implore and wail, for the conveyance with the saviours aboard has left, gone, departed, move in stunned silence – a living wall, five, ten people deep – as in a trance, towards the barbed-wire tracery to catch a glimpse of the conveyance as it travels up Limanowskiego Street.

David and I find ourselves right up against the barbed-wire. We stand next to each other – I to the right of him. We each have a mesh, like a picture frame, to ourselves. As I hardly reach his shoulder, his face is framed within the mesh above mine; mine within the mesh below his.

We wait patiently and numbly for the conveyance to appear along the Limanowskiego Street thoroughfare. In the end the primitive equipage heaves into view.

A tired, old horse, brown and lean with moulting flanks emerges from the morning haze pulling a square wooden platform rimmed with steel. Three Jewish policemen are aboard – one of them, whip in hand, is encouraging the weary animal to trot more briskly. Everyone of the upper meshes of the barbed-wire is framing a face and every mouth in every face starts, at the sight of the equipage, mumbling, repeating a name, a string of names . . . David is calling out: 'Anna, Anna Rostal,' I am calling out 'Joseph, Joseph Fischler . . .' Not a single one of those names can be heard, can reach the policemen's ears; mingling, the names rise in one gigantic tide of sorrow, of unintelligible lament . . .

The sight of that horse, that wooden platform, those three Jewish policemen driving out to rescue – whom? The train left Plaszow the previous evening, at about seven o'clock, 28 October, and has been hurtling, direction East, through the Polish countryside all night to deliver its cargo of men, women and children . . . Not even upon me is the dreadful irony lost – the horse, the platform, the three men against the power of the Third Reich, against the most ruthless machinery of destruction. Who has spread the rumour that the train is still in Plaszow? Who has made so little of our despair and torment as to give us vain hope? Even a shred of it!

Slowly we drag ourselves away from the barbed-wire and

disperse. I lose David in the crowd. I walk along Józefinska and Targova Streets and take a short cut across the Square of Peace to reach our doorway.

In the square I see Helcia's husband and daughter. I go up to them, but I do not greet them. They do not greet me. The watchmaker is a big man, tall and broad-shouldered. He must be in his middle-thirties. He is holding his daughter, Halinka, by the hand. She is about eight years old and big for her age, tall and strongly built, a very pretty child with large dark eyes and thick, ash-blond hair. They stand there, in the Square . . . orphaned . . . unseeing . . . I raise my eyes to the watchmaker's face and I know. He says, 'They have taken Helcia, my wife, and Jack, our little boy . . . they have snapped us . . . in half . . .' I said earlier that one had stopped sharing other people's grief, for one's heart was brimming over with one's own. But I felt all the compassion I was capable of for the watchmaker and his daughter. She was wearing her light-beige coat neatly buttoned to the neck. The large, red bow in her thick, ash-blond hair, always so straight and crisp, was a little crooked and rather limp . . . I never saw them again.

When I entered our room, my brother, Joseph, was stretched out on his bed – eyes closed. His face was scratched and bruised. He had a white, blood-stained rag tied round his head.

23 • *The Chosen One*

Aunt Regina, the last of the four Weinreb sisters, became very ill after the October action in which she lost her mother and sister, Anna. She lay on the narrow iron bed gradually losing all power of movement, speech and consciousness. The Ghetto around her was like a throbbing, open wound whose lips would never meet, but she was already oblivious of it, lost in the deep, dark pool of her own suffering.

Her body grew so thin and emaciated that if it had not been for the dark head against the white pillow, one would have thought the bed empty. Joseph and I were the only close relatives she had left. But her glazed eyes no longer saw us; her numbed mind no longer recognised us.

The woman doctor whom we called in to her, came in the late morning. There was nobody in the room except Regina and me. A short, thick-set woman, mannish in appearance, blunt in speech, she seemed to me singularly unfeeling, almost callous. She examined Regina with meticulous care and great gentleness however. She then addressed herself to me. 'How old are you?' she asked. 'Twelve,' I replied. 'Are you her daughter?' 'No, niece.' 'There is nothing I can do for her. She is beyond help. Let her die in peace.'

I protested. Surely, there was something she could do to alleviate her suffering, to prolong her life . . . She looked me full in the face, her small, shrewd eyes holding mine, and said: 'Ah, she is one of the chosen few. To die in one's bed, oblivious of the misery and heart-break around one, is a luxury and a privilege accorded to very few. Would you have her get well so that she can march, on her own two feet, to her death as your loved ones, and mine, have done?'

I felt a searing pain in my breast. She knew. And, now, in November 1942, I, too, knew. She had said in a calm, steady voice – 'they had marched to their death . . .'

Regina's bed stood close to the window. It was a murky, wet

190

November day. The air, seen through the dirty glass pane, looked like grey, used-up cotton wool. 'Will you not cheat them of at least one victim?' the doctor asked. Dumbly, I nodded assent. She picked up her bag and left.

Regina was the very last link with a world and a way of life that would never again be ours. As long as she lived, an adult, we remained a family. We were very conscious of her presence in the room, fragile though it was.

The days were long and cold and grey. The stove was rarely lit. There was no fuel and no food to cook. And there was nothing to sell . . . I was sitting on Grandmother's couch which she had made and covered in her usual neat fashion before leaving the room on the morning of 28 October. I drew back the pink, tufted cover. The bed-linen looked so clean and crisp – hardly a crease in it. She must have changed it shortly before the 28th. I slipped my hand under the pillow and there it was – her long, white, plain, much washed night-dress neatly folded. I pressed it with both hands to my breast, to my face, my eyes streaming with tears.

Regina was very still, her eyes closed. The room was filled with grey, November shadows. I stripped the couch of its linen, fine quality, home-spun sheets and a pair of pillowcases with hand-embroidered scalloped borders to match. I would sell them and buy some bread and apples for us, and something special, a treat, for Regina. I folded them up neat and small and made for the barbed-wire tracery on one side of which was the Józefinska Street Ghetto thoroughfare – on the other – the Aryan pavement. Every child-smuggler knew the precise spot in which the wire had been cut. It was a raw, blustery November day; the low sky was sombre; the grey streets deserted. Cautiously, I drew the barbed strands apart and slid out. Standing, now, on the pavement, my parcel inside my coat, I pulled them to, in compliance with the unspoken, unwritten smugglers' code of honour.

I sold my wares in 'Tandeta' – Cracow's vast, war-time black market. The buyer, a suburban housewife, inspected the linen very closely and said, 'They are old, your sheets and pillowcases.' 'No, Ma'am,' I replied, 'they are antique'. A flare of covetousness lit her eye; still, she drove a hard bargain, as I did. We enjoyed the haggling.

Having disposed of the bed-linen, I wanted to buy some rare delicacy, some delicious morsel for Regina. I walked up and down the food section of the market, carefully examining the fresh fruit stalls. On one of them I spotted a small round wicker basket lined with a snow-white napkin, in which about half a dozen fresh lemons glistened palely. I let my gaze feast on them. Timidly, I put out my hand and lightly, with the very tips of my fingers, touched one. The vendor's eyes were riveted to my hand.

I picked out my lemon and paid for it. I had not seen a lemon for a long time. Its cool, pitted peel made my fingers tingle with pleasure. Its delicately tangy fragrance was intoxicating. I had hardly ever been outside my native Cracow. I knew no geography. 'Politics' was just a word to me. I understood no military tactics, statistics or movements. The lemon, I thought, came from a country where people were free and unafraid; where oranges and lemons ripened slowly under the sun's hot breath. I put it in my pocket, my hand closed round it, and started on my return journey to the Ghetto.

Regina was lying on her back, her eyes closed. The room was silent except for the sound of her breathing, which came and went in short, shrill whistles. Gently I took hold of her transparent, inert hand and said, 'Regina, look what I have brought you.' I tried to close her fingers around the lemon, but they were both too rigid and too weak.

I prepared a small jug of lemonade for her, taking great care not to let stray a drop of the precious liquid which the fruit yielded under the pressure of my fingers. I then placed the peel in a small bowl. It was a great treasure. We would flavour our hot water drinks with strips of lemon peel.

That evening, when my brother came home from work, we tenderly lifted Regina up in her bed. He held her up, her head cradled in the crook of his arm, while I carried the liquid to her lips. They had no strength, no will to accept it. Most of it dribbled down her chin and fell in thick, opaque tears on to the towel. Though a tiny flicker of life still remained in her body, her spirit was already joining, in distant, shadowy groves, those she had loved and lost . . .

A few more cold, dark, November days went by. The room was filled with long, grey shadows. Fenia went daily to her parents. She did not want her child to witness the agony.

Nobody came to see us – not David, not Aunt Josephine, not Ella, Regina's best friend. They were all immersed in their own grief and pain, pitting their much reduced strength against a hard day's work . . .

When we woke up on the morning of 11 November 1942, exactly a fortnight after the deportation of her mother and sister, Regina was dead. She had died in the night whilst we slept. I looked at the long, wasted corpse, the grey, pain-scarred face and remembered the doctor's words: 'She is one of the chosen few . . .'

I filled a glass with water, as I had seen Grandmother do, and placed it on her bedside table, so that her soul might lave itself and appear cleansed before its Creator.

24 • The Yellow and the Violet

After Regina's death, I dismantled my head-board-pallet and took over her bed. I also appropriated her meagre belongings. I remember, particularly, a brown silk blouse with a flat, pleated collar, a blue and black, check cotton blouse and a small, green lacquer box in which I found her amber brooch, hand-carved, in the shape of a small rose-flower.

Fenia returned to normal – resuming her previous routine – staying in the room, lighting the stove in the morning, cooking Irene's lunch, heating water for drinks and washing.

In the late autumn, sometime in November, yet another hardship was brought into our lives. Every afternoon the Ghetto's electricity supply was cut off for two hours. Fenia and Irene would set off, shortly before it was due to be turned off, to visit the grandparents – to keep them company during the time when the Ghetto was plunged in darkness. I would slip into my bed pulling the covers tightly around me to keep out the cold, the dark, the loneliness . . .

One rainy November afternoon, when I had thus taken refuge in my bed, the covers drawn up to my chin, the door to the room opened and a young Jewish policeman appeared on the threshold. He stood there peering into the dark interior; it may have appeared to him, for there was no sound, no movement in it, that the room was empty. And then, still remaining by the door, he saw my dark hair spread on the pillow and the slight curve of my body under the covers. The gloom blurred all shapes and outlines. Momentarily, as he caught sight of me, he seemed to put aside the purpose of his call and a strange, ingratiating smile played round his lips. It made me feel uncomfortable . . . I propped myself up on my elbow and he saw the slight, childish shoulder, the small, child-like hand.

He then asked me: 'Does Joseph Fischler live here?' 'Yes,' I replied. 'Is he at work?' 'Yes, I think so.' 'Will he be home in the evening?'

'Yes, I think so.'

Neither of us was very communicative. He walked away not having asked my name; not having given any indication as to why he was making this enquiry; not saying if he would be returning . . .

Joseph and I groped and searched and racked our brains, but could not even begin to fathom the reason which had brought the policeman to our room. Joseph, a naturally sensitive boy, had become very nervous since the death-train escapade. Having a perfectly clear conscience, as we had, was not an asset in those days. One could not explain or justify one's conduct – nobody would listen. There was no law to protect us Jews. We had been condemned, wholly and irrevocably, having committed no crime, no offence, no misdemeanour, to suffer the ultimate penalty.

Our cousins and the Kalfuses, whose opinion and counsel we sought, seemed to think that it was some trifling matter. 'A young policeman, on his own, asking if you live here,' they told Joseph, 'can't be anything serious, don't worry.' But Joseph was profoundly worried. He let a day or two elapse and then, in the evening, went to the Jewish Police Headquarters, in Józefinska Street, to find out the reason for the enquiry. Neither of the two policemen on duty in the office was able to shed any light on the matter. Eventually, a senior policeman came over to speak to Joseph. He was holding a type-written letter in his hand and was well able to shed light on the matter – light blinding with terror.

'Look here,' he said, 'we have received a letter from the Kriminalpolizei at Szlak. It's your mother, Eva Fischler, whom they want to interrogate' – the very word made one's flesh crawl with fear – 'but our records show that both your parents were "re-settled" in June . . . Well, they know, and we know' – and a bitter grimace twisted his lips – 'that she can't be brought back . . . Next of kin, that's you, will have to do . . . Apparently your mother worked for a German woman, a Frau Berger, did some sewing for her . . . The woman claims that your mother is holding onto two dresses belonging to her, and she wants them back finished or unfinished. She maintains that there has been no sight of, no sign from, your mother since the summer . . . That, of course, would be right. She was 'resettled' in June, as we know . . . Do you know anything about the dresses?'

A bolt out of the blue that went sizzling through Joseph like a live high voltage wire, but he replied: 'All I know is that my mother took the two dresses with her, hoping to finish and return them to Frau Berger and to be paid'. 'Yes, I see,' replied the policeman. 'Makes perfect sense to me . . . Tell them at Szlak exactly what you've told me and it'll be all right. Nothing to worry about. We'll be in touch. It'a routine enquiry. Nothing to worry about.'

When Joseph returned, his face leached of all colour, and related the story to Kalfus, the latter's comment was; 'That's women for you. Two dresses and she's reported you to Szlak where they kick the shit out of a chap. Yeah, that's women for you.'

Joseph waited, in the grip of extreme anxiety and distress, to hear when the interrogation was to take place. But life goes on and we made the habitual, daily gestures to preserve ours until . . .

On the Friday evening of that same week, there was a knock on the door. There were only the four of us in the room, our cousins and ourselves. Fenia and Irene were taking their evening meal at the grandparents' who still observed the Sabbath. Joseph and I looked at each other chilled to the very bone with fear . . . It was Sophie who called out: 'Come in . . .' The door opened and two tall women – warmly clad, soft blond curls tumbling from under their head-scarves – entered the room. It was immediately obvious they were Aryan. 'We are Aryan. We are from the other side', one of them said. 'Have you anything to sell? We pay cash.' We were taken a little aback, but we understood from their somewhat agitated voices and movements that a speedy transaction was required. They did not wish to linger in the Ghetto.

One of the women said to Sophie: 'I do like your dressing-gown. Would you sell it?' Sophie, not batting an eyelid, replied, 'Yes, certainly.' She opened a wardrobe door, and hiding behind it, slipped off the dressing-gown and slipped on a dress. She came forward the warm, striped bed-time garment slung over her arm. 'Have you anything else?' asked the same woman. Joseph opened the door of the wardrobe and took out our Mother's heavy, black winter coat. It had once had a modest fur collar. Mamma had unpicked it and I had handed it in at 'the Fur Depot' early in the winter of 1942 . . . Parting with the coat was a formal acknowledgment that our Mother would never need it again.

Joseph and I wanted to live. We accepted, like everybody else, quietly and submissively, our plight and our pain; I never heard my brother say anything that would indicate that he felt sorry for himself. Neither of us was rebellious or hot-headed. Neither of us would, for a single moment, have considered himself or herself courageous. Yet, Joseph was. Driven by an overwhelming desire to live, we made split-second decisions, we performed split-second actions which stemmed from my brother's innate courage; both were dictated by the most perilous, life-threatening contingencies. We lived from day to day – one could not plan or think ahead. We had no family, no means – just two youngsters – a boy of nineteen and a girl of twelve. And yet, each of us seemed to be endowed with an instinct for self-preservation, for survival . . . One had to be alert and wide-awake, for the element of surprise was present in all their dealings with us. We never knew when the blow would be struck, from which direction, and with what force. Until now we had been nonentities; heads in a countless herd. It was the only way to be. Not to possess any distinguishing features; to submerge one's personality; to blend quietly and unobtrusively into the greyness of the crowd.

'The Frau Berger affair', however, had assumed proportions terrifying beyond anything we could have expected or envisaged. Joseph was being sought as an individual, with a name and a face . . . He would stand before them – a terrified, vulnerable young boy – and they would unleash their fury upon him. They would kill him. Much as my brother clung to life, it was not so much death as the savagery that terrified him. Although he did not say much on the subject, it was the thought of the savagery that haunted him day and night. Neither of us, we had acknowledged it to each other, without shame or sham, would be able to withstand brutality. We were just not made of that stern stuff.

During those few days, when Joseph was waiting to hear from the Jewish Police and when utter despair made him see, with sharp clarity and undoubted certainty, that which awaited him at the hands of the Kriminal-polizei, he called on the lady-doctor who had ministered to him after his escape from the death-train; who had washed and dressed the cuts and bruises on his face and hands, and stitched the gash in his forehead. Luminal was a poison widely used in the Ghetto – cheaper and more widely available than cyanide or strychnine . . . He explained to the doctor the predicament he found himself in. She listened, she sympathised, but she was not willing to procure what he wanted. She said to Joseph, 'You are nineteen years old, healthy and strong. You escaped from the death-train. I believe you are meant to live . . . You will survive . . .'

I did not know about the call on the doctor at the time. My brother did not tell me. It was as many as fifty years later, in the course of a conversation about those dark, far-off days – which we both remember so vividly – that he let it slip out . . .

It never rains, but it pours. The very next week a family of five moved into our room – just like that from one day to the next and not so much as 'By your leave . . .' A family of five entirely intact – the parents and three teenage children . . . We could hardly credit their good fortune. Like the Kalfuses, they were provincial Jews and total strangers to Cracow. They brought in their bundles, wads of bedding, kosher cooking pots and kitchen implements. They had no furniture. They had had to leave it behind. They spread themselves out on the floor and immediately claimed their right to the 'amenities' – first and foremost the cooking-stove.

Exceptionally swarthy and Semitic in appearance – the children looked almost Oriental and were rather attractive, especially the girl – they were, all five, singularly unfeeling, inconsiderate people. Among themselves they communicated exclusively in Yiddish. Their broken, sloppy Polish was most painful to hear. They were selfish, aggressive people with whom it was impossible to establish any form of dialogue, for others simply did not exist for them, did not count. They suffered no shortage of 'the readies' – a crude word which was constantly on their lips. Yes, they had money and they ate very well: chicken broth with butter beans or noodles, boiled chicken with vegetables, prune cake or stewed fruit and bread and tea. The mother took great care over the preparation and cooking of the food, but once on the plate they devoured it like animals.

Totally devoid of a sense of propriety, not to say shame, they performed their most personal, most intimate acts in front of others without batting an eyelid. Long gone were the days when Grandmother used to erect a screen round her invalid daughter to wash her. The only person who could keep them in check was Kalfus. Oddly enough, one look of cold contempt and total revulsion from him would make them simmer down, draw in their horns. All five went daily to work, but the mornings and evenings were hard to bear. They reigned supreme in the room when Kalfus was not there. Their name was Banach, but I came to think of them, eventually, as 'the Carpet-Baggers'.

That same week I bumped into Regina Traubb in the square. I did not know she was in the Cracow Ghetto. A woman in her late forties, she was married to my mother's cousin. They had been farmers in 'Kościelniki' and used to invite us over, to the farmhouse, when I was staying in the country with Anna and David in the summer. It seemed such a long time ago . . .

Regina Traubb was on her own. She did not know where her husband and two grown-up sons were, if they were alive. Her eyes, once piercingly blue, looked colourless, faded, as if the blue-ness had been washed away through weeping. She, too, lived in the square about three doors away from us and, yet, I had never met her before. She asked where I lived and I said: 'Here, in the square, at No. 4.' I mentioned that we had just had a rather trying family of five billeted upon us. Regina Traubb said, 'I live on the second floor, in a two-room flat. There is a couch in my room, very clean and decent, with all the bedding. The girl, a very nice girl, who had slept on it, did not return on the evening of 28 October . . . It is not being used . . . If you want to, you can sleep on it . . . You knew Natan [her husband] and my boys . . .' Her eyes filled with tears. 'It would be nice to have somebody to talk to. I don't know any of the other people in the flat.' I thanked her and we parted. I did not mention the 'Kriminalpolizei' affair. Joseph had said, 'The fewer people know about it, the better.'

A Jewish policeman came in the dead of night, when everyone was asleep, to deliver the summons to Joseph. He was to report to the Headquarters at eleven o'clock the next morning whence, accompanied by a Jewish policeman, he would be escorted to Szlak . . .

Gripped by icy cold fear because of the nearness, the grim reality of it, it was during those anguished hours of waiting for the dawn, knowing himself to be doomed, that the notion of not presenting himself at the Headquarters at all occurred to him. The idea not to answer their summons, not to accede to their request, was inconceivable, mind-boggling in its audacity, its daring – and its possible consequences . . . Of the two options, by far the greater courage was required not to submit . . .

My brother, rightly, did not confide in me. I was only a child. He did not wish to burden me. I was not aware of the very cogent analysis of the situation – I did not know what it meant to analyse a situation – carried on in his mind, nor of the images of stark horror swimming before his eyes. He had understood, he had assessed, perfectly correctly, every aspect of his tragic predicament. I only understood the isolation, the helplessness of his position, and the scorching fear they had engendered in him.

In the morning, washed, shaved, but scantily dressed for the cold, late autumn weather, for he had left his winter coat in the cattle-truck on 28 October, he walked out of the building. It was only about nine o'clock in the morning. A few steps and he was in Targova Street.

Deputy-Chief of the Jewish Police, Mr Michael Pacanower, warm and jaunty in his regulation greatcoat and peaked cap set at a rakish angle, was strolling along Targova Street digesting, no doubt, a solid breakfast. We did not know, at that time, that he was in the service of the Gestapo. Joseph went up to him and said, 'Excuse me, Mr Pacanower, my name is Joseph Fischler. I am to report to the Head-quarters at eleven o'clock for an interrogation at Szlak. I . . . to put it bluntly, I feel scared stiff . . .' Pacanower, adopting a soothing, paternal stance, replied: 'Nonsense, my boy, nonsense . . . I am familiar with your case . . . Quite straightforward . . . Nothing to worry about . . .' That did it!

Joseph returned to the room, picked up a few personal things and left. He walked briskly down Józefinska Street, to the other end from the Headquarters, entered a tenement, crossed the passage leading to the courtyard and went down a short flight of steps to a basement room. The door was opened before he had had time to knock. 'Come in, Joseph, come in.' The door closed. Joseph had gone into hiding with two friends – a father and son.

25 • Winter 1942/43

I was on my own now. Nobody felt responsible for anybody. There were very many children in the Ghetto, many much younger than myself, who had no family. I could have knocked on the door of the Ghetto Orphanage and I would have been admitted.

On 28 October the Ghetto Orphanage, in Józefinska Street, was emptied. They marched in – the armed men in green uniforms – and drove the children and the staff, looking after them, to the Square. A long procession of sad-eyed, docile children clinging to those who taught them, who looked after them, and who were now shepherding the youngest of them, 'the little ones,' walked under armed escort, the short distance from the Orphanage to the square. Although I did not see it – this, the Ghetto's most tragic procession – with my own eyes, I had heard it described, and I would not forget the fate that had befallen the Orphanage. A fresh crop of orphans replaced those taken away in October, and equally dedicated staff replaced those who had accompanied the children on their last journey . . .

I held my independence very dear and I had an innate dislike of regimentation. I was not, really, a suitable candidate for the Orphanage. I would find it very hard to knuckle down, to conform, to surrender my independence. And yet some years later I took, like a duck to water, to the cloistered, austere conditions, and close vigilance of a Scottish boarding school.

I was wary of the Orphanage for I bore in mind what had happened to it, and who was to say that the tragic events would not be repeated as, indeed, they were.

The Jewish Police came to our room time and again, at various hours of day and night – these visits were, really, like sporadic raids. They came, in number, looking for Joseph Fischler. Nobody volunteered a word of information concerning Joseph, but when they asked, directly, the answer was always the same: 'I don't know . . .' which was true. Nobody knew. After a few days and nights of

Joseph's absence, the Banach family wanted to 'requisition' his bed, but Kalfus would not so much as hear of it. He said: 'This is Joseph's bed, he may come back. We don't know.' Nor would he allow them to take over my bed when I disappeared, now and then, to sleep on the very comfortable couch in Regina Traubb's room.

We slept in the smaller of the two bedrooms. At the far end of the room, right under the window, there stood a double bed in which a young couple slept – Mr Wnuk and his companion. Mr Wnuk, who did not survive the war, was a born aristocrat. The only son of cultured, wealthy parents he was, every inch, a gentleman and strikingly handsome into the bargain. A tall, slender young man with thick fair hair, large blue eyes and fine, chiselled features; he had a heart-melting smile. Although there was not the palest suggestion of Jewishness in Mr Wnuk's appearance or manner, he was, nonetheless, the product of a strictly Orthodox home. His physical attributes and his charm rendered him quite irresistible to the ladies. But Regina Traubb who, like everybody else, had a soft spot for him felt that it was not 'nice', not 'proper' for him and a young lady, who was not his wife, to be sharing a bed. She liked to have a good grumble about 'Those two'. Still, there was a respectable distance between the bed and our two couches, which stood opposite each other. She liked to talk in the evenings. She would return from work quite exhausted, but after a wash, a rest and a glass of hot tea she would get 'a second wind' and remember, aloud, her husband, her two sons, their home, their family life . . . It did her good to talk and I liked to listen. She always shared with me a piece of bread and a pickled cucumber. She had a weakness, she admitted, for pickled cucumbers. I looked forward all day to that almost, but not quite, midnight feast!

The flat emptied in the morning. Everybody went to work. It was a cold, draughty flat with a windowless kitchen. After everyone had gone, I would scour the two rooms, the kitchen and the cupboard in the entrance hall for food, but I never found so much as a crumb or a grain of anything edible.

One day Fenia told me, for I was not in the room at the time, that a plain-clothes detective sent from Szlak had walked into the room looking for Joseph. The Jewish Police, by the Kriminalpolizei's high standards of efficiency, must have appeared, to the latter, a lamentably incompetent bunch. Szlak took the matter into their own hands by sending one of their own men to investigate the lie of the land. It must have been a galling experience for him to return to his masters empty-handed, for he met with no joy, finding a woman and a child in the room who were quite unable to help him in his enquiries.

The year 1942 – the saddest year of my life – was drawing to a close. I was alone. Times were very lean and cold. Regina Traubb, Fenia Kalfus and my cousin Sophie – each held out a helping hand to me.

I still had one relation left – Uncle Izydor – Mamma's younger brother. He, his wife and small daughter, together with his numerous in-law relations, had moved, in the autumn of 1942, into the Bochnia Ghetto. It was a very small Ghetto – just a few streets, in the poorest area of the town, had been assigned to it. As I remember it, there were no gates to cross, no form of control to submit to, in order to enter or to leave the Ghetto. Just a concentration of a few thousand Jews being overseen by the Jewish police carrying out orders from 'above'.

I visited Uncle Izydor and his family, staying with them for two or three days, several times during that autumn. They lived in a large, dilapidated bungalow, which contained several rooms – the largest of which was used, in the daytime, as a dining room – a table running the full length of it. The house was swarming with people of all ages; the whole of the vast Infeld clan (my Aunt Annie had been a Miss Infeld) seemed to have gathered under its leaky roof: elderly parents, middle-aged children with their spouses, grand-children big and small, aged aunts, uncles, cousins . . . Conditions in the bungalow were quite primitive and many of us slept at night on the rough, wooden floor, but there was food – good, nourishing, homely food. It appeared on the long dining-table three times a day – soup, noodles, potato pancakes, barley with vegetables, different varieties of beans and bread and tea.

Mr and Mrs Infeld, Uncle Izydor's parents-in-law, were in charge of the kitchen and, as I later discovered, the household budget. I saw little of my uncle and aunt, for all the able-bodied people living in the house went daily to work. Mr and Mrs Infeld spent the entire day in the kitchen cooking. He, a tall, bearded man, who was always sucking on his pipe, was gruff and taciturn. She, a plump, yellow-skinned woman dressed entirely in black, a black cotton headscarf knotted, peasant-fashion, under her chin, shouldered the burden of life with quiet acceptance. They both sat in the kitchen right next to the stove for warmth, a sack of potatoes on one side of them, an enamel basin for the peel between them, and a bucket half full of water, into which they threw the peeled potatoes, on the other side of them.

I liked spending a few days at the Infelds'. The food was good and plentiful and I had made a friend there – an elderly relation. She was a large lady, still dark-haired, very neat in her person, very mild in her manner. She was beautifully spoken, although her taste in literature, even I recognised that, was not high-brow. 'Penny-Dreadfuls' was what she read with the utmost absorption, and talked about with great enjoyment. She had an enormous stack of them, all neatly arranged in numerical order, and when she lent me one she would jot down its number, 'so as not to lose sight of it'.

I found I had another friend in the Bochnia Ghetto. It was Hannah, Aunt Josephine's sister, to whom I used to take Sunday lunch when she was imprisoned in Cracow, early in the year. I called on her during one of my sojourns with the Infeld family. She, and her two children – a girl my age and a much younger boy – received me with great warmth and affection. They were so eager and, at the same time, so sad to hear the news from Cracow. Both children cuddled up to me and Hannah kept stroking my hand whilst plying me with bread and tea. When I left, she handed me a parcel saying, 'They may come in handy . . .' It was a parcel of second-hand clothing, mostly undergarments and stockings, all spotlessly clean and well looked after. She could hardly have given me anything more precious. I never saw Hannah and her children again.

The weather was already very wintry when I paid my last visit to Bochnia. I arrived one day and the very next, just as my thoughts were turning to lunch, Mr Infeld asked me to come into the kitchen. He came straight to the point. They were finding it hard to make ends meet. His capital was dwindling. He did not expect the war to last so long. They were being as frugal as possible, but with so many mouths to feed . . . Would I leave now, straightaway, and go home to Cracow and not come back any more . . . Mrs Infeld did not look up once from her task of peeling potatoes, but a strange sound, like water gurgling in a pipe, was issuing from her eyes, nose, mouth. Mr Infeld had already fetched my things and, now, passed them to me. Hurriedly, I put them on and left the house. It was not far to the railway station. I would catch a train to Cracow. I would slip into the Ghetto – home.

A cold, sharp wind was tearing through the dingy streets. It propelled me forward, in the direction of the station. I wanted to cry so badly, so whole-heartedly that the effort of suppressing the sobs within me almost made me choke. I knew I must not draw attention to myself. I knew I must have a pleasant, carefree expression on my face. But I had never experienced such deep, such scalding humiliation before. Its taste, utterly bitter, filled my mouth, spread through my whole being.

The year 1942 slipped almost unnoticed into the year 1943. There was no thought of festivity in our hearts. The fourth winter of war came – long, cold and hungry. The Cracow Ghetto, now in the throes of death, had been whittled down to a small island, triangular in shape. Its original population, reduced by two-thirds, had come to understand that slow torment and unnatural death were its destiny. A walled-up, doomed city awaiting a fearful death in terrible anguish. But we continued to perform those everyday, habitual gestures, for it is hard to resign oneself to death when one is young and healthy and when one believes life, in spite of great hardship and sorrow, to be a very precious gift.

The Jewish police had stopped searching for Joseph. The diurnal calls and the nocturnal swoops had ceased. Joseph came out of hiding and returned to our room, to his corner in the Ghetto, for where else was he to go? He set about reorganising his life. He was still only nineteen years old. To become allocated to a solid Labour Contingent was his first priority. He succeeded. He was assigned to work in a lime quarry and we managed to keep our most immediate enemy – hunger – at arm's length for a time. We sold the last and the only object of value we still possessed – Mamma's 'Singer' sewing machine; the proceeds enabled us to keep body and soul together for a while.

I describe the following incident, as it was related to me by my brother, for I was sleeping that night at Regina Traubb's, and therefore did not witness it with my own eyes and ears.

It was well into the evening and everyone in the room at No. 4 the Square of Peace had long gone to bed, except Kalfus and his three cronies who often played cards late into the night. The four card-players were seated round the table in the centre of the room, directly under the naked electric bulb, cigarette smoke from distended nostrils and over-flowing ashtrays rising and twisting above their heads. The far corners of the room were submerged in the night's gloom and there was no sound except the sleepers' breathing, the occasional scraping of a match and the snap of one playing card against another.

205

The four players were totally absorbed in their game, when the door flew open and Spira – The Chief of the Jewish Police himself – accompanied by two of his lieutenants, burst into the room. Joseph's bed stood in the furthest, darkest corner of the room. He was instantly wide awake – his motionless, rigid body flattened against the mattress, his breath suspended. 'They have got me, this time . . .' thought Joseph. They came, no doubt, in a last, desperate attempt to exonerate themselves and to propitiate their angry masters. The three policemen approached the table and Spira rapped out to the four card-players, 'Your papers!' With swift, obliging fingers they produced their documents spreading them out on the table. A cursory glance was enough. None of the players bore the name they were looking for. The Chief strutted out. His lieutenants followed. Joseph, glued to the mattress by cold, clammy sweat, allowed the breath to leave his body. They never came again.

26 • The Conversion

I return, once more, to the Kalfus family through whose personal drama we witnessed a particularly poignant aspect of the Ghetto tragedy.

After the diabolically cruel October 'resettlement' *Aktion*, there was hardly a family left in the Ghetto that had not been torn asunder or maimed. We, the remnants, bludgeoned, stunned, licking wounds which would not heal, kept to our lairs, venturing out only when it was strictly necessary. The agony, the torment of mind seemed beyond endurance. Yet, even then, one's mood vacillated between black, incontinent despair and faint, barely glimmering hope. Perhaps, after all.

As after every 'resettlement' *Aktion*, a sizeable wedge of the Ghetto was sliced off. By the end of November 1942, there were twelve people living in our one room. Although it was large, having once been a bookbinder's workshop, it was not large enough to accommodate us all and our possessions. These we had to keep to the barest minimum, if we were not to trample upon each other in the room which, now, resembled a disorderly, makeshift hospital ward. Among the occupants was the Kalfus family – one of the few families to emerge from the October action unscathed, consisting of husband, wife, child and Mrs Kalfus's elderly parents.

The Kalfuses' chattels consisted of a double bed, a bedside cabinet and a wooden cupboard in which they kept their clothes and food supplies. The cupboard had been fitted with a special lock. Fenia, the wife, wore the key to the padlock on a length of greasy, hempen string round her neck.

The Kalfuses were an oddly assorted couple. Fenia was the only daughter of wealthy cotton-mill owners from the Bielsko region. Her husband had no background, profession or trade. He lived by his wits and seemed to be doing very well out of it. Fenia was an exceptionally ugly and ungainly woman. She possessed none of the

charms that are associated with the fair sex, nor any of the intellectual accomplishments that render plain, but intelligent, women
interesting. Tall, round-shouldered, with bulges in all the wrong
places, she shuffled, tirelessly, on her long, narrow feet, in her very
restricted territory, between the double bed and the padlocked cupboard.

I would sit on the edge of my bed contemplating Fenia's unwhole-
someness and clumsy movements as she bent down to open her
'granary'. She was about about to prepare Irene's lunch. As I
watched her, enviously, arrange the provisions on the table, I could
not prevent myself from audibly swallowing my saliva. Her motto
was, 'Nothing but the best for Irene.' She was very frugal and
sparing, however, when it came to herself. Her husband rarely ate at
home.

Her face bent over the small, communal stove, she looked, in her
spinach-green dress, like a gigantic toad patiently stirring a nourishing concoction for her little toadling.

I was only twelve, but I could not help pondering the enigma
which everyone in the room, in spite of our daily trials and tribula-
tions, tried to unravel – 'how did the Kalfuses come to be married?'
We were all agreed on one point, 'he had married her for her money;
she had married him for love.' Our sympathy lay with Fenia. She
had got a bad bargain.

Her face, if anything, was even more unattractive than her body.
Her widely-spaced, protruding teeth would not allow her to close
her mouth. The thick, mauvish lips were thus permanently apart.
Her nose broken and askew, like a boxer's, spread itself across the
best part of her face almost hiding her small, lash-less eyes. Her
thick brown hair, which could have been her crowning glory, was
unkempt and speckled with dandruff.

She was courageous and realistic; long-suffering and uncomplain-
ing. She did not bear fate a grudge. She had quietly accepted her
ugliness, her philandering husband, her frail, anaemic child.
Although she had been accustomed to a life of ease and plenty, she
had adapted herself to her present living conditions of squalor,
drudgery and complete lack of privacy, with practicality and a sort
of cheerful resignation. Nor was she insensitive to the needs and
sufferings of others. She could never bring herself to give Irene her
lunch without offering me a piece of bread and an apple or a carrot.
Sometimes, she even gave me the left-overs from Irene's lunch.

Irene spent most of the day sitting at the foot of the double bed.

She was a quiet, timid child. Her face and her large eyes, the colour of greengages, were mostly grave. She looked lonely and was an onlooker rather than a participant in the life of the room. She had never been to school and could not read or write. She liked music and was very sensitive to it. She possessed a large repertoire of Yiddish songs which she would chant to herself, in a soft, plaintive voice, all day long.

Sometimes she would come and sit by me and I would tell her about 'school' – I had received two years of primary education when the war broke out – or read her an amusing story or poem. She enjoyed this and would momentarily brighten up. The moment I had finished, she would return to the foot of her bed, like a rabbit to its warren, for that was where she felt safest. From about seven o'clock in the morning till six, or so, in the afternoon, the three of us had the run of the room to ourselves. Every one of the inhabitants of this gloomy, overcrowded room belonged to a labour contingent and went daily to work outside the Ghetto. On their return the room would become a hornets' nest. Everybody was short-tempered and tetchy, and things were said and done that people later regretted and felt ashamed of.

The moment of supreme happiness, that Irene had been, sub-consciously, waiting for all day, was nigh. A patch of colour in each cheek, fists clenched, gaze riveted to the door – she waited for her father to enter the room. In one wild leap she would cover the distance between the bed and the door where he stood, arms out-stretched, waiting for her. He would catch her and hold her close to him whilst she, pressing her face against his and twining her arms round his neck, would snuggle up to him, kiss him, sniff at him, nuzzle against him all the while squealing with delight. Kalfus would acknowledge his wife's existence with a slight nod of the head in her direction.

We all liked the look and the smell and the touch of Irene's father. Our hearts were oppressed with misery past and misery to come. Our minds were clogged with dreams of food and escape. The stench of squalor and hunger clung to our tattered clothing. The walls which sheltered us were grimy and dank. The very air on this side of the barbed-wire seemed tainted and clammy. Thus, the sight of a man like Kalfus gladdened our eyes, distracted our minds, made us remember times and places . . . He was so incongruous with his surroundings that I used to think: 'if I close my eyes, he will disappear; he is a mirage evoked by my starved, parched senses . . .'

209

Kalfus almost never dined at home. He would remove his coat, silk-lined inside out, and carefully place it over the bedstead. He possessed a fine physique. He was tall, well-proportioned and, under present conditions, shamelessly healthy. His grey eyes sparkled; his skin was fresh and tightly drawn; his well-shaped head with curly, closed cropped hair made one think of a Roman warrior. When he smiled, which, unlike his little daughter, he did often, he revealed two rows of strong, gleaming teeth. His clothes were beautifully cut and pressed; his linen of fine quality and immaculately laundered. He smelt of cleanliness, of woods in autumn, of life itself . . .

His wallet always bulged with a thick wad of banknotes. We all assumed that he was some kind of a financial wizard; much speculation went on in the room as to his source, or sources, of income, but it was all pure guess-work. The general verdict was that Kalfus was 'cagey and close'. He certainly never volunteered or imparted any information regarding his person or activities. Being 'an unknown quantity' constituted, in fact, one of his charms. It was, nonetheless, in the bookbinder's workshop that he showed his most human and softest spot – his love for Irene.

He would sit down on his bed with Irene on his lap, his arm round her shoulders and whilst she nestled comfortably against him, give himself, body and soul, to entertaining her. He possessed an inexhaustible fund of Yiddish stories and jokes. He had a homely, warm manner of telling a story and always succeeded in making his daughter burst into peals of laughter. He would sit by her whilst she ate her supper and paint pictures with words of the places he and 'his little princess' would visit when the war was over. 'A boat gently bobbing upon the calm blueness of a lake; a golden, sun-baked strand. The fresh, minty smell of the eucalyptus tree. Enchanted castles and mysterious caves. Express trains thundering through continents; majestic ships gliding across oceans. There is a country called Palestine . . .' And the yearning in his voice was such that it made one catch one's breath. 'And music, Daddy, will there be music?' 'Oh yes, darling, there will be music everywhere we go. Daddy will see to it.' When she was ready for sleep, he would tuck her up in bed and kiss her again and again saying, 'Daddy has to go out to attend to some important business.'

'The important business' lived within a stone's throw of his own abode; his mistress was the very antithesis of Fenia. Slender, but alluringly shaped, with lovely soft eyes and dark, glossy hair she

210

was all woman – charm, grace, subtle, but irresistible, magnetism. Fenia, like everybody else in the room, knew about her, but closed her eyes to her, as she had done to many another in the past.

Come what may, the Kalfuses were inextricably bound together. They were governed by an all-demanding, inexorable force – their love for Irene. There was no sacrifice, no hardship, no burden they would not undertake if it ensured Irene's happiness and, above all, survival.

Kalfus would return home about midnight, produce a pack of cards from his pocket and he and his three cronies would sit down at the, now, cleared table to play. They would tie a very primitive shade, made of crumpled, plum-coloured tissue paper, round the naked bulb – their only gesture of consideration towards the other inhabitants of the room – and embark on a game of bridge. The game went on, and on, and on, and there was no end of complaints and grumbles – to which the quartet, passionately absorbed in the game, turned a deaf ear – about not being able to get 'a wink of sleep'. It often seemed that Kalfus went on playing in order to postpone the moment when he would have to lie down by his wife's graceless, uninviting body.

We were well into winter now. The Ghetto had been divided into two sectors – 'A' and 'B'. In 'A' lived the young, the healthy, the able – those who could work. In 'B' lived the aged, the infirm, the orphans.

In the meantime, in Plaszow, a large, undeveloped suburb of Cracow, a Labour Camp, later to become a Concentration Camp, was fast taking shape. It rose up, it spread out, it was being overlooked by watchtowers, it was being encircled by barbed-wire. We knew that the liquidation of the Ghetto was imminent – a matter of months, a matter of weeks . . . The inhabitants of Sector 'A' would be transferred to the Labour Camp; those of Sector 'B' would be despatched on a journey of no return . . .

The Kalfuses started holding long, whispered conversations punctuated by words like: 'Irene', 'safety', 'Catholicism', 'kind people', 'Irene', 'money', 'Aryan', 'good home', 'Irene', 'baptism', 'prayers', 'jewellery', 'nice family'; 'Irene', 'preparation', 'dollars'; 'Irene . . .' We all knew something was afoot.

One evening in December 1942 (the Ghetto was not to be liquidated till March 1943) Kalfus, after coming home and going through the usual evening ritual with Irene, produced a small, thick book bound in white satin, with gold-rimmed pages and a discreet cross embedded in the snowy cushion of its cover. When Kalfus and Irene knelt down by the bed and he opened the prayer book a deathly hush fell over the room. We all froze in our tracks, just like the characters in the famous fairytale.

Whilst Kalfus was very slowly and distinctly reciting prayers as unfamiliar to him as they were to his child, Fenia sat at the table, her back to the bed, the man and the child. She had planted her elbows on the table and had covered her face with her knobbly, red hands. Although her whole body was being cruelly racked by suppressed sobs not a sound, not a whimper escaped her; only the tears, side-tracked, as it were, coursed down her chin and fell, like pure crystalline raindrops, onto her arms, onto her dress . . . Kalfus had in the meantime, with Irene repeating the strange words after him, gone through The Our Father, The Hail Mary, The Credo.

Irene's religious education and general grooming for the day when she would leave her parents, to be placed with an Aryan family, went on for about a month. Towards the end of January 1943, she was judged to be ready for the transfer. She had stopped chanting Yiddish songs; she knew all her prayers off by heart; she was able to recite, parrot-fashion, without a whit of conviction, the story about her dead parents and her new uncle, auntie and cousins.

She was a child who made very few demands on those around her. She loved her mother and adored her father. She was so gentle, docile and placid that one was hardly aware of her presence. In the last month, however, that is, since the beginning of her conversion to Catholicism and once the realisation that she would live away from her parents had taken root in her mind, she withdrew into her shell completely. All life seemed to have seeped out of her. The tiny triangle of her face grew paler and smaller still. Only the expression of total incomprehension and mute terror in her sad, old eyes gave one some idea of the turmoil in her mind and the anguish in her heart.

We could not bear to look any of the Kalfus family in the face. The agony they were undergoing was excruciating. Each of them separately and all three together were being crucified.

Our days in the Ghetto were numbered; mine particularly. I was only twelve and small and childish in appearance for my age. I knew, and so did my brother, who was older and qualified for Sector 'A', that I would never get transferred to the Labour Camp at Plaszow. It would be Sector 'B' for me . . . We had lost all our family; we were as poor as church mice; we had nothing and nobody, but each other. Now the last thread was about to snap. I envied Irene; she had parents and grandparents who loved her, who cherished her; they were making preparations for her escape and survival. They had the wherewithal with which to pay for such luxuries. She would live . . . I, too, wanted to live!

For days Fenia had been getting her things ready. She had made her two very pretty new frocks with generous hems 'to allow for growth'. On Irene's last evening in the Ghetto, the inmates of the bookbinder's workshop were strangely silent and subdued. We had all got to love Irene. She was the youngest occupant of the room; also, the most innocent and the most vulnerable. The Ghetto had not sullied her spirit; it had remained perfectly pure in spite of what she saw and heard daily. She epitomised, for everyone in the room, the tragedy of the Jewish children.

Fenia, who was almost distraught at the thought of the parting which the morning would bring, managed to appear calm, even cheerful, on the surface. Everything was ready for Irene's departure. For once the three of them sat down to an evening meal together. Somehow the food was not going down. They did not seem to be able to swallow. It was offered to me, and sharing it with my brother, I made very short work of it; though I felt, on this occasion, ashamed of my insatiable appetite.

Fenia poured a saucepanful of warm water into a basin. She undressed Irene and stood her in it. Carefully and tenderly she soaped the little white body, caressing with her fingers every fold, dent and crease in it. Kalfus was warming the towel by the stove. He wrapped it round his child and started drying her delicately, lovingly, his fingers lingering over her small body as if he, too, wanted to retain its shape and feel in his hands forever.

Early the following morning, Irene was smuggled out of the Ghetto and placed with an Aryan family.

Kalfus hardly came home at all now. There was no longer any need for preserving appearances. Fenia, her eyes puffy and red from crying, all life and colour drained from her face and body, was uglier than ever. Time hung heavy on her hands. Her grief was almost palpable. She would either spend hours fingering and fondling the various objects the child had left behind, or sit at the table, her gaze vacant, her whole being numbed by pain and sorrow, staring into space.

A fortnight went by. We were in the middle of February; the Ghetto would be liquidated in a month's time, although we did not know this. Irene was hardly ever mentioned. The line between life and death had become so fine as to be hardly discernible. Life on the other side of the barbed-wire seemed as beautiful and desirable, as it was distant and unattainable.

In the third week of February, Kalfus returned from work holding Irene by the hand. Fenia, when she saw her child, gave a sob which contained all the mother-grief since the beginning of creation. She knelt down before the child and clasped her to her breast. Their faces pressed against each other they wept and their hot, unstemmed tears mingled. Irene looked very wan and thin. Her face was as white and transparent as the Host which the priest places on the tongue of a communicant. She had undergone a gruelling ordeal. She had no words with which to describe it. Three whole weeks among total strangers. She was very tired and soon fell asleep. Fenia and Kalfus sat on the edge of the bed gazing at the peacefully sleeping, evenly breathing child. Fenia knew her husband. She knew that he had been dealt a mortal blow. Timidly, she covered his white, well-kept hand with her rough, work-worn one. Their eyes met and their thoughts were one. Wordlessly, they acknowledged to each other that their child was doomed.

Kalfus opened the grip which contained every single item, neatly folded, that Irene had taken with her, as well as a foolscap envelope packed tight with dollar bills. And a handkerchief, its corners knotted together, containing a handful of jewellery. Fastened to one of Irene's frocks was a note written in a crude, untutored hand on a page torn out of a child's exercise book. Irene's 'auntie', a simple, honourable woman, wrote to say: '. . . that it broke her heart to watch the child waste away. All day long she sat on her bed crooning softly to herself in a strange, foreign tongue. She ate less than a little fledgling bird. She was returning all the money and jewellery . . .'

The Ghetto was now but a handful of faintly glowing embers, which would soon turn to ashes. The Kalfuses resumed their 'pre-conversion' mode of life. Kalfus still played with his little daughter in the evenings, but his stories and jokes sounded flat. His eye would become dewy. His voice would quaver. He would get lost in mid-sentence. His vitality, briskness and self-assurance were almost visibly ebbing away. His child no longer knew how to laugh; some inner mechanism seemed to have broken down within her. Sometimes she would smile – a forlorn, mysterious smile – to please her daddy; a smile compounded of the most refined suffering. Her father never again mentioned what he and his 'little princess' would do when the war was over.

The Ghetto liquidation action began on 13 March 1943. Most of the Ghetto's children perished in that action. A 'privileged' handful, Irene Kalfus among them, was transferred to the Camp at Plaszow. At what price? I do not know.

There was a *'Kinderheim'* in the Camp. It had a charming garden. The children themselves tended the flowers and the shrubs. Fourteen months had gone by since the children's arrival at the Camp. It was the month of May; the garden would soon be at its best, a blaze of colour, a bouquet of delicate fragrance.

Fenia and Kalfus were already dead.

On 13 May 1944 the Camp children were rounded up and escorted to an isolation barrack.

On the bright, sunny morning of 14 May whilst the inmates of the Camp were standing to attention in the 'parade' ground and the loudspeakers were pouring forth a then popular, sentimental song – 'Alles geht vorüber, alles geht vorbei . . . nach dem Dezember kommt wieder ein Mai . . .' a lorry drew up in front of the isolation barrack. The last of the Cracow Jewish children, Irene Kalfus among them, were led out and helped to climb into the vehicle. They were driven to the train standing on the Camp spur-line.

The journey from Plaszow to Auschwitz was only a short one.

27 • The Sewer

It is March 1943. The once bright-burning flame that was the Cracow Jewish Community has been stamped out forever. The Cracow Ghetto, now in the last days of its two-year agony, is like a guttering candle whose pale flame vacillates – it rises, it dips again; it provides neither warmth nor light. It is dying.

On Friday afternoon – 12 March – Fenia and Irene went to the grandparents', who continued to observe the ritual of the Sabbath, to share their evening meal with them.

On Friday evening – 12 March – Mrs Banach placed two candles on the table – a hush fell over the room. We bowed our heads in thought and remembrance. She lit the candles and covered her face with her hands. From behind those hands issued a prayer, a lament . . .

On the evening of 12 March I left our room at No. 4 saying to Joseph: 'I am off . . .' and walked the very short distance to Regina Traubb's flat. It was already dark, and I saw no one in the streets. As usual, she shared a modest supper with me, and we talked for a while before going to sleep. Neither of us mentioned the Ghetto, the present or the future. Although the word 'liquidation' was being bandied about, and I understood the meaning of it in a sense – I knew, for example, that when a factory was liquidated, it ceased to function, to employ people and to produce its wares – both of us, as if by tacit agreement, turned to the past. We talked about that other world, the one that was so fresh in our minds, the one that we had been part of, the one that now appeared as 'Paradise Lost'. And then we bid each other 'goodnight'. The room was very quiet. The March night very dark. I was warm and comfortable on the young woman's couch. I had never seen her, but I remembered what Regina Traubb had said about her and I knew that she had gone to her death on 28 October . . . I closed my eyes and went to sleep on her couch.

When I awoke on Saturday, 13 March, there was not a sound in

216

the flat. In our room, Mr Wnuk and his companion were still fast asleep, as was Regina Traubb. I lay there, not moving, relishing the warmth and comfort of the bed. There was not much incentive for getting up. There was no breakfast to look forward to . . . My couch faced, as did Regina Traubb's, the curtainless window. It was a grey, dismal morning. It was drizzling.

Drops of rain, as tiny as pin-heads, were silently shivering against the window-pane. I always had a book under my pillow; I had one today – a poetry book – but the light was not good enough to read by . . .

A woman, a stranger, totally unhinged, flew into the flat shrieking in blood-curdling tones: 'We are surrounded . . . We are surrounded . . .' and flew out again like a bird of ill-omen. Mr Wnuk and his companion were already kneeling on their bed, their faces turned towards the window. Regina Traubb and I moved with the speed of light towards the window, and squeezed into the narrow gap between the foot of the bed and the wall, pressing our faces against the rain-bespattered window. The view from that window was of the finest – a Royal Box at the opera . . . It stretched, before our eyes, over the entire Square of Peace, right up to the barbed-wire perimeter and beyond it. On the outside, but close to the bristling partition, facing the Ghetto, facing the Square – the green-uniformed, steel-helmeted, rifle-carrying troops, tall and straight, were to be seen perfectly clearly. '. . . it's the liquidation, it's the liquidation . . .'

They had caught us napping, literally, for as a grey, chilly dawn was breaking over Cracow, a lively division of SS officers, ably supported by Ukrainian and Latvian auxiliaries – men who could be counted upon, men who would not baulk at the task before them – goose-stepped across streets from which the shadows of night were only just receding, and the echo of their rhythmic footsteps rang the death knell for men, women and children . . . In semi-darkness, they threw a cordon around the tiny area of the Ghetto whilst its population slept. As Cracow church bells began to toll calling the faithful to mass, to prayers, they took up their positions for a hard day's toil – the slaughter of the innocent . . .

I do not know how I came to be dressed, but the next thing I remember is leaning out of the window looking down into the street and there walking along the pavement was my brother, Joseph. I yelled down: 'Józek, Józek . . .' He looked up and, seeing my face at the window, stopped. I remember, very distinctly, racing down the

217

two flights of stairs my feet hardly touching the ground. 'Józek, Józek?' I gasped out, and he answered: 'It's the liquidation, it's the end . . .' There were people scurrying about close to the tenements, close to the square, but there were no Germans except for the tightly drawn ring by the perimeter, but the whole of the Square of Peace stood between us and them . . .

Joseph and I tarried in front of the doorway from which I had just emerged for a minute or two, not knowing what to do, which way to turn. Then, not saying a word, but of like mind, we turned back to go to our room at No. 4.

We entered the room and found it empty – its inmates having left in a hurry to be with their Labour Contingents – the tell-tale signs of abrupt leave-taking were everywhere; the unmade beds, the scattered clothing, the half-eaten food, the half-drunk tea, personal belongings abandoned . . . But the most material, witness-bearing evidence of life having been severed from one breath to the next was the cooking stove in the right hand corner of the room. On coming in we automatically turned towards it – not only was it a source of warmth on this raw March morning, but the several saucepans standing upon it contained food. Neither of us had a watch, but it must have been around midday, for the Banachs' family lunch was not only fully cooked, it was over-cooked. The stove was hot, but not red-hot; the food was hot but not scalding. I lifted a lid and there was the chicken-broth. The bird itself – its legs sticking out of the golden liquid – so tender that the meat was coming away from the bone. Like two famished predators fallen upon a carcass, to strip it clean, we tore at the succulent meat with our fingers and our teeth, stuffing it into our mouths, barely chewing, swallowing whole large pieces of it. Then I lifted another lid, and there were the butter-beans cooked to perfection – soft and plump and sweet. We fished them out with our fingers pushing them into our mouths. Sated, for once, we left the room not giving it, or its contents a second glance . . .

On coming out of the tenement we turned right and holding hands proceeded along Targova Street. The Ghetto's entire population, driven out of doors by uncertainty and fear, seemed to have assembled in the Józefinska Street thoroughfare. It presented a blood-curdling sight. It was packed, jam-tight, with a terror-convulsed human tide – surging and riding up and down the thoroughfare – wild and all-engulfing. Joseph and I were sucked in by it and we rode with it up and down, up and down the street. And there, on the right hand-side pavement, two young SS officers – calm, unaffected – were standing shooting blindly into the boiling human tide. Driven by sheer terror, the tide swept down the thoroughfare again and just as it had sucked us in, spat us out. We were in Krakusa Street, the upper reaches of it, closest to the Vistula. It was quiet and deserted.

We saw at the top of Krakusa Street, about three yards away from the red brick, crenellated Ghetto wall, a group of people crouching round some object . . . We approached. It was a man hole. The cover had been removed and was lying on the ground at the side of it. Men and women were disappearing down the man hole one after another . . . We understood, instantly, that this was a route of escape . . . I recognised two persons squatting round the edge of the man hole – a widow, whose husband had been my Father's friend, with her young daughter, Danuta, a child of eight or nine.

Some man holes are cylindrical; this one was square. Some man holes have steps leading down; this one had none. The sewer was well underground; the leap was deep. When our turn came, Joseph jumped down without a moment's hesitation, held up his arms for me to jump into and I leapt in. I felt my knee being ripped by a metal hook sticking out of the man hole wall, but it was nothing . . . I felt no pain. Joseph caught me, set me down on the narrow, stone ledge – the sewer floor. We moved immediately – I in front, Joseph behind me, following the line of people ahead of us, and already a line was forming behind us . . . The further we got away from the open man hole, the darker it became. Progress was slow. We were carefully stepping along the right-hand ledge of the sewer. It was narrow and greasily, moistily slippery . . . There was not room enough on the ledge to put both feet down one alongside the other. One foot in front of the other was how we moved forward.

The sewer – a narrow, still stream filled with dense, black matter like melted tar – I do not remember being conscious of a stench – was caught between the two narrow ledges and almost on a level with them. It lapped the ledges, and our feet, leaving them wet and slippery. Every so often one lost one's footing on the ledge and one's foot slipped into the thick, sticky gunge of the stream. I do not remember anyone speaking, not even whispering. We moved forward in darkness, our senses stretched by it, not knowing if we would see the sky and the light of day again.

I remember only one thought, a kind of prayer, really, spinning round and round in my head, 'Dear God, if we come out of here alive, I'll always be good . . .' A promise which, sadly, I have not kept. I do not know how long we had been in the sewer when a narrow sliver of daylight sliced the darkness. The moving file came to a stop and a message travelled from one person to the next, 'We have come to a man hole . . .' The file stood stock still whilst a man climbed the flight of steps – there were steps this time – to the top, placed his hands, palms up, under a man hole cover and cautiously, soundlessly lifted it up just enough to peer out and find our bearings. He soon replaced it, just as cautiously, and returned to his position in the file. The word travelled down again: 'We are outside, but close to the Ghetto, it is too risky . . .' The file set in motion again. The water squelched in my shoes. My feet, my legs, the lower part of my body were soaking wet . . . My mind registered the fact, and dismissed it as of no importance. I felt no discomfort. 'Dear God, if only . . .'

I do not know how long we were in the sewer altogether – maybe an hour, maybe two . . . It seemed a long time. I continued to put one foot in front of the other and to follow the person in front of me. I cannot say, today, if it was a man or a woman. It was not a child. The only other child whom I remember seeing in the sewer was Danuta, but she and her mother were well ahead of us. We continued, single file, to move forward. After a time, a shaft of grey light filtered, again, into the pitch-black darkness. Another man hole. Again the file froze. Again there were steps. Quietly, cautiously a man climbed up. At first he lifted the cover just a crack. But he remained at the top of the steps for some minutes, moving, inaudibly, the cover away from the man hole. A stream of pale-grey light poured into the sewer. The word went round. 'We are in Zabłocie . . . It is safe to come out . . .' Zabłocie, as we knew, was well outside the Ghetto walls. It had been the same long, dark tunnel from the beginning to the end of the journey, and now there was light, natural light, at the end of the tunnel . . .

Silently, on tip toe, one after another, we climbed the flight of steps. A dense, cold drizzle fell on our faces from the pale-grey, overcast sky – an endless stretch of it above our heads . . . The rain-soaked air, so clean, so sharp, like a balm to our nostrils, to our lungs – was there – for everyone . . . 'Dear God . . .'

The man hole in Zabłocie, through which we emerged, was situated next to a disused railway line. There was not a soul about except us – a small group of drenched, slime-covered Jews – perhaps

as many as thirty. I cannot be sure . . . The Jews vanished so quickly
that one minute they were there, the next they had gone . . .

The air, the rain, the wind were pungent with the odour of
the Vistula, as we stood there, Joseph and I, saying a brief, unsenti-
mental good-bye. He had to cross the whole of Cracow to reach the
lime quarry night hut . . . I was on my own, but he had led me out.
He had kept faith.

28 • On My Own

It must have been early afternoon when the handful of us, Jews – men and women – drenched, covered in slime, shivering with fear and cold spilled out of the sewer through the manhole in Zabłocie. It had all happened with such stunning rapidity and such paralysing, visceral terror, that I did not fully realise or appreciate that I had only been a hair's breadth from death . . . I was twelve years old. I could not imagine myself dead . . .

We had scattered so fast. Everyone made off, speedily and unobtrusively. My brother had gone. I was on my own. I had suddenly become a criminal through my very desire to live. I made my way along the muddy, unmade road – on the left a row of shabby, mean dwellings; on the right the Vistula hissing and foaming angrily, its tumbling waters swollen with winter's ballast of snow and ice. I had to cross the Third Bridge and only then would I leave behind the proximity of the Ghetto, and the horror that was being perpetrated in it; having crossed it I meandered along Starowiślna Street. There were people walking along its pavements, briskly, purposefully. They had a family, a home to go to. But I? I was on the run. A fugitive from justice. My shoes were soaked right through. The black gunge sloshing and squelching around in them. My stockings, panties, the skirt of my frock were clinging, sticking damply to my skin. I was cold. The icy drizzle falling from the sky was as sharp as pinpricks.

I glimpsed, on the opposite pavement of Starowiślna Street, Mrs Banaszek and lagging a good few paces behind her, her teenage son. They, too, had emerged from the sewer. They, too, like my brother, worked at the lime quarry and were hoping to reach the night hut without mishap. I knew the parents and the boy. They were well-to-do business people. Mrs Banaszek – a tall, powerfully-built woman, usually heavily made-up – was very Semitic in appearance – both the thick, coarse, black hair and the large crooked nose were unmistakable. And her son strongly resembled her. Mrs Banaszek was now swaddled in a voluminous headscarf. It covered her head and most of her face, ostensibly to protect her from the cold and rain, almost like a yashmak. The boy, too, had pulled the visor of his cap well over his eyebrows and, like his mother, had buried his face in a muffler. Mrs Banaszek's handbag was dangling from her arm. I thought to myself, 'Goodness, she must have so much money in it and I don't have one złoty on me. What am I going to do?'

I turned right off Starowiślna Street and soon found myself walking along Kopernika Street – the street of hospitals, surgeries, medicine. Here, doctors and nurses fought to save life or to make it bearable. 'Ah me, they are slaughtering my people . . .' But who would believe it here, in these deserted, peaceful streets where it was customary to walk soundlessly, to keep one's voice down to a whisper out of consideration for other people's suffering, other people's pain?

Leaving Kopernika Street, I realised that I had, instinctively, taken the route leading to the 'Officers' Village' where I had once lived with my parents and brothers. I had reached the tall wrought-iron gates of the Old Cemetery in Rakowicka Street. To reach the Village, I would have to turn right opposite the Gates. But I knew the Village was out of bounds to me. And I could not think of anyone in it on whose door I might knock asking for shelter, for help . . . To go there would be courting very grave danger. I shuffled past the New Cemetery, towards Olsza – a suburb next door to the Village where my father's family and a number of Jewish friends had lived in the early 1940s.

There had been a sizeable Jewish Community in Olsza. They were all dead – their ashes scattered to the four winds . . . But I felt safer, more hopeful about Olsza. I crossed the creaking, wooden bridge over the 'Białucha' river, more of a stream, really, than a river, and found myself in Olsza proper – a poor, working class outer suburb of Cracow. It was late afternoon; it was still drizzling – a dreary, miserable day . . . But what struck me as I trudged along the unmade road, by the shallow, winding 'Białucha', was the quietude, the tranquillity, the stillness of the suburb. It filled one's being. It penetrated one to the very bone like the cold and the gloom. Not like the boiling, stampeding, howling Ghetto in which I had woken this morning . . .

There was a grocer's shop in Gdyńska Road, run by a young Pole. The Jews used to buy their groceries from him. He was well-disposed and helpful, always cheerful and smiling. I entered the

223

shop. I am not quite sure what I had in mind, but he and his wife were nice, kind people. He was busy serving from behind the counter, but he noticed and recognised me instantly, although daylight was waning. I stood quietly against the back wall. I felt scooped out physically and emotionally – so weary, so cold. The grocer continued to serve the two or three customers in the shop, but kept glancing at me. When they had gone, he came over. He was a nice-looking young man, healthy and clean. Having looked me up and down, his gaze returned to, and remained on, my shoes and stockings. An expression of utter repugnance came over his face. He motioned, with his head, towards the door, as one might towards a filthy, importuning beggar or a mangy stray dog . . . I crept out. It was piercingly cold; the air as sharp as a whip.

There, at the bottom of the paved pathway leading from the shop to the road, stood a man. Although daylight was dwindling, I fully recognised him as, I believe, he did me. We knew each other by sight. Everybody in Olsza knew him. He was a man in his fifties – tallish with a rugged face and light, clear eyes. He was bare-headed, his hair greying. He was known to be a bit simple. And maybe he was . . . I think, if anything, he was a little too friendly in his eagerness to be treated, to be accepted, as one of the community in which he lived.

'Don't be frightened, girlie, I've never hurt anybody . . .' The voice was low, timid, the speech a little mangled. 'Don't be frightened . . . Are you in trouble, girlie? I live close by . . .' His home was a ground floor room. He pushed the door open. The room was warm. Very warm. There were two single beds in it – one at each end, and a small cylindrical stove, almost red-hot, with a pile of chopped up wood by it in a corner. It was nearly dark outside. He went in and lit a candle. An enormous, shifting shadow appeared on the wall. 'Come in, girlie . . . It's warm . . . Don't be afraid . . .'

I went in and closed the door behind me. There was no chair in the room. I went and stood over by the window. He said: 'Sit down, girlie . . .' I sat down on the edge of the bed furthest away from the stove.

I had lived in the Ghetto for two years. I knew all about relations between a man and a woman – from the most sublime to the most sordid. I was outside that orbit. I was a child. I was not frightened of him in that way, I don't think – my imagination, my understanding could not encompass these things in relation to myself – but I was nonetheless petrified. Rigid with fear.

He had some provisions on a shelf. He filled a mug from the kettle on the stove and flavoured the boiling water with a spoonful of jam. He brought the mug over to me. He then sat down on his bed by the stove. 'I've got some bread here on the shelf. I'll cut you a slice.' I shook my head. My vocal chords would not, could not, function. I closed my hands round the mug trying to warm them against its sides. I sipped the scalding liquid very slowly, through clenched teeth – unable to unclamp them.

He drew an enamel basin from under his bed, filled it with hot water from the kettle on the stove, added some cold water from the bucket, tested it with his hand and, judging it right, brought it over to where I was sitting, placed a sliver of laundry soap and a greyish cloth by it and said, 'I'll be off now . . .' He left the room.

Nobody, ever, has done me as great a courtesy as that man did on the evening of 13 March 1943. I had more than finished my ablutions when he returned. The water in the basin was black – a layer of earthy sediment at the bottom. He said not a word, but picked up the basin and went out to empty it. He refilled it with warm water and again brought it over to me saying, 'There's a washing line above the stove' – a length of string stretched from one wall to the next – 'Your washing'll be as dry as bone by the morning.'

I knelt down by the basin and, with my back turned to the man, I rinsed my stockings as best I could. I cannot, to this day, describe my feelings, except that my body was being torn apart by inner anguish and the need to sob my heart out. He went on talking: 'That's a good pair of shoes, that is . . . You want to look after them. I'll put them by the stove, not too near, mind . . . They'll be nice and dry in the morning. You'll be all right, girlie . . . I'll clean them for you . . . A speck of cart-wheel grease. You'll be all right, girlie. There's always work to be found . . . There's always work for willing hands . . . You can go into service . . . And the farmers'll be taking on casual labour now that spring's nearly here. Mind you, they'll lay you off in the autumn. The cows'll soon have to be taken out to pasture; weeding to be done; lots of jobs around the farmhouse; babies to be minded. The Lord never abandons an orphan. He's got a soft spot for them orphans.'

I do not know the man's name and if I ever did know it, I have erased it, perhaps very consciously, from my mind. But the images and the sounds of that dark, cold March evening – the crackling stove, the guttering candle, the man's poorly enunciated speech drifting towards me have remained with me . . .

Many years later, when I had the good fortune to be a student in London, I came across a play by Jean-Paul Sartre entitled *La P . . . Respectueuse*. In a small American town a Negro is fleeing from injustice . . . The only person in the town to show him humanity, to offer him shelter in the hour of his greatest need, is the local prostitute. I, too, was shown humanity and offered shelter, in the hour of my greatest need, by the 'Simple Man' of a Cracow suburb – Olsza.

29 • Easter 1943

Situated on a minor tributary of the Vistula, 'Mogiła' – for many years now 'Nova Huta' – was a village of about 300 inhabitants. It nestled in a shallow hollow, its homesteads and outbuildings dappling the verdant countryside with pale, washed out smudges of red, gold and grey.

A fairly prosperous village, lying in the shadow of Cracow, it could boast of such amenities as a school, a church, a co-operative store and much to my terror, a police station.

It was in this village that I found shelter in the early spring of 1943. The time of the year was propitious. It was in spring that the farmers took on casual labour; it was in the autumn that they dismissed it. My mind did not run that far ahead; I had learnt to live for the day. I knocked on many doors offering my services, as was the custom, as an itinerant farm-hand, a child-minder, a general dogsbody. The farmer and his wife would appraise me, shrewdly, at a glance. It was quickly borne upon me that my size was against me. They were looking for brawn, a commodity I sadly lacked. I was slight and pale and undernourished. I did not even look my twelve years. If only I had been tall and strapping, with rosy cheeks and large, capable hands . . .

It was a raw March day; a cold, dense drizzle had set in; my jacket was soaked right through and I shivered with cold and fear as I trudged along the sludgy, rutted lanes. A burning-hot tear slid down my nose. I was feeling very tired, hungry and heavy-hearted when, at last, I was invited inside a farmhouse. Mistress Kucharczyk was on her own; her husband and daughter had gone to the mill. She asked no questions beyond my name, age and where I came from. I added that I was an orphan, which was true, and she nodded her head in compassionate understanding. She glanced at my down-at-heel, mud-caked shoes and said I could sit down. She did not even ask if I was hungry, but cut a thick slice of bread from a round home-baked loaf and poured some milk into a mug and offered them to me. Whilst I ate and drank, which I tried to do not too voraciously, we took stock of each other.

She was tall and gaunt, and seemed very old to me. Her face had a greenish tinge to it. She was suddenly seized by a fit of coughing and averted her face to spit into a rag. Her breast was racked by a violent, raucous cough which lasted some minutes, and which left her perspiring and breathless. There was a tiny scarlet bead in the corner of her mouth. She said she was not well and would be glad to have a 'girlie' around the house to help with the work. I could stay.

The old farmer and Kasia, the daughter, returned at dusk. They, too, seemed to welcome my presence. Kasia asked me to come with her to see to the livestock. She showed me round the byre and I watched her prepare the animals' fodder. She measured out, mashed, mixed, watered-down, gingered-up and filled the troughs. Her movements were quick and sure and I watched them with a hawk's keen eye; I wanted to learn and learn fast. She carried a sort of hurricane lamp around with her. The flame was screened from the wind and draught by a fine wire-mesh going all round it. She impressed upon me, time and again, how important it was to keep the lamp well away from the straw and hay. When the cows, pigs and poultry had been comfortably settled for the night we returned to the farmhouse. The farmer had, in the meantime, seen to the horses.

The evening meal was on the table and a place had been set for me as if I were one of the family. We had borscht and boiled potatoes. I had never before, nor since, eaten such delicious potatoes. They just crumbled and melted on one's tongue, and one could have as many as one wanted. Afterwards Kasia and I washed up and put the utensils away in the dresser.

The family motto seemed to be 'Early to bed, early to rise . . .' One reasons for this being that paraffin was hard to come by and very dear. During our rounds and the washing-up operation, I greatly wanted to ask Kasia where I would sleep, but I did not dare, in spite of her friendliness. I was frightened that I might have to sleep, on my own, in the barn or shed. The mistress, as if reading my thoughts, said that I would sleep in 'the best room' where she and Kasia slept. The farmer fetched a generous armful of creamy, rustling straw and spread it in one corner of the room, alongside the wall on the other side of which stood the long, old-fashioned cooking-range. It kept the wall lovely and warm all night long. The mistress gave me a couple of rugs to cover myself with. They were a bit threadbare with age and use, but soft and snug around my body and inside it – a feeling of such blessed repleteness as I had not known for years. At the last moment the door creaked and the farm mongrel slid in. He made straight for my palliasse and curled himself, at my very feet, into a ball of warm, living shagginess.

The Kucharczyks were simple, good people. They treated me as one of the family and never asked me to do work which was beyond my physical strength. The mistress had taken to me and looked upon me not only as a help, but also as a companion, in spite of the disparity in age. She thought me sensible and quick to learn.

I had struck lucky in this, my first venture at keeping 'adrift' on my own, for my assets were meagre. Blue eyes, straight nose and speech in which there was not the slightest hint of a Yiddish intonation. My most outstanding asset – one that had so often landed me in trouble with my parents and teachers, but that was in another world, in another lifetime – was the ability to invent, if necessary on the spur of the moment, water-tight stories. The Ghetto had provided excellent learning ground in that respect, and had offered no end of opportunities for perfecting my technique. I would spin out my story in a leisurely, not over-colourful, even somewhat hesitant manner, as if groping for words as experience had taught me. It seemed all the more credible and convincing for it. These were the tenuous foundations on which I was building my hopes of survival. There was also my passionate love of life. Somehow my indomitable, almost savage, desire to live seemed to guide my instinct, unerringly, towards the attainment of that goal. My liabilities outweighed my assets so preposterously that I did not have the courage to look them squarely in the face. It was easier to ignore them, more reassuring to live in the land of make-believe.

One afternoon, early in April, the mistress and I were busy in the farmhouse kitchen. It was a long, narrow room, plainly and sparsely furnished with a wooden dresser, a table, directly underneath the room's only window, with a bench and a couple of chairs standing by it. One corner of the room was wholly occupied by an enormous, tiled cooking-range. Standing on it was a solitary, cast-iron pot in which a pork-rib stew, richly spiced with herbs, was gently simmering for the evening meal. The palate-tickling aroma issuing forth from under its lid filled my tummy with pleasant anticipation. It was warm, cosy and safe in that kitchen.

The mistress and I were sitting at the table podding last year's beans into a small enamel bowl. The pods were very dry and crackly and as we broke them open, the light mauve beans, flecked with a darker mauve, spilled into the bowl with a light pattering sound. Neither of us said much; I was still feeling my new surroundings and savouring their freedom and ease. Although like most children, I could prattle on endlessly, I did not, in truth, know how to start a conversation with the mistress. To her, on the other hand, words did not come easily and she used them, when she had to, sparingly. Just her very presence was a comfort to me, as mine seemed to be to her.

From time to time I would steal a surreptitious glance at her old, deeply furrowed, almost lipless face. She reminded me of neither of my grandmothers. They had been better looking and nicely plump, whereas she was painfully thin and haggard. Yet, she was as kind to me, a stranger, as they had been. Now and then she would set her fleshless lips in motion, for it was her habit to 'rattle off' innumerable 'Hail Marys' and 'Our Fathers' in the course of the day. My gaze would then wander from her face to the scene outside the kitchen window. The sky – an endless stretch of blue unscarred by barbed wire; the cherry trees – smothered in fragrant pink blossom; the farm mongrel, basking in the early spring sun. It was good to be alive.

Not quite a month had elapsed since the liquidation of the Cracow Ghetto and I, who should have shared the fate of the hundreds of children whose lives were ended that day, and whose blood meandered freely among the cobblestones of the Ghetto's little square, was feeling with every vein and fibre of my being the precious and exquisite gift of life. I was jolted out of my musings by a crunching, rasping sound reaching my ear; my eye travelling to the gravel path whence it came – I saw him. A navy-blue uniformed Polish policeman approaching the farmhouse on a bicycle. The earth careered madly on its pivot and went pitch-black; then, like a Catherine wheel, burst into a shower of dazzling sparks. My eyes, which were not deceiving me, saw him dismount, lean the bicycle against the barn wall, test it to make sure he had planted it firmly and then, with a springy, military step make for the farmhouse. The mistress had seen him too; she stopped working and her old, work-worn hands were a-tremble. She, too, had a crime on her conscience, but of a very different type and magnitude from mine – mine was that I had not submitted to slaughter, whereas she had committed it.

A sledge-hammer was pounding in my breast. My throat felt parched and constricted and I seemed to be choking on my own too large, swollen tongue, my arms covered with goose-flesh, my whole body chilled to the bone. I raised myself from the bench by holding onto the edge of the table, the palms of my hands clammy with sweat. Automatically, I tried to wipe them dry against the sides of my skirt, but they just fell limply against me. I was drained of all strength. All routes of escape were cut off and yet, as if making a bid for freedom, I started to shuffle towards the blind wall, my sturdy, quick-footed legs having turned to jelly. One thought only was throbbing in my fear-crazed mind: 'He has come to get me . . .'

Giving a light rap on the door he entered, the age old greeting used among the peasants issuing from his lips, 'Praised be the Name of the Lord' – 'For ever and ever, amen', came the mistress's reply in a steady, even voice. She passed the corner of her apron over the seat of the chair and indicating it with a gesture of her hand, bid him sit down. Having seated himself – stretching out his long legs shod in lustrous black leather – I had seen such fine boots before, bespattered with human blood, and associated them with the utmost terror, his close-set, shifty eyes proceeded 'to take the room in' and the mistress, seeing them alight on me, said in a perfectly natural, matter-of-fact voice, 'This is Yanka, my new help, I don't know what I would do without her; she is a good girl, she is.' He smiled at me benignly and from then on, to my indescribable relief, did not honour me with another glance. I sank onto the hard, beaten-mud floor, tucking my legs under me, and felt life, warmth and hope slowly, droplet by droplet, seep back into me.

The mistress, having offered him a coffee with the words 'The officer will have a coffee . . .', was now busy pouring hot, frothy milk into a mug, adding a spoonful of 'ersatz' coffee and a saccharin tablet which dissolved itself with, what to my tattered nerves sounded like an explosion, but was, in fact, a tiny sizzling 'plop'. She placed the steaming liquid before him, and he, thanking her with the words 'May the Lord reward you', put it to his thin, greedy lips. She then sat down on the bench, facing him, and the old, old battle of wits between the peasant and the police began.

Current topics were discussed: the war and the news from the Russian front; the work in the fields; last year's crops and the expectation, with God's help, of a better harvest this year. And then touching upon the subject of Easter, he let drop a few well chosen words, in a sly, smart alec manner, which revealed the object of his visit. 'Er . . .' he said, 'It has come to our ears that a great deal of pig slaughtering is going on in the village in preparation for the Easter festivities . . . The farmers know, only too well, the Authorities mean business . . . Every head of cattle is to be accounted for – dead or alive. No slaughtering without permission! They will take risks – goodness knows we, the police, are on the side of the farmers. Still, we have a job to do, to see to it that the law is upheld. We close our eyes to all kinds of goings on, whenever we can . . . but . . .' There was a moment's uneasy silence. He had run out of platitudes and was taking a breather before the next round.

The mistress and I were well aware of the specially bred and fattened pig which had been slaughtered and turned into beauti- fully smoked hams, sides of bacon, sausages and meat cheeses – all neatly arranged in a wooden trough and stowed away up in the hay-loft . . . But the mistress had no means of knowing whether the man facing her had come, like the fox that he was, on the off-chance, or whether he really knew. Suddenly his nostrils up-curved, his eyes riveted to the pot on the cooking-range, he was delicately sniffing the air, saying, 'Makes one's mouth water, that smell does . . . just like a pork-rib stew . . . spiced to a treat . . .'

The mistress knew when she was beaten. Turning round and addressing herself to me, she said in a cool, fearless voice; 'Go up to the loft, "girlie", and fetch the officer a nice ham.' I did as I was told, and crossing the room caught sight of his unctuous smile. No doubt, he was well pleased with the outcome of his 'social call' and was, once again, obligingly closing his eyes.

Putting my foot on the very first rung of the ladder leading to the hay-loft, I was stopped by the mistress. She put her mouth to my ear and I heard her impassioned whisper, 'Make sure it's the smallest one, the perisher . . .'

30 · Lola

When I think of Lola, who belonged to a world which vanished, never to reappear, over half a century ago, I see her sitting in our kitchen across the bare pine-wood table from my mother. She would place her capacious, lidded wicker basket within easy reach of her hand. The first objects she drew from it were a fluffy pastel-coloured hand-towel and an immaculately laundered, stiffly starched narrow strip of white linen – not unlike an altar cloth. She spread the latter on her side of the table smoothing it out with her soft, plump hands. Lola's movements were deliberate and measured – rather like those of a high-priestess in the performance of a religious ritual – and though time was of the essence, she never gave that impression. She then produced a heavy, grey flannel bundle fastened with white cotton tape. Reverently, ceremoniously, for it contained her livelihood, she untied the bow and then slowly, solemnly, she uncoiled the long strip of grey cloth; on the inside pockets of varying sizes and shapes contained the tools of her trade, some of which looked quite lethal to a small girl. She proceeded to lay them out neatly, in order of use, upon the white cloth in a row of gleaming steel. These tools, as I well knew, for she had told us often enough, had been made in Germany of the finest Essen steel. Then came the last object – my favourite but one – a small square tray fitted with sample phials and chunky, little bottles containing brilliantly-coloured, viscous nail varnish. Lastly, she produced a small porcelain bowl, with a scrap of scented soap at the bottom, which I would half fill with warm water for her; she was then ready to start plying her trade – for Lola was a home-manicurist.

With a generous bud of cotton-wool soaked in colourless liquid, she would remove last week's varnish from Mamma's nails. Mamma would then dip her fingertips in the milky, warm water – the soap having in the meantime dissolved. Lola was already holding Mamma's left hand with the fingers outspread like a fan, in her own, gently but swiftly shaping the oval nails with a long, ivory-

233

handled nail-file. Mamma and Lola had known each other since they were girls. Lola, who was several years younger than Mamma, had been tending Mamma's nails ever since I could remember, but she only started imprinting herself on my mind as an interesting, I would even go so far as to say a fascinating, individual during the late 1930s and of course, during the years of her physical blossoming and economic prosperity – the early war years.

Lola liked to chat and she did so in a firm, resonant voice, yet her concentration, her attention never wavered. What she was saying as she shaped the nails, massaged the hands and fingers with a fragrant cream, delicately removed the cuticles, buffed and finally, lacquered the pale, opalescent nails, did not in any way detract from the quality and precision of her skills. I think that Mamma enjoyed listening to Lola's tales. Basically, they were the same tales as those of last week, last month, last year and although the foundations, well and solidly laid, remained the same, the castles she built upon them varied in structure, ornamentation and landscaping . . . I understood, after a time, that she varied somewhat the details of her accounts out of sheer consideration for her audience. She did not wish to bore. I, for one, was never in the least bored by her narrative, but often puzzled. I was an eavesdropper by nature, but I understood from Mamma's comments on the subject that it was a lamentable character trait to possess . . . I was in a quandary, for having retained certain words and phrases – some of which clattered around in my head sometimes for years because I did not understand their meaning – I was not able to seek explanation or elucidation since that would have been tantamount to an admission of guilt.

One of the phrases which Lola used regularly, week in, week out, was: 'Because he's done me wrong . . .' I was well into my teens before I managed to decode that one. The utterance was used in connection with a swain, a nice Jewish boy, the neighbours' son who, having deflowered Lola, had not done the honourable thing by her, but had gone elsewhere to look for a life's companion. That loss of virginity, with hindsight, appeared to Lola quite purposeless and wasteful. It never stopped rankling with her, and the worst part of it was that he had been 'a nice Jewish boy . . .'

Lola, also, liked to discourse, with a degree of pride and satisfaction, on how she had acquired and paid off her set of fine Essensteel manicure implements. Although she had bought them second-hand, they were in splendid condition and of superb quality

– 'the finest Essen steel', she would again remind us. They, certainly, looked impressive, weighty, immaculate. They had cost her, she never failed to mention, 'an arm and a leg . . .' She had purchased them on the instalment plan from a Jewish dealer in second-hand surgical instruments. 'A thief and a liar if ever there was one – Easy terms . . .' And a strange sound, not unlike the hiss of a wild cat would issue from her full, rouged lips. 'Easy terms, my foot! It took years of sweat and toil to pay him off, to free myself from the bondage. How I had to scrimp and scrape. No dripping on my bread, counting every grain of barley, splitting a match in four . . .'

Lola always said to Mamma, and I am sure Mamma never tired of hearing it, when she had finished her ministrations, as Mamma's freshly polished, glossy nails were drying and she was packing her basket, 'You've lovely hands, one doesn't often see alabaster-white hands like yours!' It was from Lola that I learnt that word 'alabaster'. I can remember, to this day, from whom and under what circumstances, I learnt certain words, certain expressions, though it may be as many as sixty and more years ago. It was from Lola that I first heard, and through her made my own, that lovely word – 'alabaster'.

Mamma's hands were busy hands. She looked after her family and her home. She earned a living – sewing. The skin unusually pale, almost lily-white, was soft and delicate. They were small, graceful hands with slender, nimble fingers and beautifully shaped, strong nails. Pampered and cosseted – she had a number of 'recipes' for maintaining their pallor, delicacy and softness, one of which I still remember. It was to rub a drop of paraffin oil into them and slip on old, white cotton gloves. They may have looked like idle hands, but indeed they were not. Mamma was vain of her hands.

One day, I may have been about eight or nine years old at the time, Lola offered to show me her home. I remember she lived in Podgórze (the future German-designated Ghetto area), at No. 11 Wita Stwosza Road. It was a dingy, dreary one storey building situated in a harsh, treeless road. Lola lived in a sort of lean-to in the courtyard. I was a little disconcerted, I thought she was leading me to a hen-coop. She inserted a large black key into a large black key-hole and there it was – her home. A small room with a sloping ceiling and a narrow window. It was the cleanest, neatest, most thoughtfully arranged little home. The truckle-bed under the window was covered with a sky-blue cotton bedspread and on the small bedside-table, right next to it, covered with a daintily crocheted white doyley, there stood a candle in a bright red enamel holder – Lola had no electricity. It was a dollie's room and Lola was of good medium height and strongly built. She offered me a glass of cherry cordial and carefully drew back a corner of her bedspread, so that I could sit down, but not crease it . . . Lola liked children.

And then the war broke out and our world toppled. We lost sight of Lola for a while. We thought that she may have left Cracow. That she may have crossed over to the Russian side. People were secretive about such activities. She was a loyal friend. She came once a week, regular as clockwork, through our fat years (such as they were), through our lean years, through the hopeful and promising, as well as the hard, painful trajectories of life. A good friend, we missed her.

After an absence of well over a year, she suddenly appeared, but without her basket, without that air of submission peculiar to downtrodden people and, brazenly confident, without the Star of David armband which had become by then compulsory. A metamorphosis had taken place. It was not Lola the manicurist who was sitting at our kitchen table, but a woman fully conscious of the power of her femininity and in full command of that power. A chic suit, in Prince of Wales check, moulded her strong, generously-proportioned body. She had had her hair hennaed. Today, a woman turns from a deep brunette into a golden blonde from one day to the next and nobody turns a hair . . . But in those days to change the colour of one's hair marked one as a female bold as brass, a pioneer, a revolutionary – almost. A mass of fiery, coppery, glinting waves and ripples. We were speechless with wonder and astonishment at the audacity and splendour of that transformation. A rose in full bloom sitting at our kitchen table. And the longer she sat there – her beautifully tended hands, with their long vermilion nails, quietly relaxed – telling us about the changes in her life, full of *double entente*, the more I marvelled, the more puzzled I became. Lola had gone 'Aryan'. Her documentation, she assured us, was 24-carat, absolutely full-proof . . . 'Not cheap, mind you', she added, but worth every penny she had paid. Sterling work!

Lola no longer lived in Podgórze. She now had her own flat in Dietla Street, at the more salubrious end of this quite central street. She still maintained her relationship with her pre-war friend, Staś, a middle-aged bachelor of good Aryan stock. They were genuinely fond of each other and it was an alliance of many years' standing. He had greatly prospered, economically, since the outbreak of the

236

war. He was a generous man and the prosperity was rubbing off on Lola . . . She, not content, however, with her present good fortune, chose to play for very high stakes. She was, also, bestowing her favour upon a German *Wehrmacht* officer who was, from what she said, very smitten with her. Describing the officer, she said, 'There he is telling me that the Jews are a putrid, degenerate race and at the same time stroking, caressing, kissing my Jewish hand . . .' I remember her uttering those words perfectly clearly, for the officer's strongly held beliefs in juxtaposition to his amorous activities struck me as strange, but, of course, he did not know he was stroking a Jewish hand.

Lola was 'two-timing'. The latter is not an expression I knew at the time; indeed, I do not know if it exists at all in my native tongue. I was very much a mature woman when I first heard it in English. A friend, speaking about a mutual acquaintance, said to me one day, 'I'm worried about Stacey, she is two-timing . . .' I looked at her blankly and asked. 'What do you mean?' And then, later on in the day, the expression came back to me, and as I was dwelling upon it, it suddenly struck me: 'Oh, that is what Lola was doing back in 1940 . . .'

Again, Lola invited me to her flat in Dietla Street. She said to Mamma that once I had discovered her treasure trove I would want to stay the night. Would Mamma allow me to do so? Mamma gave her permission. All things being relative, it was a modest flat, but I still think, today, that it was well and comfortably appointed. It consisted of a room and a kitchen. The latter, through which one entered the flat, was large, well equipped and sparklingly clean. The room, in essence a dining-room, with a divan in one corner was comfortably and solidly furnished in the idiom of a modestly prosperous merchant. But it was the view from the room's tall window which made one catch one's breath. It commanded the most magnificent view anywhere, ever . . . Right opposite it, across a long expanse of trimly maintained meadow, slightly to the right, there stood on its rock, behind ivy-clad fortifications, the Royal Castle – Wawel. To the left of the Castle, wide and peaceful at this point, flowed the river – the Vistula – its dark, sleepy waters murmuring soothingly . . . Lola enjoyed the same breath-takingly beautiful view as had, over the centuries, the Kings, Queens and Princes of Poland. The room had a curious aura – bourgeois, yet artistic. There were delicate, dreamy thumb-nail sketches of Cracow in gilded, slender frames on the walls and fragile lovingly nurtured plants in colourfully glazed pots. A heavy, solid dining-room table with a set of matching chairs occupied the centre of the room. There was a massive wardrobe with an oval mirror set in one of its doors and opposite it, against the other wall, there stood a tall two-tier, rather buxom, sideboard. It was in this sideboard, in a cupboard on the left hand side, that the treasure reposed. Books, books and yet more books for a child aged somewhere between ten and thirteen, more likely a girl . . . I was overwhelmed with joy. Lola said, 'Take them out, look at them.'

Lola told me, in confidence, that she had taken the flat over, fully furnished and functional, from a Jewish family – father, mother and daughter – who were desperate to leave Cracow, but were very reticent about their plans and future whereabouts . . . 'It was a bargain, a real snip,' she said.

It is, I know, too much to hope that this couple and their book-loving young daughter escaped the cruel sentence passed upon us all, but if we can judge people by their possessions, they were a happy family who did not live by bread alone. Many delicious meals had been cooked in that homely kitchen and eaten in calm enjoyment at the solid table . . . The conversation must have flowed – books, pictures, scholastic success, flowers, gardens, plans for the future . . .

I visited Lola a number of times in Dietla Street. She always allowed me to take a book home. She continued to drop in on us from time to time, but as the Jewish situation worsened, became more unstable, more danger-fraught she spaced out her visits more and more. In the end she stopped coming altogether having understood, no doubt, that it was imprudent for an 'Aryan' to be seen associating with the Jews. The last time we saw her was, I think, in the summer of 1941. Although she looked very well, was elegantly attired and, she told Mamma, was financially secure, she felt – since the establishment of the Cracow Ghetto, not that far from Dietla Street, in March 1941 – she was treading on very soft ground. She was on edge, frightened, she said. She wished she had left Cracow, 'but where am I to go, now . . .?'

After we had moved to the Ghetto, in December 1941, I found myself, one day, walking along Wita Stwosza Road in which my Mother's aunt and cousins lived. I remembered that Lola used to live, before the war, at No. 11. I thought to myself, 'Lola would not have needed to move, she would have found herself living within the Ghetto area . . .' But I was wrong. Wita Stwosza Road had been sliced in half by the crenellated red-brick Ghetto wall. The Ghetto half of the road ended at No. 9. The Aryan half started at No. 11. After all, Lola would have had to move.

My brother, Joseph, ran into Lola by sheer coincidence, not far from her flat by the Vistula, in the spring of 1943, after the liquidation of the Cracow Ghetto in March of that year. Joseph was being marched through Cracow's streets with his Labour Group; as they were being guarded by Jewish overseers, and there were few pedestrians about, he detached himself from the group and approached Lola. Recognising Joseph instantly, she asked, 'How is your mother, how is everybody?' He shook his head saying 'There is nobody left . . . all gone . . .' She opened her handbag, took out a 20 złoty note – the price of a loaf of bread – and pressed it into his hand. Before he even realised what she had done, before he had had time to thank her, she was gone . . .

In the summer of 1943, when I had been working and living at the Kucharczyk farm for two or three months, the mistress asked me one day if I would make a weekly trip to Cracow to sell some of their farm produce. The prospect half-frightened me, half-gladdened me. Cracow – where I might run into someone I knew and who knew my origins. Cracow swarming with German uniforms and bristling with pitfalls and snares. Cracow, which was the very breath of life. The companion and witness of the joy and grief of my twelve-year old life.

One early summer morning, the mistress and her daughter helped me prepare for my first black market, for black market it was, venture – a trip to Cracow.

A large square of strong, coarse cloth was placed on the kitchen table; two aluminium milk churns, containing about five to six litres of milk each, were placed in its centre; two corners of the cloth were tied firmly into a large knot which was then wedged in between the two cans, so that they would not rattle or knock against each other. The pack was then hoisted onto my back. I would tie the other two corners into another sturdy knot in the middle of my chest. My hands were free. I would carry a small wicker basket which contained a nice lump of butter reposing on a bed of fresh, green leaves; a dozen eggs buried in a canister packed with sawdust; a wedge of soft cream cheese wrapped in moist snow-white muslin.

The mistress was pleased with the outcome of these expeditions. It was easy enough to sell fine, fresh dairy produce in Cracow and I was fully able to account for the takings I brought back.

One day, it may have been about May or June 1943, and must have been only weeks after Lola and my brother had run into each other (I only learnt of this meeting after the war when Joseph and I were swapping war experiences), that I called at her flat in Dietla Street.

I had sold all the farm produce, except for a little milk at the bottom of one of the churns. I thought Lola might have it. I would see her, speak to her. She had been part of that other life. My heart was already filling with warmth. She had known my parents, my brothers. It was already a year . . .

I entered the building and climbed the stairs to the first floor, walked along the railed balcony and knocked on her door. There was no answer. I rapped again, applying my knuckles hard. There was no answer. The next door neighbour appeared in her doorway. 'I have a little milk left over. The lady in the flat would sometimes buy milk from me. I was wondering . . .?' 'She doesn't live here any more. She was a Jewess.' I opened my innocent, blue eyes wide . . . 'Yes, a Jewess. '*Granatowi*' [the navy-blue uniformed Polish police] came for her – at night. Someone had denounced her. Yes, a Jewess . . .'

31 · A Farm Hand

Life on the farm at Mogiła was monotonously even and predictable and thus contained an element of security, of safety, which I had not known for many years, and which I now savoured and relished.

By April, with spring all around – in the sky, in the fields, in the farmers' hale faces and brisk movements – it was time to take the cattle out to graze.

The family on whose farm I worked and lived were neither rich nor poor. Although they only had one cow, they also had a horse, a fact which placed them on the upper echelons of village society. They not only did not need to hire someone else's animal to work their land, but were able to rent out their own in exchange for young manpower. Manpower was what they lacked, and for the farm to thrive and prosper a great deal of it was required.

Both Mr and Mrs Kucharczyk were of advanced age. She was particularly frail. She was suffering from tuberculosis and spat blood. Her illness had never been officially diagnosed. It was not mentioned and certainly not treated or considered in any way. Although she had brought seven children into the world, she had never spoken to, or been examined by, a doctor in her life. Medical help, in any form or shape, had no place in their life. Heavenly aid, divine intervention was all they recognised and called upon.

The farmer was a big man – gentle and spare of speech – and must have once possessed great physical strength. He still carried himself ramrod straight and toiled away as the day was long. He was the first to rise in the morning and the last to retire in the evening. He and his horse shared the stable at night. The mistress, in spite of her frailty, also kept pegging away and never allowed herself any respite from the daily grind. One moved from one task to the next without a moment's rest and nobody, in that world, had ever heard of a tea-break. Nor had I.

Of the farmers' seven children, two were still on the farm. Kasia, the daughter, well into her thirties and unmarried, carried a heavy

241

burden on her shoulders. She was tall and thin and physically very tough. A dutiful daughter – she was very devoted to her parents; next came the animals. She understood their needs and language well. Mooing, neighing, bleating, grunting were as clear, as natural to her as human speech. She was deeply religious, but highly practical and beavered away from morning till night. Her work output was that of a healthy, strong and thoroughly dedicated young man.

Then there was the youngest son – 'The Benjamin' I called him in my mind. His name was Vladek. Because he was the fruit of old, tired loins, his physical attributes were all the more remarkable. Tallish and well built he had clean, regular features, light-blue eyes and flaxen hair. He was then, in 1943, in his late teens . . . He would disappear for days on end. Turn up, unexpectedly, stock-drunk, stagger around the farm for a while, swear at the dog and kick it when it got under his feet – he knew some really horrendous swear words – and, eventually, crawl up the ladder into the hay-loft, bury himself in the straw and hay and sleep for many hours. It was said that he had fallen into bad company; that they brewed their own vodka which was pure poison, lethal.

It seemed such a shame – a fine physique and no mind at all. He was not unkind to any of us. The person he was harming was himself. He never did a stroke of work. He just about knew a rake from a scythe . . . His parents and sister were very fond of him and his unnatural conduct was accepted as God's will. I learnt, many years later, that he had died, still in his twenties, of delirium tremens.

The family were kind to me, for I was neither big nor strong for my age. The daily task of clearing out the byre lay very much within the province of my duties. A heaped pitchfork of soggy straw dripping with the animals' urine and enriched with their excrement was very heavy. I could not lift it. The first time the old farmer saw me struggling with it, he spat into his hands, rubbing the spittle into his palms – an indication that he was about to tackle a gigantic task – and, winking at me, took the pitchfork from me. Before I had time to get over my astonishment the job was done. I would then pick up the twig broom and neatly sweep the byre floor. Next, I brought in fresh, golden straw, tomorrow's precious manure, by the armful and spread it under and around the animals. Once a week, we hosed down the byre floor, and that meant endless buckets of water from the well. It was hard work. Kasia and I tackled it between us. She liked to clean the animals herself, but I, too, became quite competent at looking after them. Eventually, the cow became my responsibility which was, in a way, a promotion, and I learnt to keep her clean and comfortable and, in due course, to milk her.

The Kucharczyks' grazing grounds were a long way from the farmhouse – at the other end of the village and beyond. The area was known as 'The Knoll'. It was, indeed, a grassy hillock surrounded by flat, arable land. I would cross the whole village, stick in hand, driving the cow before me. It was a peaceful, docile, black-and-white animal. The stick was part of the stock-in-trade, but I never did need apply it. The loosely woven, jute sack also formed part of the image. I always carried it with me, for it came in handy in a number of ways. It was especially useful when it rained. I would fold it double, so that it made a sort of cape and hood which protected my head, shoulders and back. It was also good to sit on, for the grass was cold and wet with the dew first thing in the morning and even more so after a shower of rain. I went about bare-foot, as did pretty much everybody else, except on Sundays when I went to mass. I would then carry my shoes, tied together by the laces, over my shoulder and only put them on when I was in sight of the church. The soles of my feet became very hard and calloused, but in spite of the odd bruise and cut, remained perfectly healthy. My hands, too, became very rough and chapped. Only in winter did I experience discomfort when the chapping led to open sores and bleeding.

Day in, day out, I spent many hours at the Knoll with only the cow for company. It was yellow-brown country, with the odd patch of green, like the hillock on whose slopes the cow grazed. I felt, during those long hours on my own, lonely, abandoned. I would have liked to chat and to listen; above all, to read. Yet the air around me was so fresh and pungent with the good, true odours of the countryside. The sky, more often than not, was blue and the sun warm and golden. Suspended between heaven and earth, out of the eye of the terrible global storm, the sounds of the raging tornado just beyond the purple-silver mists did not reach me, and the deep silence of the fields and meadows was soothing – comforting.

On one side of the Knoll, there was a shallow ditch, and one morning I discovered that its sides were covered with tiny, ripe-red wild strawberries . . . I have never forgotten that day. It was like Manna from heaven – they were so sweet and juicy and fragrant. This is one of two happenings I remember from my days at the Knoll. The first sweet, the second infinitely sad, but I did not fully understand its implications then. One day I found a double news-paper sheet come adrift from the *Krakauer Zeitung* lying on the grass at the foot of the Knoll. The wind must have brought it a very long way. I snatched it up and smoothed it out. It was grubby and creased, but perfectly legible – the precious, printed word. It turned out to be an endless list of Polish officers' names. It was the summer of 1943 – Katyn Forest had yielded its secret. The *Krakauer Zeitung* was expressing the Germans' utter horror at the discovery in the strongest possible terms. I recognised one name on the list – Cjankiewicz – a well known Cracow military family. Mme and Mlle Cjankiewicz had been Mamma's clients. They lived in one of Cracow's loveliest squares – Plac Jabłonowskich . . .

One late afternoon, as dusk was already approaching, the mistress asked me to take some newly-laid eggs to an outlying farm in acknowledgment of help received with harvesting. It was an isolated farmhouse situated in the midst of meadows. It had been a beautiful summer's day. The countryside, in its full plenitude, was preparing for a night's peaceful rest under a cloudless, silver sky. I skirted a large, freshly-mown meadow, taking my time, for it was very pleasant to be strolling along, in the early evening's coolness, in this bountiful, green land.

I was already in full view of the farmhouse, when I became aware of a low, but persistent growling . . . I saw a huge, black shape leap-ing towards me and managed to emit a piercing scream before it descended on me, knocking me down and burying its fangs in the calf of my left leg. I continued to scream with all my might. The dog was dragged away from my person and I was helped to my feet – very frightened and shaken – the blood dripping from my leg.

I was led into the farmhouse, sat on a stool and offered a tin mug of cold water. The eggs were perfectly intact; not so much as a crack on their shells . . . I sat there for a few minutes dazed, yet instantly aware of my predicament and very fearful. 'What if I can't walk? What if I can't work?' The family at the farm were very upset at the incident. They said the dog, a good, faithful animal, had been loosened from his chain rather earlier than usual. They were not expecting any callers this late in the afternoon. It was a clean, healthy animal and my leg, as I was young and fit, would heal in no time. I ambled back, shocked and frightened, but not really aware of the possible consequences of this misadventure. The mistress, the family, were waiting for me with the evening meal. We sat down to eat. 'What's taken you so long?' asked Kasia.

I related the incident and although blood was oozing from the two patches where the skin had been ripped out, I ate with my usual hearty appetite. Everybody said it was a good sign. Disinfectant, iodine, cotton-wool, bandage, aspirin – I knew there were none and I felt it was best not to make too much fuss. I washed my feet before going to sleep and bathed the leg with cold water. It seemed to assuage the throbbing which had already set in.

Very fearful at the sight of my leg, I dragged myself off my pallet in the morning. The leg was swollen, deep-pink in colour, pus and blood bubbling at the edges of the broken, tattered skin. I felt ill and weak all over. I hobbled into the byre and bumped straight into Kasia. 'Are you poorly? Let's have a look at that leg . . . I'll get a rag to tie round it.' I went on with my various tasks, but every gesture, every step was an effort. The leg throbbed painfully. I took the cow out to graze and, somehow, managed to hobble as far as the Knoll. Totally exhausted, I lay down on my sack under a tree. I had to fight hard the desire to sleep, for although the cow was nibbling contentedly, an eye had to be kept on it . . . it was my responsibility. At mid-day, Kasia said she would do the milking. I drove the cow back to the Knoll for the afternoon's grazing.

A few days went by; the swelling was not going down. The discharge continued. My work output had steadily diminished and I was no longer able to make the weekly trip to Cracow to sell the farm produce. Kasia was not pleased. It was coming to the end of July. Another few weeks and autumn would be upon us. Kasia started dropping hints that they had always managed, over the winter months, without outside help. The elderly farmers' attitude towards me did not change. The mistress would slip me a tomato or a pear – I liked pears very much – as the cow and I were setting off for the Knoll, for even though the trees and the bushes were laden, bowed down, with fruit, it was not done to help oneself.

A few more days had gone by since my accident. One morning, as I was limping through the village behind the cow, placing my weight on my right leg and foot and dragging the left one behind me, an old woman, very tiny, very bent, stopped me asking, 'Is that leg still giving you trouble?' I told her that it was and described the symptoms. 'Ah' she said, 'you want to apply a dock-leaf to it. It'll draw out the poison.' 'A dock-leaf?' I asked. She shambled to the nearest ditch and plucked a large, fresh, clearly veined dock-leaf. 'Wash it before you place it against the sore spot. Keep changing it. Make sure it's fresh and clean.' She was the village *sage-femme*. . .

When I got to the Knoll, I wiped the leaf thoroughly against the dewy grass. A few more days went by and the swelling went down, the colour of the skin became natural, the suppuration diminished . . . I started feeling much better in myself.

I had been at the Kucharczyks' farm for over four months. I knew it was time to move on.

32 • *The Sisters*

By the summer of 1943 most of the Officers' Village had become a 'Nur Für Deutsche' residential area. Of the pre-war Aryan residents only the caretakers were permitted to remain in their dwellings to continue to perform the duties devolving upon them.

I found 'a post', in August 1943, on the very outskirts – still inhabited by pre-war Aryan residents – of the Officers' Village. Two ladies, two sisters who used to buy the dairy produce I brought weekly from Mogiła to Cracow, had offered to take me on. They did not want a fully-fledged servant. An adaptable, willing 'girlie' whom they could train in their ways . . . I appeared eminently suitable . . . I liked them. They lived in a comfortable, very well-appointed ground floor flat.

When I crossed their threshold, on the appointed day, I was instantly whisked off by the two ladies, neatly aproned, to their immaculate, sweet-smelling bathroom. I was immersed in a tub of warm water and they set, with considerable gusto, to scrubbing me. My hair, my nails, every inch of me tingled and glowed with friction and cleanliness. My washable clothes were put in a small cauldron to be boiled. I slept, that night, on a folding-bed beautifully made up with crisp, fresh linen.

They were two kind, civilised and extremely fastidious ladies. Both were married. The elder sister was a rotund, plain lady; her husband, a portly gentleman, went daily to his office. The younger sister was slight, finely-boned and still very pretty. Her husband, a tall, distinguished gentleman, was a businessman. I only saw him once, for he was permanently on business in Warsaw. There were no children. Both sisters loved them. Both were past child-bearing age.

It was a very good post. I was kindly and scrupulously fairly treated. Every day, I had a certain amount of free time when I could do 'my sewing', at which I was hopeless . . . There were books in the flat, plenty of books, but I did not dare. I hardly ever set foot outside the flat, for the sisters would not trust anyone to do their shopping.

When they bought a loaf of bread, it was immediately passed over a gas flame, in case it had been handled by less than clean hands . . . I only went as far as the courtyard, for the carpets had to be beaten every day and the refuse was taken out twice a day – 'before it started exuding an odour . . .' Only once was I sent out, in an emergency, to buy some curd cheese seasoned with paprika in Mogiłska Road. I flew to the shop and back, my feet hardly touching the ground, almost terrified out of my senses that I might meet somebody who would recognise me from 'the olden days . . .'

The two ladies found my ways crude and primitive; I did not chop the onions finely enough; I sometimes mixed up the different tea towels – for glass, china, cutlery; my ironing was far from perfect. They were patient, forebearing teachers and I was a willing, attentive pupil. I never received an unkind word from either of them.

There was a calendar on the kitchen wall – a thick pad of small, square white pages – bearing in large black letters and numbers the day's date. On the back of each page, there was an adage, a ditty, hints on this and that . . . The previous day's page was torn off first thing in the morning. One morning I was asked to do it. Automatically, I turned the page over and started reading out loud practical hints for the day's housekeeping. The two ladies, in great astonishment, exclaimed almost simultaneously, 'You can read!' I had let the mask slip. I had given myself away. I had the presence of mind to say that I had learnt at the village Sunday School – the priest, Father Dominic, had taught us. I was immediately allowed access to 'suitable' books.

I knew I could not remain at the sisters'. The geographical situation of their home formed an insurmountable obstacle. I feared it might prove to be my undoing. Anywhere else in Cracow, but here. I lived daily, hourly in the most terrible suspense – am I going to be discovered, recognised, denounced. . .? I also realised from hints, remarks, half-finished sentences that they, too, as a family, lived in dreadful fear. The elder sister's husband, the white-collar worker, had been a regular army officer before the war. How he had evaded detection I do not know, but I knew that he had not registered, as was compulsory, with the German Authorities. They, too, lived in daily fear of discovery. There would be a very high price to pay.

I was often left in the flat on my own, when the sisters went shopping or made their social calls. They always left me work to do.

They went out early that afternoon – the younger sister looking so pretty in her silk frock, her soft brown hair curling around the brim of her elegant navy straw hat, her bracelets tinkling delicately.

As soon as the front door had shut behind the two sisters, I got down to my work. I had been asked to clean the kitchen window. It gave onto the road in which we lived. A quiet side street, virtually traffic free, except for the odd bicycle, pram or push-chair. Now and then, a pedestrian or two sauntered by. It was a clear, bright summer's afternoon. I assembled my window-cleaning kit, placed it on the sill and drew a stool up to it. I did not like cleaning the windows. I did not like being in full view of the road. Someone might catch a glimpse of me. But it had to be done. I climbed onto the stool and started rubbing away.

A woman appeared on the opposite pavement, waddling sedately, looking straight in front of her – her thick dark plait coiled on top of her head; Mrs Wadowska – our one time caretaker. She did not see me. Her gaze did not waver. She was looking straight ahead. I slid off the stool and lay down on the floor. The panic, the fear were so intense I could not breathe. Mrs Wadowska was a kindly woman; I am sure she would not have reported me to the police, denounced me, and she had not seen me. I crawled up to the kitchen sink and holding onto its edge stood up. I turned on the tap, splashing my face with the cold water and letting it trickle over my hands.

After a while I felt calmer, more composed. My breathing became regular again. 'She did not see me, she won't go to the police . . .' I kept mumbling to myself. I opened the kitchen cupboard where I kept my possessions – my precious shoes and winter jacket. I slipped off the overall and put on the new frock – black cotton sprigged with small, white flowers. It had a gathered skirt and puff sleeves. The elder sister had made it for me from an old dress of hers.

I tied my things into a bundle, together with the bun and the handful of plums the sisters had left for my tea, but on reflection, I thought that a bundle was conspicuous, might attract attention. I took the string shopping bag from the larder and stuffed my things in it. It was the only thing I took. I walked out of the flat closing the door quietly behind me.

33 • Winter 1943/44

I did not know the countryside around Cracow except Mogiła and its immediate surroundings. The village of Pleszów was about an hour's journey, on foot, from the latter. It was bigger and busier. I was looking, this time, for a tucked-away, barely accessible hamlet. A real hiding-hole. 'Kujawy', situated within walking distance of Pleszów, was not even a hamlet, just a straggle of cottages – about a dozen. It was a warm, peaceful September afternoon. I knocked on the door of a prosperous, double-fronted cottage with a tiled roof. Nobody answered. I knocked again. A young woman, gathering her shawl about her, a baby at her breast, appeared. I greeted her and she returned my greeting. She had extraordinarily beautiful eyes – very dark and lustrous with flecks of gold dancing in them. I asked if she needed a live-in help. After a moment's thought, she made the usual enquiries – name, age and where I came from. She looked me up and down, up and down. 'You're small for your age,' she said. 'Yes . . .' 'Will you work hard?' 'Yes.' 'I've three boys . . . could do with help . . . There's a tub of nappies, there, in the corner . . . Get 'em nice and clean . . .' There was a lot of them and they were heavily stained. I did my best. She said I could stay.

Thus began the harshest, the leanest, the most emotionally arid period of my two-year odyssey.

The Świders were the second richest family in the tiny community. They had five cows and two horses. The byre, the stable, the barn and the outbuildings had been built in the last few years – they were modern and solidly constructed. The farmhouse itself was old, but dry, spacious and well-maintained. It was a prosperous, thriving household – most efficiently managed, meticulously overseen.

The farmer – Świder – was a flinty man. He was tall with the flesh tightly drawn over his bones. The clean shaven face, hard; the mouth, a slit; the small, pale eyes, cold; the thinning hair, ginger. Maria, his wife, was a woman of extraordinary beauty with her fine

250

eyes, thick silken hair, as black as a raven's wing, and pale, delicate complexion. She was a hard, tight-fisted woman. The boys – Staś, Joe and baby Charlie – were three spit images of their father. Staś had poor eyesight and wore thick lenses. He was not bright. Joe, when a baby, had fallen off the kitchen table onto the hard, beaten-mud floor. He had banged his head. Now, at the age of eight, he had almost no speech and was generally backward. Charlie was a fine, bouncy baby.

The Świders' extensive grazing lands were close to the farm-house. I took the five cows out to pasture.

I had only been at the farm for about a week when I fell ill. I woke in the morning feverish and aching all over, but I got on with my tasks and took the cattle out to graze. In the course of the day, my neck became stiff, my head drooping onto the right shoulder. When I brought the cows back to the byre, in the late afternoon, I was feeling very poorly indeed. My temperature must have been quite high, for I felt burning-hot all over. It was getting dark. All I wanted to do was to lie down . . . to sleep . . . I crept into the cart-shed and climbed into the farm-cart. It was nicely lined with straw. I closed my eyes. I was out like a light. It must have been some hours before Staś discovered me there and rudely woke me with, 'Mum wants to see you.'

I stood with my head to one side, inwardly trembling, before the sloe-eyed beauty. 'If you're poorly, you'll have to go. We can't keep you, feed you.' I assured her I was already feeling much better, that I would carry on with my work . . . 'We don't want to take on a grown lad, though Heaven knows the work's there, but they eat you out of house and home.'

By the middle of October, when there was already ground frost, and the long succulent grass was silvery with hoary dew, I still took the cows out to graze on the near by embankment. It was the last stand, a special treat, as it were, before they were penned for the long winter months. The mornings were cold and misty and the dampness in the chilly air penetrated one to the very bone. By about nine o'clock in the morning, when I had been up for nearly three hours, Staś would bring me a piece of bread to the embankment. How I waited for it . . . How slowly I chewed it . . . made it last . . .

About an hour later he came and relieved me for a while. I went indoors where the daily mound of potatoes needed peeling. I was very fast at it. Whilst I peeled away, I was given a mug of hot coffee – watery milk coloured with a little brown ersatz powder – bits of skin floating in it. I would close my eyes and drink it in one fell swoop.

Once winter had set in and I stopped taking the cattle out to graze, the daily routine changed. I was the first to rise in the morning. It was still dark. I had my own little room – it contained a bed and a built-in stove, which was never lit, nothing else. I only slept in it. I never entered it in the daytime. The farmers' sleeping chamber was across the passage, right opposite my cubby-hole.

Just after six in the morning the farmer would yell out, 'Yanka!' Although he could not read a watch, he was endowed with an exceptionally acute, and accurate, sense of time. I drew my stockings on, slipped my feet into the lace-up ankle-high shoes in which I had escaped from the Ghetto, wound a kerchief round my head and fastened my winter jacket – the one in which I came out of the sewer. I was ready to face the elements and do a day's work. As I came out of the farmhouse, our little world was still being held within night's ample black bosom. I went straight to the byre to pick up the empty tin pails. I took them to the well sending them down, one at a time, hooked onto the chain. I hauled them up, filled with water, and carried them to the byre. It took many buckets to quench the animals' morning thirst. The water was icy-cold. I, too, had a drink. It was cold, bitingly cold out in the open, but the byre was warm.

Apart from the cows and the horses, there was a large litter of pigs, poultry, rabbits. To keep them all fed, watered, clean and comfortable required ceaseless, hard work all day, every day. All the animals' fodder had to be well and carefully prepared. The pigs' diet, as I remember it, was potato-based. The potatoes had to be washed nice and clean before being boiled. There was a trough out in the open in which they were washed in cold water. The temperature around was not infrequently below zero . . . Although I had a stout, wooden club with which 'to stir the potatoes around,' it was not possible to get them nicely clean without immersing one's hands in the freezing water. They were odd sizes, odd shapes . . . Many had patches of frozen soil or sand sticking to them – the club, which was heavy and awkward to manoeuvre and, really, too large for my small hands, would not dislodge the dirt, would not do the job properly. The potatoes were washed and boiled twice a week – on Tuesday and Fridays. I truly dreaded those days.

Now that his presence was not required on the land and in the fields – for the countryside wrapped in a snug, white coverlet, was dreaming a long white dream – the farmer made a weekly trip to

Cracow. The first time I saw him striding towards a harnessed sledge my heart stood still. He was wearing a long, black coat of the finest wool, lined with silk-soft beaver fur. A matching fur cap, beautifully crafted, covered the sparse strands of ginger hair. Where was the original Jewish owner of that sumptuous ensemble? Naked, behind barbed wire? Ground to dust in the East?

The year 1943 was drawing to a close. I had been at the Świders' farm for nearly four months. My physical condition was steadily deteriorating. My hair was teeming with vermin. I had no comb. There was nowhere to wash myself . . . no soap . . . no rag . . . Abscesses started appearing on my legs. My gums became very tender. The only person to whom I related and who, strangely enough, related to me was little Joe. He would come to the byre and sit down on a bundle of straw whilst I got on with my work. He, too, was a kind of Lazarus. He was affectionate with the animals stroking and patting them, and he wanted to say many things, his little mouth working and twisting painfully, but the sounds it emitted were unintelligible.

I remember 1 January 1944 – a piercingly cold day – a church holiday. The snow and ice bound countryside stretched like a long bridal veil into infinity, and above it floated, strong and vibrant, the music of church bells. Their joyful pealing reached the byre.

At the beginning of February, whilst treading the path from the well to the byre with two full pails, the sole of my right shoe came adrift from the upper – it had not come off, just opened up like a pair of jaws. The shoe had, instantly, filled with snow. I made it to the byre, put down the pails, slithered onto the straw and started to cry. I must have been crying for quite a long time, because, eventually, Staś appeared saying, 'Mum is cross, the potatoes need peeling . . .' But I would not leave the byre and could not stop crying. He went and fetched his mother. She rarely set foot in the byre. She said, 'You know how busy I'm in the mornings, having to come all this way: What's happened to your shoe? Staś, you'll just have to lend Yanka your boots. Father'll be going to town next week, he'll get her a new pair.' Staś started wailing, 'Do I have to, Mum?' 'Well, if you want to do her work, don't.' Staś brought the splendid, knee-high leather boots and put them down next to me. They fitted perfectly.

The following week, as promised, I received a new pair of lace-up shoes. The uppers were made of very hard, unyielding leather and the soles of wood. It is a curious thing, if I had not experienced it at first hand, I would not know about it. If one walks in snow, or soft soil, on wooden soles, the snow, or soil, will collect in a huge, uneven lump under the shoe's instep. It is very hard, and uncomfortable, to move about with the lumps stubbornly clinging to one's shoes.

By the early spring of 1944 – it was already a year since I had escaped from the Ghetto on the first day of the Liquidation Action – I started experiencing an itching sensation on the inside of my forearms. It was confined to that area only. In the evening, when I lay down, I would fall asleep instantly. I was very tired. Having slept for some time, having become warm, I would wake up every night, at the same time, with a maddening itching sensation in my arms . . . I could not stop myself from scratching, from tearing at the skin. I had scabies.

For every month of service Maria bought me an item of clothing from the travelling pedlars . . . two pairs of lyle stockings, two pairs of knickers, a headscarf, a vest and, of course, the wooden-soled shoes. When the weather became warmer, I started washing myself in the byre, a bit at a time, but I had no soap, no cloth to dry myself with. I knew that my situation at the Świders' farm would never improve. I made up my mind to leave.

It would be very difficult to find a post, a good post, in my present physical condition – that much I understood. I knew nothing about the progress of the war. I had lived in a total vacuum for eight months. I believe that I had not even heard the name 'Stalingrad' and would not have, even most vaguely, understood its significance. 'The Germans being pushed back, the Germans retreating . . .' that would have made sense, but I did not know. It never occurred to me that the Germans might win the war. But on what evidence, on what grounds I held that belief? I had no understanding, no knowledge whatsoever of the mighty global struggle which had claimed my family, my people among its countless victims. I had no idea how much longer the war would last. What I would do if it ever ended.

I left the Świders' farm, carrying my few possessions in a string shopping bag, on 5 May 1944. I must have looked like a walking scarecrow.

34 • The Goat Family

It was a bright May morning. I trudged as far as Pleszów and beyond. I could see, in the far distance, the outlines of a village, but did not know how to reach it, except across country. It took a long time reaching the village, my wooden-soled shoes impeding movement, burdening me down. I remember crossing a freshly ploughed field – it was wide and long – the soft soil piling up into huge lumps under the soles. I thought it would never end . . . when it did, I was very, very tired. I sat down on the grass verge by the roadside, as much to rest, as to dislodge the lumps of clay, with the aid of a stick, from the shoes. I took them off, resting my feet, wiggling my toes and scraping the mud away as best I could.

It was well past midday, I could tell by the sun, for I too had learnt to tell the time, although not as accurately as some, from its position in the sky. I was sitting on the edge of a quite wide, quite deep road-side ditch. It was too wide to jump over. I slid down, then climbed up. It was the tail-end of the village; the narrow road bone-dry. There was a brick bungalow – a small front garden between it and the road. A woman came out of the house. She was dressed like a town-dweller – her fair hair, a little dishevelled, not hidden under a headscarf. She was holding an earthenware dish, with a lid over it, in her hands. I said, 'Praised be the Name of the Lord,' and she replied, 'For ever and ever, amen . . .'

'It's groats,' she said – 'it's still warm. I was taking it to the bunker to keep it fresh. Would you like it? I'll fetch a spoon.' I sat down on the steps. A golden-brown Labrador stepped out of the house and made straight for my string bag poking it about with its muzzle, sniffing it suspiciously. 'Wait, I'll fetch a mug of whey. I've got some even though we don't have a cow. It's nice and cool.' I ate and she watched me, somehow pleased to see me eat. 'We're from Cracow,' she said. 'We've only been here a couple of years. We like it. My husband works in Cracow. He commutes. It's quiet here. And there's plenty of food. My little boy is only eight. There's a school in

255

the village. He's got a lot stronger since we came to live here. He's getting quite tall for his age. It's the food and the air. I miss my neighbours though, there's nobody to talk to. What's your name?'

'Yanka . . . I'm looking for work. My Mum and Dad have passed away.' 'Oh, you're an orphan. I thought as much. We don't have a cow, just one goat – the milk is good, healthy. It's got its own byre; white as snow it is. And there are chickens and rabbits. Behind the house, there's a vegetable garden and a bit of an orchard, lots of fruit trees and red and white currant bushes and gooseberries. And there's plenty to do in the house, even though it's only small.'

That same evening, after the little boy had gone to sleep, and the husband had disappeared with his *Krakauer Zeitung* – for he brought a copy home every evening – the wife said, You'll want to have a good wash. Give us a hand with the bath tub.' We brought a round, wooden tub into the kitchen. Water was already being heated on the stove. I was so ashamed, so mortified, and so terribly frightened. I had not yet removed my head kerchief. She said, quite matter of fact: 'I've got to cut your hair short but it'll grow again, it'll be nice and clean.' We went out into the tiny entrance hall. She placed a tin bucket on the floor. We knelt by it. I bent my head right over it and she started snipping away. She did not mind touching my head, my hair.

When I had stripped and got into the tub and she saw my arms and legs, my filth encrusted body, she closed her eyes for a moment and sucked in her breath, but I think it was out of pity, not revulsion. She washed me as if I were a little child – so careful not to hurt my arms . . . 'We'll have another go tomorrow,' she said.

She must have told her husband how it was, she asked him to buy the necessary ointment and lotion in Cracow. The following evening, after the bath, she gave me the ointment – 'Smear it gently over your arms . . .' Then the lotion – 'Rub it well into your hair . . . The legs will heal up once we've fattened you up a bit.'

The next two or three weeks were, I think, the easiest, the best in that long two year trek. My physical condition ameliorating speedily, I fully understood my great good fortune in finding this really nice, close-knit family. The little boy was the apple of their eye, but not spoilt. I ate with them. I ate the same as they did. I was not an outsider. The little boy let me help him look after the rabbits. They were his pets. As for the Labrodor, he followed me around wherever I went.

The village, apart from the school, also, had a co-operative store.

One afternoon, the wife asked me to go to the store to buy a bag of washing-soda powder. She would add a handful of it to the water when boiling her household linen.

I set off – the Labrador trotting happily by my side, wagging his tail in enjoyment. The moment I entered the store, the dog at my heels, I saw him and he saw me – our regular, one-time milkman. We knew each other so well; I used to hold out the saucepan for him to measure out the milk into. He made not the slightest gesture of acknowledgement, of having ever seen me, of having ever known me . . . My mouth went very dry . . . arid. Having transacted his business, he picked up his parcel, walked past me, gave the dog a pat on the head and left the store. Eveybody in the village knew the dog. It was such a beautiful animal. It was referred to as 'the Town Folk's dog'. The milkman knew which house I had come from because of the dog.

When I returned from the store placing the bag of soda powder on the table, I knew, instantly, that something was wrong. The wife was very quiet, thoughtful and, it seemed to me, frightened . . .

In the evening, when the husband came home, we sat down, as usual, to eat our evening meal. There was an uncomfortable silence in the room, at the table. After dinner, whilst I got on with the washing up, the husband and wife closeted themselves in their room. I was on tenter-hooks, so fearful . . .

They came out after a while and it was the husband who spoke – he was angry, but calm: 'You've lied to us; you've deceived us . . . The milkman ran over, this afternoon, to warn us, to tell my wife – she's frightened. You must go . . .' 'Shall I leave here and now . . .?' It was the wife who replied. 'Where will you go now? It's almost night-time. No, in the morning, in the morning will do.'

35 • The Fortune-Teller

By the time I found myself on the road again, it was June 1944. The Allies had already landed in Normandy. But I don't think I had ever heard of Normandy, nor did I know who the Allies were. I understood well enough, however, that I must now change direction – look for work and shelter in a different corner of Poland, not South, not too close to Cracow.

I walked, barefoot, all the way to Cracow. It was nearly a year since I had last seen it. I was astonished, then, that I could stay away from it for a whole year and not wither, not shrivel up from yearning, from longing for it . . . I loved Cracow. I still do.

As I trudged along, I was mentally reviewing all our pre-war Aryan neighbours and acquaintances. On whom can I call? Whom can I trust? Who would be brave and good enough to help me? Mrs Kopiec – with whom I had once left my Aunt Regina's winter coat for safe-keeping – was a kindly, generous woman. The incident with the coat? These things happen . . . An aberration . . . She lived in central Cracow – in Krakowska Street. She may not be able, she may not wish to help me, but she would never denounce me.

When I had reached the outskirts of Cracow, I slipped my shoes on. There it was – my lovely city, intact, crawling with military uniforms. There they were securely moored, it seemed to me, forever; and no less arrogant, cock-sure, lordly . . . Their days were numbered, the Third Reich's slow agony well advanced, but I did not know that. Countless lives would be lost in that gap between June 1944 and January 1945 when the Russian armies marched into Cracow. There again, I was totally ignorant, unprepared.

Mrs Kopiec came to the door. 'Come in, come in . . .' she whispered and quietly shut the front door. She was already heating up the soup, slicing the bread, when I asked her quite bluntly if I could stay the night. She, equally blunt, replied, 'One night . . . I'm too scared . . .'

I slept, that night, on an old blanket on the kitchen floor. It was

June, the nights were warm. She gave me an old navy-blue coat to cover myself with – Regina's coat. So what? She had forgotten all about it. Her charity, her courage had no price. The following morning, after breakfast, she put a few złotys in my hand and Heaven knows she, herself, was not living in abundance.

In Starowiślna Street, some distance before one reached the Third Bridge, there was an old block of flats with a discreet, brass plaque, to the left of the doorway, affixed to its facade. It said: 'Madame Sabina – Medium.' Fortune tellers, seers, mediums were busy people in those days. Business was brisk. The services of persons deemed to possess extra-terrestrial powers and connections were in great demand. One clutched at straws. In the grip of utter despair, one sought any means of succour, above all, hope, however slender. I had known a number of people, before my world had crumbled, who made no secret whatsoever of being in touch with the dispensers of hope, as they were sometimes referred to. I have heard it said that having recourse to such persons, believing in them was a sign of intellectual obtuseness. Maybe . . . It was a high-falutin phrase, I did not precisely understand its meaning, but even if I had, it would not have troubled me.

I was truly at my wits' end. Desperately alone. I wanted to talk to someone, to an adult, about my predicament . . . I needed help to resolve it. I was admitted into the medium's presence – a middle-aged woman with a colourless face and colourless hair. She was mild and softly spoken. There was an aura of spirituality about her. I told her at the outset that I could not pay, that I had no money. Her reply was: 'Ah, but you must be in sore dismay, you a child, to be knocking at my door . . .' There was another woman in the room, slight and thin with a lined, prematurely aged face. I felt constrained by her presence. But the Medium said: 'This is Leonora. My friend. We have no secrets from each other. Whatever you say will remain here, in this room.' And so I told the Medium and Leonora who I was, what had happened to me and how I had survived up to now, and that I had no inner or outer resources left.

'Let me reassure you,' the Medium said, 'their days here, in Poland, are numbered. Their reign is over . . . a few more weeks . . . The Russian armies are moving forward fast apace. Leonora, my dear, you're so practical, what do we do to help, to save the child?'

And so Leonora, a maiden lady, a shrewd, experienced black-marketeer took me under her wing. We boarded a tram. I sat by the window. We crossed the Third Bridge – the Vistula's pewter-grey waters flowing on, dark and mysterious, in calm indifference. We entered what was once the Ghetto area – the Square of Peace on my right, now fully Aryanised . . . We hopped off the tram at the top of Wielicka Street and joined a motley group, mostly women, waiting for their regular transport, a lorry, to Gdów, a small town north of Cracow. The passengers were regulars, black-marketeers in the most anodyne sense of the word, who plied their trade between Gdów and Cracow. The lorry drivers, two sharp-witted young men, ran a twice-weekly service between Gdów and Cracow. We climbed in. We drove along the dusty, white Plaszow route – the railway station on the left, the Concentration Camp, which I had not seen before, and behind whose barbed-wire I believed Joseph to be – on the right. The camp stretched on and on . . . I could see rows of huts – barracks, but, in truth, I had no inkling what the words 'Concentration Camp' signified . . . except that it was shut off, dark, fearful.

Our journey took us through the salt-mining town of Wieliczka. On and on we drove – the road sloping gently up hill till we reached Gdów in the late afternoon. There, by the church, we disembarked. From Gdów to Strychowa, the small village where Leonora lived, was a goodly walk, all the way up a steep hill. Whilst climbing the hill, Leonora told me a little about herself. She had lived most of her life in Strychowa. She had been orphaned young – her father killed in the First World War; her mother died soon after. 'I can read and write,' she said proudly. 'I've a good head on my shoulders. My Mum and Dad sang in the church choir. I've always wanted to get married, to raise a family. I've had no luck. Madama Sabina has helped me to cope with disappointments, accept my lot. That's how we became friends. I rent a room from a farmer, tiny, poky it is, but I'm at nobody's beck and call, nobody orders me around. I make a living. I'll help you.' I wanted to ask why, but I never did.

We found lodgings for me in the village – the space in the corner of a room, in a tumble-down cottage, on which to place a straw mattress. My landlady, a widow with two young children, had no land at all and found it hard to make ends meet, but she was naturally provident and frugal and made a little go a long way. The very modest rent which I paid her came in very handy.

Leonora was a good friend and an invaluable counsellor. She helped me to find lodgings and 'establish' myself in the village. Through her good offices, through her recommendation – for she was on good terms with all the wholesalers in the village – I was given my first lot of 'wares' on credit – coils of sausages, neat cuts of smoked bacon and thick pads of white pork fat for rendering. One of the most precious tips she gave was not to carry fresh meat in the hot weather.

On the days when I travelled from Gdów to Cracow, I got up and left the cottage in the dead of night. The village very peaceful – people and animals all fast asleep – lost in dreams . . . The whole-salers had been up and working all night by the light of oil-lamps and tall, thick tallow candles – their produce 'mint' fresh. And so I carried two well-filled baskets from Strychowa to Gdów twice a week. Fortunately, when laden with merchandise, the on-foot part of the journey was downhill.

There was a handful of us, all women, wives and mothers, Leonora and I the only unattached ones; we descended the hill in darkness, laden like beasts of burden, and in silence. Yet there was warmth and solidarity. In need, in trouble, we rallied round and helped each other . . . By the time we reached Gdów and stood wait-ing by the church for our transport a fine, silvery summer's dawn was breaking over the sleeping town. I soon learnt that our drivers had our interests at heart.

The two very practical young men had constructed a hiding place, a cache, in the lorry's wooden floor. A section of the floor had been removed and a large metal container let into the cavity – the wooden cut-out fitting perfectly over the metal bin. Sacks, straw, old, tatty blankets were casually scattered over the floor. On board-ing the lorry, each passenger was allowed to lower one item of merchandise – one chose the most weighty, the most precious piece – into the metal bin. This was a very sensible precaution in case we were stopped, en route, by German patrols and our merchandise confiscated. Then, something would still be salvaged – the contents of the bin.

It took time, many weeks, to learn all the intricacies and skills of the trade, of this, yet another, way of existence. It took time to find regular customers – retailers as well as individual housewives. It took time, above all, to establish trust between those I was now deal-ing with and living amongst and myself.

One tends, on the whole, to associate vast sums, vast profits with the iniquitous activity of black market operations. It was not like that. The profits, especially at the beginning, when I was learning the ropes, were very meagre. It was hard work and I only just managed to subsist. Also, I was never free from the fear of running into someone who would recognise me from the 'olden days'. It only happened once, in October 1944. I chanced upon Mrs Szenc in Wielicka Street – an incident I describe later. It shook me rigid. It terrified me.

One of the first purchases I made with my hard-earned złotys was a comb and a bar of laundry soap to keep myself clean and neat – my appearance having become more wholesome, my hands less rough. Food was cheap in the village. My diet, which included no meat whatsoever – it was too dear – consisted of groats, potatoes, milk, fruit, which I loved, tomatoes and, as a special treat, cottage cheese. The widow made fresh soup every day and there was a bowlful for me. On Sundays I had my favourite dish – 'frumenty' is the nearest I can get to it in English. I believe it was in great demand at country fairs in Thomas Hardy's day . . . I made a small ball of dough with wheat flour and an egg and then crumbled it into tiny, oval shaped noodles which I would boil in watered down milk with a little sugar and home-grown spices. I loved it.

The months flew by. The Warsaw Uprising broke out and was quelled . . . I only learnt about it because a handful of Warsaw refugees had been billeted upon the farmers at Strychowa. It was autumn again – the sixth autumn of war . . . Four times a week the lorry drove past the Plaszow Concentration Camp. All my senses were on the *qui vive* from the moment the barbed-wire, the watch-towers and the indistinguishable, anonymous huts appeared till they were, again, lost from sight. Only once did I catch a glimpse of a handful of Jews – the camp inmates.

It was late in the year, perhaps December, and only weeks before the Germans were routed by the Russian forces. The air was frosty and sharp – tiny snow flakes, like a sprinkling of salt, whirling in it . . . I was waiting at the top of Wielicka Street with my travelling companions, all warmly wrapped up and looking more like bundles or parcels than women, for our transport to pick us up at the appointed spot, when an open military lorry carrying about a dozen civilians in it came into view. One of the men, his face turned towards the pavement on which I was standing, was Mamma's younger brother – my Uncle Izydor. He did not see me. He was wearing a thick navy-blue shortcoat and his face looked the same as I remembered it – healthy and sun burnt. How I managed not to cry out, to control my emotion I do not know . . .

Early in the New Year, in January 1945, I made my last 'business' trip to Cracow. We knew, I knew, that the Russian armies were forging ahead fast, that any day now the Germans would be in flight.

The town of Wieliczka, as we slowly drove through it, on the return journey, was in a state of great turmoil; people, panic-stricken, running hither and thither in the bitter cold. Sirens were howling, aeroplanes were circling overhead in the wintry sky, but I cannot say whether they were Russian or German ones . . . I do remember, very clearly, a young German soldier, perching at the very back of an open peasant cart, his legs dangling, almost touching the ground. His hands were wrapped round the stock of his rifle, its muzzle pointing downwards, right in front of him. What struck me, and has remained with me, was the expression on his face – a mixture of animal fear and abject humility. I had never seen such an expression on a German face before . . . Was he hitching a lift all the way to Germany . . . home?

36 · Return to Cracow

The atmosphere in the village was heavy with tension and uncertainty. The farmers were fearful – for themselves and their families; for the livestock; for the accumulated stocks of food, grain and fodder, as well as their homes and land . . . By far the majority of the villagers, although they had lived under the German Occupation for nearly six years, had never seen a German uniform, had never heard a shot fired. They now expected fierce fighting, on their very doorstep, for the possession of Strychowa.

The rumblings from the East were no longer wishful thinking . . . They had become detonations. They came with clear regularity and their reverberations made the very earth tremble and shudder. The sky, far out, towards the East, blood-red at the edges, was a gamut of colours with bursts of gold yellow and emerald-green that turned the nights into brightly lit days – the hot, copper flames consuming the darkness . . . We waited . . . There was no news from the outside . . . only the icy winds whistled more shrilly round the houses and the flurries of snow-flakes, driven by them, span round and round in the frosty air.

The widow and I gathered a few provisions to last us through the days when it would be too dangerous even to set foot outside the house. Those days, which it was thought might stretch into weeks, even months, were but three. On the fourth morning, around noon, they started pouring into the village in a disorderly file, in clumps of three or four – thick-set, sturdy soldiers. Their heavy brown great-coats sweeping the ground, trailing in the snow. Their faces almost hidden by fur caps and ear-muffs – a little red star twinkling amidst the bristling fur. Their hefty boots treading over the solid frozen land with a weary step. Not a shot was fired, for there was no need – there was no enemy to fight or drive out; they just took possession of the village and the farmers extended a welcome in which relief mingled with fear.

Thus, the moment for which I had waited for nearly six years had come – I had survived. How differently I had imagined its coming, although there were many times when I did not think I would live to see it. Never did I think that this 'moment' and I would come face to face on a peaceful winter's morning, in a village that even a year earlier I had never heard of, amongst people who were total strangers and who knew nothing of the joy and despair that it brought. The vision of this day, kept so close to my heart, yet so long awaited in time, was full of loved, familiar faces – my father's, who used to say: 'Oh, we'll celebrate, how we'll celebrate . . .' at their centre. I had won a victory, but a victory bereft of all glory, a victory tainted with the bitter taste of defeat . . . There was no one to share it with.

I waited a few days, and when the soldiers moved out of the village, went on their way, and the fear and excitement having subsided it returned to its everyday life, I knew it was time for me to return to Cracow to search, amid the rubble and destruction of war, for a life and a family I had once been part of.

I got up very early that morning and made myself as presentable as I could by carefully plaiting my hair and putting my best Sunday clothes on. I packed my few possessions into a wicker basket and gathered the provisions I had purchased a few days earlier and gave them to my landlady.

It was a fine, very cold January morning – the countryside so tranquil and snug under its thick, fluffy blanket of snow. When I reached Gdów and joined the main road leading, through Wieliczka, to Cracow, I saw a strange sight. Russian soldiers, fully dressed, their fur-gloved hands under their heads, their knees drawn up to their bodies – brown bundles – fast asleep, in that bitter cold, on road verges, on paths, in ditches . . . I walked for many hours along the slippery ice and snow-bound gently curving main road. It was afternoon by the time I reached the outskirts of Cracow. The nearer I drew to the city, the fresher the signs of recently fought battles. In a field to my right lying on the snow, as if on an immaculate shroud, fully dressed, his arms by his sides, his feet neatly together, his swastika branded helmet just a little askew, a dead soldier – the mask of death hidden by a handful of snow which the wind had blown off a branch of a near-by tree onto his face. I tramped across the snow right up to him thinking: 'He must have a watch on his wrist . . .' The sleeves of his grey-green soldier's coat went over his wrists onto his warmly gloved hands . . . I could not bring myself to touch him, to push up the sleeve . . .

265

Further on, a large, chestnut horse, stretched out full length on his back in a ditch, his hind legs bent inwards as if to push back into his shrapnel-torn belly the congealed mass of his spilling out vitals. Two men with sharp knives had already set upon his flank and were busily carving it, for he had not died of old age or disease, but a good, natural death and his flesh would be tasty and tender.

Part of the way I walked with a middle-aged woman who was also making for Cracow. She prattled on and on about her son. He had spent the war years in the service of the enemy denouncing his fellow-countrymen, so I gathered, right, left and centre, not because he was a bad lad, but because he had no trade or skill of any kind and there was no other way open to him of making a living. She kept assuring me that he was a good boy and had meant no harm, but now that accounts were already being squared all over the country she feared for her boy. We almost stumbled into a stark naked male corpse already stripped of his earthly possessions, but his helmet lying by – the only key to his identity. A fine young soldier with short-cropped thick black hair and strong white teeth bared in the agony of pain. My companion said: 'Don't look, it's not nice . . .'

It was well into the afternoon when I found myself walking along Wielicka Street; its continuation was Limanowskiego Street – the one time Ghetto area. The walls which had enclosed us and within which we had lived and perished were still there, otherwise there was no sign of the tragedy once enacted within them. I entered the dingy, four-storey house in which we had lived – 42 Limanowskiego Street. I came to keep the promise which we made, as a family, that whoever survived the war would return to that house to await the return of the others.

I tried to open the door to the basement room in which we had lived and which, in the end, had proved but an ante-chamber to death. It was locked. I sat down on the flight of stone steps below the room's grime covered window. With my sleeve I rubbed a little clear patch in the pane and peered in. My gaze was met by slimy green walls and rotting floorboards . . . I sat on the steps for a long time; dusk had gathered round me and the cold was numbing, but the tears that rolled down my cheeks were burning hot. Yet, even then, I did not know that my entire world had been turned to dust and ashes.

37 • *Awakening*

The streets were dimly lit. I reached the Third Bridge. It was impassable. It had no middle. It had been blown up and had caved in. Huge slabs of cracked concrete and twisted metal were suspended over the frozen river. I joined the long line of people, some of whom were carrying torches, some of whom were pulling laden sledges, and crossed the hard-frozen Vistula into central Cracow.

It was very cold. The air was icy. The street lamps cast an eerie, dirty-yellow light.

I went to 27 Dietla Street. Crisp white snowflakes had settled on my head and shoulders. I crossed the courtyard and climbed the narrow stairs to the second floor. I knocked on the Niedzielskis' door. I was admitted into their warm kitchen and, in no time at all, a plate of hot soup was placed before me.

Mrs Niedzielska, née Zastępa, had a brother, Karol, who long before the war had married a Jewess – my mother's cousin Hanka. She had converted to Catholicism on marriage. She was looked upon by the family as something of a black sheep. I had met Mrs Niedzielska at the Zastępas' early in the war. She was a kind, motherly woman. I liked her. I renewed the acquaintance during the last few months of the Occupation. My religious denomination was never mentioned.

My hostess, the mother, must have been in her middle-forties at that time, but looked much older. Her husband, an insignificant man except for the fever and hatred that blazed in his eyes, kept to his room night and day. His days were numbered. He was dying from tuberculosis. They had two sons – both university students – and a daughter a year or so younger than myself. The girl, Barbara, was tall and shapely. A long, black braid swung down her back. By my standards she was worldly, accomplished, even sophisticated. The war had not touched her. She looked upon me as a little country bumpkin. The mother said I could stay with them in exchange for domestic help.

Nothing much had changed and everything had changed in my life. I no longer lived in fear. I had returned to Cracow. I was alone and I was again a kitchen skivvy.

The flat was small and one room in it was out of bounds, as the husband's disease was transmittable.

The building, the doorway, the courtyard, the stairs and passages at No. 27 were so squalid, fetid and dark that when I thought of them in retrospect the word 'Zolaesque' attached itself to them in my mind.

The family lived very modestly. They had no fixed source of income. The mother, who was an unselfish, generous woman, kept the family going. Kept it fed. But only just. She dabbled in 'commerce'. She ran a kind of *Exchange and Mart* enterprise – mostly clothing, wool, shoes – performing an extraordinary juggling act daily, but making very little profit. Potatoes formed our staple diet.

Almost within days of the Liberation, a Jewish Council came into being. It was housed in a tall, large building in Długa Street. One of its very first acts was to set up an orphanage. A handful of Jews – adults and children – had crawled out of the woodwork.

As soon as I learnt of the Council's existence, I went there to register. The clerk behind the desk asked me to fill in a form. I found, there and then, that after nearly six years of not putting pen to paper I could not write. Only with tremendous effort, very slowly, could I produce a scrawl. The clerk helped me. She said, 'We already have an orphanage. We already have a handful of children in it. You can join them – now. But I had an in-built fear of orphanages and an innate dislike of pity. Could I think about it? I asked. 'If you decide not to join us, we'll pay you a monthly Orphan's Pension – starting right away.' I presume these were Joint funds.

It was a very modest pension, but my status *vis-à-vis* my hosts rose considerably. 'Of course, the Jews look after their own . . .' said the husband.

Not a single member of my family had returned. Nobody. My brother, Joseph, had been held at the Plaszow Camp. I knew that. But the liberating army had found the camp cleaned out, empty. No inmates. No guards.

I knew that our parents and little Bartuś would never come back . . . But Joseph! I hoped. I prayed. But not conventionally. My grief, my loneliness, my yearning were my prayer. Nobody was glad, nobody was pleased that I had survived. Nobody wanted me – someone else's child.

A number of my mother's cousins had survived, had come out of hiding, but no one offered me a home. No one made a gesture of affection towards me. They were all so busy re-building their shattered lives – making plans for the future. They hardly noticed that I had survived except that, for some reason, my survival caused a reaction of mirth. 'Smart, canny, cute' were the adjectives used. I understood that except for the element of fear I was in the same position as before. Alone. Unwanted. The realisation dawned upon me gradually, but unshakably.

I had, really, not the vaguest idea what had been done to the Jews, where and on what scale. I needed to possess a vast trove of knowledge to understand the circumstances, the reasons, the methods, the final tally of our tragedy and I had none. For me the war had ended. I did not know how fiercely it was still raging elsewhere. That it would be another five months before the monster was brought to its knees.

There were lots of books in the flat. My ability to read, unlike my ability to write, was not impaired. Books became a source of solace and escape and, in spite of everything, delight. There was no rhyme or reason to my reading. I read whatever I happened upon – from Sienkiewicz to an old cookery book.

I made up my mind to return to school. My hostess and her children were very much in favour of the idea. She came with me to help me enrol at the local primary school, just round the corner from Dietla Street, in Stradom. The Headmistress said she would give me a try in the 5th Form. I had lost nearly six years of schooling, she pointed out. She was giving me three years' grace.

On 12 March 1945 I sat down on a form behind a desk. School lasted from eight in the morning till one in the afternoon. At the mid-morning break we received a mug of sweetened black coffee and a thick slice of rye bread spread with jam.

Spring came to Cracow once again. And with it hope.

I visited the Jewish Council centre every few days. With the Allies' penetration of Germany and the discovery and liberation of Concentration Camps a thin trickle of Jews started passing through the Council.

One of the first people I met was Ela Reinfeld – Aunt Regina's best friend. She had lost everyone. Palestine was her dream. I also ran into Mrs Emmer. Her daughter, Renia, and I had been classmates before the war. She had changed and aged so greatly that I did not recognise her. But the hollow-eyed spectre gripped my shoulder tight. 'Yasia . . . Yasia . . .! Do you remember my Renia? Do you remember my Helenka?' 'Mrs Emmer!' 'Do you remember my children? Do you remember my Renia and my Helenka . . .?'

I also met at the Council the beautiful Sonia Brandeis. The last time I had seen her was in the Ghetto. She was trying to wash a very large sheet in a very small basin. She belonged to my cousins' and brother's group of friends. She had a little purple number tatooed on her left forearm. She was one of five children. All five had survived. She told me she had been an inmate of the Auschwitz camp and was only passing through Poland. We sat down on a bench in the park and talked for a while. She had no news, no knowledge of my brother's fate, but she confirmed that he had been in the Plaszow camp.

I called on the Zastępas from time to time. They lived next to the Plaszow railway station. Uncle Karol, a thoroughly decent man, but badly hen-pecked by his wife, was a railwayman. The Plaszow Station was his workplace. Accommodation in a bleak, drab block of flats – the Railwaymen's Flats – went with the job.

When I called on them in the spring of 1945 they had Aunt Hanka's niece staying with them. I remembered Hala from the Ghetto; a slight lissom young girl with long, brown hair. She had been released from a German concentration camp. She was gravely ill. Her swollen, distended body was covered with open, running sores. She had almost no hair – just a few little tufts on her head. She kept repeating, 'Where is my Dear One? Where is my Love? Will I see him again?' The Zastępas had no children. Aunt Hanka was good to Hala and looked after her devotedly.

I did quite well at school. The Niedzielski youngsters had plenty of old textbooks, atlases, half-used exercise books, nibs, stubs of pencils – even a satchel. They generously put them at my disposal. The husband was the only one who resented my presence. I was Jewish. I had two healthy lungs. One afternoon, when I was doing my homework on the kitchen table, concentrating very hard on the writing, he crept up behind me, soundless like a cockroach, and said, 'Having difficulty with the pen, are we? We are much handier with the shovel, aren't we?'

Oddly enough another Jewish girl joined my class. She was younger than I. She was the right age for the 5th Form. We took to each other. She had carrot-red hair, a freckled face and a wide, ready smile. It was good to have a friend. She, her parents, her brother and other close relations had spent the war in hiding in considerable comfort. They lived in Batorego Street, where I was a frequent visitor – always hospitably and warmly received. They, too, had a niece staying with them. A young woman in her twenties. She, too, had been released from a German concentration camp. She did not appear to be as physically ill as Hala, but she lay on her bed all day her face turned towards the wall. She would not speak at all.

38 • Joseph

It was May, 1945. Germany had been vanquished. The war had ended. More and more Jews were passing through the Council office in Długa Street.

And now lists of survivors' names, circulated round Europe by the Red Cross, started appearing on the Council entrance walls. I scanned them religiously. Not one member of my family figured in them. No one. The information the lists gave was scanty: Name, date and place of birth, occupation. But it was a joyous confirmation of life.

School ended in June. I received the end of year report. Although it was very good, it was a modest achievement for a fifteen year old. And there was nobody to show it to, or share it with.

Now that school was over, I visited the Council even more frequently. It drew me like a magnet. Every time I went I found fresh lists on the walls and read them carefully time and again. Nobody.

One day, in the early summer, I ran into Rutka Lewkowicz. I knew her very well and we threw our arms round each other. 'Rutka!' 'Yasia!' She looked well. The same dark, lively eyes. The same dark curly hair. The same sturdy, womanly body. Rutka, the daughter of a well known Cracow artist was, also, the niece of Ralf Immerglück – the painter (Adam's and Richard's father). My parents had been friends with both families.

I remembered vividly the social gatherings organized by the Lewkowicz and Immerglück children, already in their teens before the war. My big brother was always invited and I tagged on. Nobody minded. There were poetry and prose readings. Music recitals. Dancing displays. Theatricals, charades, games – all home-produced including the lovely, colourful costumes and the imaginative scenery. When the entertainment had ended Mrs Lewkowicz, a large majestic woman, would sail into the room bearing a platter of hot frankfurters – her helper following with a basin of baked potatoes. What a splendid time we had!

Joseph

I met Rutka two or three times, but she, too, was only passing through Cracow. How well she remembered Joseph. She had no news of him at all. Yet the meeting with Rutka was to be of the greatest consequence, affecting the rest of my life.

Sometime in July 1945, I crossed the Council threshold yet again. My spirits were particularly low. People were returning. Mostly young people. People's names appeared on the lists. What had happened to Joseph? I had not heard of Mauthausen Concentration Camp, of its stone-quarries, of its 187 steps up which the Jewish rag-dolls, in their striped tatters, carried stones and boulders.

I approached the wall. There was a fresh batch of lists fastened to it. My eye automatically sought the letter 'F' . . . There it was! 'FISCHLER JÓZEF – KRAKÓW – 10.3.1923. CARPENTER.'

I read that one line again and again – droplets of tears rolling quietly down my cheeks. It was right in every detail except the 'Carpenter'. I knew that if a person's name appeared on a list, more information could be obtained about him in the office on the second floor.

The office was very crowded and the clerk behind the desk quite unable to deal with the flood of enquiries. Their urgency. Their emotion. Everyone was talking at once. She could barely hear the questions. The information-seeker could barely hear her replies.

When eventually I managed to engage her attention, she consulted her file and said: 'Yes, he is alive. He is in Italy . . . to make his way to Palestine.' This was all she could tell me.

I walked out of the office very crestfallen. My joy had given way to despondency. Italy . . . Palestine . . .? But it may be years before we see each other. Italy! Palestine! But he is alive! How are we going to find each other? Look for each other? My brother is alive!

I met 'Black Lola' in Długa Street. 'Lola . . .'; 'Yasia . . .' We kissed and hugged. She was my cousin Sophie's best friend. We called her 'black' because of her black eyes, black hair and deep olive complexion.

'We were in Skarżysko Kamienna [one of the harshest women's concentration camps on Polish territory] – Sophie and I. She is dead. We worked with chemicals which turned our faces, our flesh yellow . . . Made us ill . . . Sophie was hanging on by a thread. She was so thin and yellow. We knew the Russian Army was approaching, was very close . . . Sophie attempted to escape. They shot her. We were liberated a few days later . . .

In the summer of 1945 I used to cross the river – the Third Bridge its old self again, after having been damaged during the January 1945 offensive when the Germans were being routed by the Russians – to stroll about 'The Ghetto' streets. Sometimes I sat down for a while – on a doorstep or a stone ledge. One sunny afternoon, it occurred to me to pay Mrs Szenc a visit. The last time I had met Mrs Szenc had been on a less equal footing towards the end of October 1944, three months or so, before the Russian Armies liberated Cracow – long after the Cracow Ghetto had ceased to exist, and my people, my world had been reduced to ashes. I had just jumped off a lorry which had brought me from the country to the outskirts of Cracow. I was carrying two wicker baskets filled with a variety of sausages, chunks of bacon and other porcine delicacies.

I walked down Wielicka Street, in which I had one or two regular customers. A woman, dressed all in black, was coming towards me. We almost collided with one another, for neither of us, from the moment we caught sight of each other, could believe her own eyes. The recognition was instant on her part and mine. It was Mrs Szenc.

'Fancy that, the Jewish brat is still alive . . . well, I never!' Her voice dropped to a lower register, became a plaint: 'Did you know I lost my boy? The younger one . . . That's why I'm in mourning . . . He was only small. Going on five. It's like having a strip of living flesh torn out of your body. I'm going to the cemetery – to see to the grave; put a few plants in for next week, for All Saints' Day. There's no stopping the hurt . . .' Her eyes misted over. We stood there, for a minute or two, silent, each with her thoughts. Her attention focusing on my two baskets, her voice firmed, she asked: 'What have you got in those baskets?' She raised the lid of one, she raised the lid of the other. 'Hmm . . . hmmm . . . nice . . .' She looked the contents over with a practised eye. 'I'll have that nice long sausage . . . hmmm . . . hmm . . . and that nice piece of pork . . . there, slip them into my bag . . . next to the plants . . . a bit of soil never harmed anyone . . . Fancy you being alive . . .' And having plundered my wares, she resumed her journey.

I now walked, curious, into her building and knocked on her door. A woman, a stranger, answered it. I asked if Mrs Szenc was at home. 'Oh no, 'er don't live 'ere no more . . . 'Er lives in one of 'em posh streets.' I asked if she knew her present address. She did not. As an afterthought, she added, ''er in No. 5, 'em is friends. Ask 'er.' At No. 5, the lady of the house was most obliging. 'The Szences moved. Soon after the Germans were chased out. She's got ever such a lovely flat. Ever so posh. And her husband. Ever such a good job.'

'Could you let me have her address, please?' 'Oh yes. Are you a stranger in Cracow? Do you want it written down?' 'If you could just tell me, please.' She did. 'You're sure you won't forget it?' 'I am sure. Thank you.'

One evening, that summer of 1945, accompanied by Mrs Niedzielska, I went to call on Mrs Szenc. She was, indeed, living in one of Cracow's finest areas – so fine, in fact, that during the war it had been designated as a 'Nur Für Deutsche' area.

We rang the bell and Mrs Szenc, in person, answered the door. About eight months had elapsed since she and I had stood, mutually shocked, on the pavement in Wielicka Street. We would always recognise each other. 'What do you want?' she snapped out looking straight at me. But I, I was speechless for I was completely lost – looking over her shoulder, through the door she had inadvertently left open on coming into the hall – in contemplation of a wall covered with a tulip-strewn carpet. I made a great effort to pull myself together. I said I wanted her to return my carpet, the one hanging on the wall in the room directly behind her. I wished it done through the proper legal channels. She remained aggressive, but it was obvious that the wind had been taken out of her sails. It would have been easier to maintain a belligerent attitude, if only she had not left that door open. I said I would report the matter to the local police station. I did just that.

At the police station I was asked to fill in a form. I had only answered three or four questions on it, when a plain-clothes detective walked in. He was young, matter of fact and helpful. He understood the nature of my complaint perfectly. He said that, of course, he would have to interview Mrs Szenc. Once he had done that, he would communicate with me and that, he was afraid, he would have to bring the two of us together. He would then be able to resolve the matter there and then, at the police station, without further ado. He worked speedily. About three weeks after first speaking to him, I received a communication requesting me to present myself at the police station.

It was a fine, sunny July morning. When I arrived the detective was standing at the reception counter in the entrance shuffling bits of paper about. As soon as he caught sight of me he came over, shook hands and said: 'We are ready now.' We went into a longish, bare room in which there were two men: a uniformed policeman and a civilian. The civilian was striking in appearance. Tall, athletic with beautiful golden hair trimly cut and carefully groomed. He was wearing a pale-cream summer suit, a camera, in a neat leather pouch, swinging from his shoulder. The detective introduced him as 'Mr Szenc.' He explained that Mrs Szenc was medically unfit to attend, and that her husband was standing in for her. 'This is perfectly in order,' said the detective. 'I have the medical certificate right here,' and he waved a sheet of paper up in the air. Mr Szenc was both mild and conciliatory. He said it was difficult for him to conceive, never mind believe, that his wife was capable of such a . . . dishonourable action. She, they – as a married couple – were people of the highest moral principles. It was unthinkable that his wife could have done such a dreadful thing. She clearly remembers paying the young lady. The young lady was only a child at the time. It could be that she does not remember, that it has slipped her mind. After all she has been through . . . But if anyone were to suffer loss in this most unfortunate affair, he would be the first to volunteer to do so.

The carpet was deposited at the police station. I made a gift of it to the family I was staying with.

One day in August 1945, as I was walking along Dietla Street, an elderly man approached me and said, 'An atom bomb has been dropped on Japan.' I said: 'Pardon?' But he was gone.

Rutka Lewkowicz and her young man left Poland. They got as far as Austria – Salzburg. They stopped at a Jewish Refugee camp called the 'Regensburg Casino.' It was a stop-over for Jewish ex-concentration camp inmates.

Joseph was also staying at 'Regensburg Casino'. He had been there for some weeks. He had a cubicle all to himself and had made himself at home. The human wreck, weighing 35 kilos, liberated on the 5 May 1945 by the American Army and carried on a stretcher to their field hospital, had fully recovered. He was twenty-two years old, strong, vigorous with a prepossessing appearance and personality.

'*Haganah*' agents were scouring the Jewish Refugee camps looking for suitable recruits. The recruitment officer had approached Joseph. Would he be interested in joining the Organisation? Delicate, cautious negotiations were under way.

One evening in August as Joseph was crossing the camp compound he heard a girl call out his name: 'Józek!' 'Rutka!' Hugs, kisses, exclamations of amazement, questions. She introduced her friend. 'Look, we have nowhere to sleep tonight,' she said. 'I have a small room of my own. You will sleep on the bed. Your friend and I can sleep on the floor,' said Joseph. And so it was.

Joseph

They talked for while before dropping off to sleep.

Rutka: 'Where are you going from here?' Joseph: 'I hope to make it to Palestine.' Rutka: 'Aren't you going to Cracow first?' Joseph: 'To Cracow? What for?' Rutka: 'What about your little sister?' Joseph: 'My sister? What do you mean! My sister?' Rutka: 'Your sister is in Cracow!' Joseph: 'My sister is alive? My sister is in Cracow?' Rutka: 'Yes. Your sister is alive. Your sister is in Cracow. I saw her. I spoke to her. Several times.' Joseph: 'You saw my sister? You spoke to my sister? She is alive?'

The next morning Joseph handed his little room over to Rutka. He was leaving for Cracow.

It was the middle of August. It was hot. It was suffocating in the Niedzielskis' flat. I was nearly broke. I could not see myself eking it out till the end of the month. Should I make some enquiries about the Orphanage? They would show me around, explain how it functioned. Every month when I drew my pension I was asked if I had made up my mind to join them. I was now turning this possibility over in my mind. The price of independence was too high. I was weary. Lonely. Disheartened.

I reached the Council doorway and was about to cross the threshold when I saw a young man standing by it looking a little non-plussed. The face was instantly familiar. 'Józek!' I yelled out. 'Jaśka!' he responded. 'I have been here, in Cracow, for three days now trying to find you. Everybody said you were around, but nobody knew exactly where. Just like you to salt yourself away like that . . .'

He looked so well, my brother. Stalwart, sun-tanned, clear-eyed. And so pleased.

It was a warm, sunny August, the August of 1945, and we sat on a park bench, the summer's pleasant greenery around us, talking, talking, talking inexhaustibly. We had so much to tell each other. Two-and-a-half years. A long and painful time. But somehow our suffering was now overlaid with joy. The joy of our reunion, of being together, which we felt was nothing short of miraculous.

And so a plan was born of our endless talk, for we both knew that the Big Wound – the loss of our parents and little Bartuś – would never heal. We would leave Cracow, we would leave Poland and seek to make a new life for ourselves elsewhere – far away from places, once so much part of us, which had become images of terror, suffering and death.